MW00987605

Discipleship has turned into a buz[...]
without properly defining it. In s[...]
navigational chart to get us back [...]
provides the course correction we [...].

—*Robby Gallaty, senior pastor, Long Hollow*
Baptist Church; president, Replicate Ministries

Bill Hull is spot on. Disciples are not a special class of Christians. Bill has provided us with a challenging and thought-provoking examination of biblical conversion and discipleship. My bet is that you won't agree with everything in these pages. (I didn't.) But I guarantee you that your ministry and personal walk with Jesus will benefit greatly from wrestling with the wisdom and insights he provides.

—*Dr. Larry Osborne, author and pastor,*
North Coast Church, Vista, CA

Bill Hull believes that in receiving Christ as Lord and Savior, we also receive his lifestyle of making disciples. The two commitments go together. Not the kind of book to read lounging in a rocking chair munching on chocolates.

—*Dr. Robert Coleman, author,* The Master Plan for Evangelism

This book is a must for church leaders. It deals with the root issues, the upstream theological realities that are required to make a sustainable discipleship movement in your church and beyond. Read it, ponder it, and let it change your life and ministry. I heartily endorse *Conversion and Discipleship*.

—*Dr. Bobby Harrington, director, Discipleship.org; board member,*
Relational Discipleship Network; author and pastor

I am convinced that one of the deepest flaws in discipleship derives from our lack of understanding of the significance of repentance as an intrinsic part of a living relationship with God. Bill, as the longtime activist for the disciple-making cause, makes an irrefutable case for the relationship of ongoing conversion to a life of discipleship. A well-written book on an important topic.

—*Alan Hirsch, award-winning author; founder, Forge,*
100Movements, and Future Travelers; www.alanhirsch.org

Bill Hull has been committed to discipleship for many years and has helped to shape many of the minds who consider discipleship the core mission of the church. I admire Bill so much because he is not just a theorist but a practitioner who does what he says others ought to do. He has given those committed to discipleship a new theological tool to promote something that has been left out of the church for some time. I know you will enjoy this book as much as I did.

—*Jim Putman, senior pastor, Real Life Ministries; coauthor,* Discipleshift

I've been reading and listening to Bill Hull for years. He's been a discipleship coach in my life, and for countless others. I'm so thankful for him, his work, and his passion for discipleship.

—*Ed Stetzer, www.edstetzer.com*

Bill Hull writes boldly about how Dallas Willard challenged him to think differently about one of the key pillars of evangelicalism, the meaning of the gospel, and the natural bond between conversation and discipleship (aka apprenticeship). For Jesus' disciples, the good news was not that they could say a magic phrase and then go to heaven when they died; the good news was that they could enter into an apprenticeship with Jesus and begin living an eternal sort of life right then and there. Nothing has changed. That is still the good news.

—*Gary W. Moon, MDiv, PhD; executive director, Martin Institute and Dallas Willard Center, Westmont College; author,* Apprenticeship with Jesus

Bill Hull's lifelong journey has given him one of the most important leadership roles in the discipleship movement of the last fifty years, and makes him uniquely qualified to guide the church to true biblical discipleship. This will be a hard read for some because Bill speaks directly and with no nonsense to those who have substituted elitist programs for biblical discipleship. Read, and heed, the clarion call of this book.

—*Michael J. Wilkins, Distinguished Professor of New Testament Language and Literature, Talbot School of Theology; author,* Following the Master: A Biblical Theology of Discipleship

CONVERSION & DISCIPLESHIP

Other Books by Bill Hull

Jesus Christ, Disciplemaker

The Disciple-Making Pastor

The Disciple-Making Church

Straight Talk on Spiritual Power

Christlike

The Complete Book of Discipleship

Choose the Life

Anxious for Nothing

Right Thinking

Building High Commitment in a Low Commitment World

The Experience the Life Series

Believe as Jesus Believed

Live as Jesus Lived

Love as Jesus Loved

Minister as Jesus Ministered

Lead as Jesus Led

The Christian Leader (May 2016)

Evangelism and Discipleship (with Bobby Harrington 2014)

The False Promise of Discipleship (with Brandon Cook 2016)

BILL HULL

CONVERSION
OTHER
YOU CAN'T HAVE ONE
WITHOUT THE
&DISCIPLESHIP

ZONDERVAN®

ZONDERVAN

Conversion and Discipleship
Copyright © 2016 by Robert W. Hull

This title is also available as a Zondervan ebook. Visit www.zondervan.com/ebooks.

Requests for information should be addressed to:
Zondervan, 3900 *Sparks Dr. SE, Grand Rapids, Michigan 49546*

ISBN 978-0-310-52009-2

Cover design: Brand Navigation
Interior design: Denise Froehlich

Printed in the United States of America

HB 12.14.2018

To Dallas Willard,
the reluctant prophet who inspired
me to undertake this work

CONTENTS

The Western segment of the church today lives in a bubble of historical illusion about the meaning of discipleship and the gospel.

—DALLAS WILLARD, *THE DIVINE CONSPIRACY*

Some believe you can have conversion without discipleship. I believe that the proof of conversion is discipleship.

FOREWORD

Buzzwords abound in the church today. Sometimes they are little more than publicity stunts, sometimes they are just below shallow, and other times they are genuine attempts to get to the heart of God's mission in this world. Individual terms will take us only so far, so terms like *missional* or *formation* or *spirituality* may help, but we need them all if we want a balanced and robust theology. When it comes to the Christian life, however, there is one term that can take us to the heart of God: *discipleship*.

I found this term on a journey. As a high school convert, I was absorbed with the joy of having found meaning and purpose in life. My pastor, God bless his heart, was deeply fond of the apostle Paul and absorbed in a theology that seemed to avoid the Gospels and Jesus as a historical figure. So it was not until I was in college, both immersed in studying the whole Bible and working as a youth pastor, that I discovered the Gospels. My world was suddenly aflame with a desire to know about Jesus and the Gospels, and while this flame was burning bright, a professor recommended that I read Dietrich Bonhoeffer's *The Cost of Discipleship*. As a college junior or senior, I pored over this book, soul and body quaking and aching for comprehension of the depth of this man's great book. That journey—to Jesus and the Gospels and to the works of Bonhoeffer—changed the course of my life. When I heard anyone talking about Jesus or found a new book about Jesus, I turned in that direction; when someone directed my attention to Bonhoeffer, I discovered that he kept on that Jesus-and-the-Gospels path.

The "first day" with Jesus, if we begin with Mark, is a lesson in succinctness: repent, believe, gospel, kingdom. Put them into a single bag of ideas and you get discipleship. I wanted to grow as a disciple and I wanted to teach about discipleship and I wanted to read about discipleship.

But I learned quickly that not everyone was on board. I heard some say that discipleship sounded like works righteousness and not like grace; others said we have to balance Jesus with Paul's "life in the Spirit." I even heard some say that salvation is one thing, conversion is one thing, but discipleship is something else entirely and optional. What I heard was that you can have the one without the others—that you can be saved and not be a disciple. I was young and I was enthusiastic, but I smelled a theological rat in that claim. So I kept teaching and I kept writing, and then one day at Trinity Evangelical Divinity School, in the hallway outside my office, I met a young pastor, Bill Hull, who cared about the same thing. He had heard that I was teaching discipleship and that I was teaching you can't have one (salvation or conversion) without the other (discipleship). He thought I was right, and I thought he was right—and here we are together again.

I endorse 100 percent what Bill Hull lays claim to in this book: when it comes to conversion (salvation) and discipleship, you can't have one without the other. There aren't many books whose titles tell both the story of the author and express the heart of the book's message like this one. *Conversion and Discipleship: You Can't Have One without the Other* perfectly expresses everything I've known of the life, the ministry, and the writings of Bill Hull. Dallas Willard, if you read him carefully, wrote all of his books toward a theology of Christlikeness. Bill has written all of his books toward discipleship, or toward a church composed not of the saved but of disciples.

Bill Hull begins in the right place, with the gospel. He offers a profound word: if we get the gospel wrong, we get everything wrong. If we get the gospel right, we are on a different and holy and healthy journey into discipleship. In saying these things, however, Bill does not hold back, and he critiques some of American evangelicalism's pet (and shallow) themes about the nature of the gospel and the kind of response to which it summons us. But if we get the gospel right—and Bill Hull is on all fours on this one— what flows is the beauty of what the gospel can create: churches packed with flourishing disciples.

There is in *Conversion and Discipleship* a profoundly healthy and holy impatience—Bill has been teaching, leading, preaching, and writing about this theme his entire ministry. But churches all around the world are not listening as they should. They continue to offer the same lame excuses. "Sure sounds," they cough up, "like works righteousness," or, "It's all about grace, not discipleship," or, "You can have one without the other, but you should try to get the other." Bill's not alone in his holy impatience. I meet pastor after pastor who tells me the same thing: too many in the churches are fully satisfied with less than being fully devoted to Christ, and they bank on grace and goodness and unconditional love. But the God of grace, the God of goodness, and the God of unconditional love became incarnate in the one who calls us to repent, to believe, to embrace the gospel, and to fall head over heels in love with the King of the kingdom, Jesus.

Discipleship is about conformity to Christ, as the apostle Paul once put it: "Now the Lord is the Spirit, and where the Spirit of the Lord is, there is freedom. And we all, who with unveiled faces contemplate the Lord's glory, are being transformed into his image with ever-increasing glory, which comes from the Lord, who is the Spirit" (2 Cor. 3:17–18). Behind the apostle Paul's words about being conformed to the image of Christ himself are Jesus' words about mission-defining and life-determining discipleship. I think of Mark 8:34: "Whoever wants to be my disciple must deny themselves and take up their cross and follow me." Friends, these two words form the core of *Conversion and Discipleship*. You will find in this book not a new program but an old word: the word that says discipleship is the mission of the church.

This book is bold, it is courageous, and it is biblical. Bill has worked the Bible; he's not a pragmatist trying to load up the pews of a congregation. He knows what the Bible says about gospel and grace and repentance and salvation and that the mission of God is to transform sinners into saints. That transformation is called discipleship, and God's gift is the Spirit, who empowers each of us to become more and more Christlike. In *Conversion and Discipleship: You Can't Have One without the Other*, you will be treated to a creative combination, expansion, and renewed application of the greatest ideas of Dietrich Bonhoeffer and Dallas Willard. But behind them are the words and mission of Jesus, and in absorbing those words and that mission, Bill Hull sends us on a journey into nothing less than what can be called "Christformity."

No serious pastor and no serious Christian can ignore the message of this book. Bill is seriously right: you can't have one without the other.

—Scot McKnight, Julius R. Mantey Professor
in New Testament, Northern Seminary

ACKNOWLEDGMENTS

Special thanks to Ryan Pazdur and his editing team, who improved my work and honed the message. I appreciate the help of Bobby Harrington, Todd Wilson, Brandon Cook, Dann Spader, Michael Wilkins, and Robby Gallaty, along with the men and women involved in the Bonhoeffer Project who assisted me in the completion of the book.

INTRODUCTION

If you read the Great Commission, you may not realize that it is about world revolution. If you think it is about planting churches, as important as that may be, if you think it is about evangelization, as that is often understood—no, no, it is about a world revolution promised through Abraham, come to life in Jesus and living on in his people up to today. This is what our hearts hunger for, even when we don't know how to approach it or how to go about it.

—DALLAS WILLARD, *LIVING IN CHRIST'S PRESENCE*

"Follow me" is the substance of the call in the power of which Jesus makes people his saints. . . . We may say, therefore, that in practice the command to follow Jesus is identical with the command to believe in him.

—KARL BARTH, *THE CALL TO DISCIPLESHIP*

This book proposes that all who are called to salvation are also called to discipleship, and that there are no exceptions to this. Many Christians today, especially in the West, think they have salvation figured out. But if you were to ask them about discipleship, they might hesitate or look at you with confusion. Discipleship? Isn't that what you do after you become a believer? What does discipleship have to do with becoming a Christian? What does discipleship have to do with conversion?

In this book, I want to show you that conversion and discipleship, while distinct, are really two sides of the same coin. You can't have one without the other. But don't just take my word for it. Throughout this book, I will show you that this is what the Bible teaches and is what Jesus intended for his followers.

Let's begin with some definitions.

Conversion: For our purposes, *conversion* is "theological slang" for when a person decides to become a Christian.[1]

Discipleship: Discipleship occurs when someone answers the call to learn from Jesus and others how to live his or her life as though Jesus were living it. As a result, the disciple becomes the kind of person who naturally does what Jesus did.

A few years ago philosopher, writer, and Christian minister Dallas Willard was reflecting on the evangelical understanding of salvation and discipleship. Willard wrote, "There has simply been no consistent general teaching or practice under the heading of discipleship among evangelicals of this period: none that would be recognizable as discipleship in terms of biblical teaching or of the Christian past . . . this most recent version of evangelicalism lacks a theology of discipleship. Specifically, it lacks a clear teaching on how what happens at conversion continues on without break into an ever fuller life in the Kingdom of God."[2]

When I first read these words by Willard, they went through me like a knife. At the time, I had written three books that laid out a new template for discipleship, so I had some skin in this game. I wondered what Willard would make of my modest contribution, so one day over lunch I registered my complaint with him. "What about my books, Dallas? You know, *Jesus Christ, Disciplemaker, The Disciple-Making Pastor,* and *The Disciple-Making Church*?" I remember Dallas pausing and then laying his big hand on mine. He said to me, "Bill, I haven't read all your work, but I don't see it there." Strangely enough, this didn't discourage me. If anything, it made me even more passionate to address the problem. Dallas and I went on to discuss exactly what he meant by a "theology of discipleship," what it is and why it is needed.

Dallas has gone to be with God, and I no longer have the comfort of asking him questions at our leisurely lunches. But I have often thought of what he said that day. Now we see encouraging signs that the church is taking discipleship more seriously, especially among younger pastors and leaders. Victor Hugo reportedly wrote, "All the forces in the world are not so powerful as an idea whose time has come." It seems that moment has come for discipleship. I think the time has come to craft a common language for the growing interest in discipleship. At present we are using the same words, but we are speaking different languages. If we are not clear about why discipleship matters, what disciples actually are, the key role they play in God's redemptive drama, and how it is all tied together in the end, what the Holy Spirit has begun will disappear into the theological mist of confusion. This is why we need a theology of discipleship.

What qualifies as a theology of discipleship? First, it must address the relationship between discipleship and salvation. Present day evangelicalism gives little place to discipleship in its view of salvation. Our doctrines of grace tend to keep us from clearly defining what it means to be a disciple. We tend to treat the experience of conversion as something entirely separate from the process of becoming a disciple.

This separation has led to a common problem we face today. People profess to be Christians yet believe that they do not need to follow Jesus. We've defined discipleship as optional, a choice and not a demand.[3] For many who call themselves Christians today, being saved or being a Christian has no serious connection with an ongoing commitment to being formed into the image of Christ.

Though it was difficult for me to hear at the time, Dallas Willard was pointing out that my theology was defective in a significant way. At the level of the gospel itself, I had misrepresented what it means to be saved. You see, the gospel we preach will dictate the result; the content of what we preach will lead to the kind of person created.

My goal in this volume is not to introduce new ideas. I believe that a theology of discipleship already exists and can be found in the Scriptures. In other books, some I have written, this problem of separation is addressed in a chapter or two. But here, I want to face the issue head-on. So with fear and trembling, I'm going to lay it out for you to consider. I'm sure that my thoughts will be flawed and criticized, and that as soon as they are published, I will want to change them. But my goal is to start a discussion, and not just in academic circles. I want to see pastors and church leaders—those who are engaged in disciple-making everywhere—participate in this conversation. My hope is to help them better understand the theological basis for discipleship so they can better work to reproduce the life of Christ in others.

I will cover eight subjects:

1. The Gospel
2. The Call
3. Salvation
4. The Holy Spirit and How People Change
5. Ways and Means

6. The Church
7. The Pastor
8. The End

For each, I hope to address the challenge that my friend Dallas Willard laid out before us: "For Evangelical Christians, turning around the ship of their social reality, and *restoring* the understanding of salvation that characterized evangelicalism from its *beginnings in Luther* and periodically after him, will be very difficult if not impossible. It would primarily be a work of *scriptural interpretation and theological reformulation*, but modification of time-hardened practices will also be required. *Radical changes* in what we do in the way of 'church' will have to be made."[4]

Thus, this work has at least three dimensions. First, we need to restore our understanding of salvation. Second, we need to do the work of scriptural interpretation and theological reformulation. Here I will be relying upon the work of others, summarizing and integrating their thoughts with my own. Third, once we have looked at the Scriptures, we must address our practices and methods. One problem in the current discussion of discipleship is that while we are using the same words, we don't all agree on the meaning of those words. Unless we define what discipleship actually is, all of our talk will be about as useful as the conversations at the tower of Babel.

So these three steps are where we are heading. Let's get started by looking at the gospel.

1

THE GOSPEL

I believe the word gospel has been hijacked by what
we believe about personal salvation, and the gospel
itself has been reshaped to facilitate making decisions.
The result of this hijacking is that the word gospel no
longer means in our world what it originally meant to
either Jesus or the gospels.

—Scot McKnight

One of the perennial tasks of the church is to reexamine the gospel we preach and believe, alert to ways it has been reshaped by the idols of our culture. Martin Luther did this in his day in response to the Roman Catholic understanding of the gospel. Yet a mere hundred years after Luther led the Reformation, the gospel was contorted and the German church was an orthodox carcass. Dietrich Bonhoeffer, picking up Luther's torch four hundred years later, spoke about this corruption: "What emerged victorious from the Reformation history was not Luther's recognition of pure, costly grace, but the alert religious instinct of human beings for the place where grace could be had the cheapest. Only a small, hardly noticeable distortion of the emphasis was needed, and the most dangerous and ruinous deed was done."[1]

Even small corruptions of the gospel make a mark. And they do not often begin with big sweeping changes. Among Luther's followers three generations after him, the corruption was only a change in emphasis, a slight redefinition of grace. However, this soon became the dominant emphasis of the gospel message, and it bred passivity in believers because it replaced the emphasis on living out professed faith. Luther's followers didn't explicitly advocate cheap grace. They simply neglected to talk about discipleship.

What Is the Gospel?

The word "gospel" simply means good news.[2] The word occurs over ninety times in the New Testament and is a translation of the Greek noun *euangelion*. Both the noun and the verb form, *euangelizo*, are derived from the noun *angelos*, which is often translated "messenger." "An *angelos* was one who brought a message of victory or political news that brought joy."[3] We should note there is nothing inherently religious in the word gospel itself.

Though the word translated "gospel" can be found alone at times, it is most often accompanied by a modifier. Among the most common are "the gospel of God" (Mark 1:14), "the gospel of Jesus Christ" (Mark 1:1), "the gospel of his Son" (Rom. 1:9), "the gospel of the kingdom" (Matt. 4:23), "the gospel of the grace of God" (Acts 20:24), "the gospel of the glory of Christ" (2 Cor. 4:4), "the gospel of peace" (Eph. 6:15), and "an eternal gospel" (Rev. 14:6).[4] These modifiers give us a sense of the content of the good news, that it is of God, of Jesus Christ, of the kingdom, and that it relates to grace, peace, and glory in some way.

Yet the power of context is even more helpful than these simple adjectives. Reading about the gospel in the context of a broader description by the apostle Paul helps us grasp the meaning and content of the gospel in a person's life: "For I am not ashamed of this Good News about Christ. It is the power of God at work, saving everyone who believes—the Jew first and also the Gentile. This Good News tells us how God makes us right in his sight. This is accomplished from start to finish by faith. As the Scriptures say, 'it is through faith that a righteous person has life'" (Rom. 1:16–17 NLT).

Here we see Paul launching into a grand description of the gospel that continues until his magnificent pivot point in Romans 12:1–2. There he turns to the practical application of the gospel's power to change a person's life when he says, "And so, dear brothers and sisters, I plead with you to give your bodies to God because of all he has done for you" (Rom. 12:1 NLT). The gospel that Paul speaks about captures God's work from creation to consummation—nothing important is left out. Paul's letter to the Romans concludes with practical teaching on how the gospel's power and wisdom propel us through even the most mundane experiences of religious community life.[5]

The structure of the gospel is best displayed in 1 Corinthians 15:1–8, which serves as a helpful, concise summary of the gospel. Paul reminds his followers of the core message in light of the resurrection: "Let me now remind you, dear brothers and sisters, of the Good News I preached to you before. You welcomed it then, and you still stand firm in it. It is this Good

News that saves you if you continue to believe the message I told you—unless, of course, you believed something that was never true in the first place" (1 Cor. 15:1–2 NLT).

Paul reminds us that believing something and standing firm in it are the same thing. His words indicate that belief is more than mere agreement or intellectual assent; belief involves existential living as a demonstration of belief. Paul includes a somewhat cryptic phrase, "unless, of course, you believed something that was never true in the first place." He may be referring to a belief in the gospel without the hope of the resurrection or to belief in a different "gospel," one corrupted by his enemies or rivals. Paul then speaks of the origin of this gospel message and its importance: "I passed on to you what was most important and what had also been passed on to me" (1 Cor. 15:3a NLT). He wants us to understand that the gospel is not his, something he made up or created. He does not have permission or authority to make up the gospel or to write his own version of it. The gospel is something that is received, passed on, and entrusted to others. It is not to be edited, adorned, or removed from its proper context, here referring to the resurrection.[6] Receiving the gospel and passing it on—unchanged—is the only way to preserve it from corruption.

The skeleton structure Paul gives us in this passage has three parts: Christ died, Christ was buried, and Christ was raised.

1. Christ died. "*Christ died for our sins, just as the Scriptures said*" *(1 Cor. 15:3 NLT).* "Just as the Scriptures said" is shorthand for the writings of the Old Testament. In particular, Paul is thinking of the predictions of the coming Messiah, the promises God gave to Abraham, David, and others that were fulfilled in the birth and work of Christ. When Jesus was born and formally began his ministry, he presented the full revelation of God to the world. My point here is to remind us that before Jesus died, he lived. Ninety percent of his time on earth he lived in obscurity—not exactly a strategy designed for impact. Yet in three short years, he rocked the world in which he lived and started a movement that continues today.

Jesus' death meant something far more than most deaths because of *who* he was: God incarnate. His death had greater meaning because of his godly heritage[7] and because those closest to him considered him sinless.[8] In another passage, Paul interprets Jesus' death to mean something that all Israel should have understood: "For God made Christ, who never sinned, to be the offering for our sin, so that we could be made right with God through Christ" (2 Cor. 5:21 NLT).

When Paul proclaimed "Christ died," he meant several additional things that are a result of Jesus' death. Because Jesus was the appointed one, chosen by God as a substitute, he took the penalty of sin in place of all who are guilty by birth through Adam's curse. Why God decided on this plan is not explained here. But we have the simple revelation that Christ died for us and that his death in some way satisfied God's requirements for humans to be reconciled with him.[9] A living Christ was both chosen and volunteered to give up his life. This is where the gospel begins.

2. Christ was buried (1 Cor. 15:4). At first, this second point may seem incidental. You might think, "Of course he was buried. Why mention it?" But Paul includes this point because it establishes that Christ really was dead, locked away in a tomb with a two-ton stone wedged against the opening and a Roman guard making sure no one would steal his body. Jesus himself claimed that he would be in the earth for three days and nights and then would be raised.[10] So part of authenticating Jesus' words and life and establishing the truth of the promise he fulfilled is verifying his death. Yes, Christ was buried. He really died. And as we shall see, he was truly raised from death.

3. Christ was resurrected. "He was raised from the dead on the third day, just as the Scriptures said" (1 Cor. 15:4). Again, the phrase "just as the Scriptures said" refers to all of the messianic promises God made, starting with his statement to the serpent that the deliverer would strike a fatal blow to his head while he would wound his heel.[11] However, the fact that Jesus experienced a verifiable death and burial does not hold much meaning for us without the final act, his resurrection. And resurrection is only an abstraction without appearances and eyewitnesses. Paul chronicles Jesus' appearances to Peter, the twelve, and more than five hundred others and explicitly states that many of these five hundred could verify to Paul's original readers what they saw (1 Cor. 15:5–6). Paul even mentions James and himself as among those who saw Jesus after his resurrection (1 Cor. 15:7–8).

These three points are the skeletal structure of the gospel. The remainder of 1 Corinthians 15 is devoted to explaining the significance of the resurrection and includes the fact that Jesus will one day return and subject all things to himself.[12] The resurrection naturally leads to the return of Christ, the consummation of the gospel and the believer's blessed hope for the future.

But the story of the gospel is not over yet! The good news for today is that because of what Christ has done, we will one day see God eliminate sin, free us from the distress of living in a broken world, give justice, creating a new, eternal world. These truths, guaranteed by the resurrection, should bring great joy for all who have placed their hope in Christ.

The Gospel Elevator Speech

The skeleton I've sketched out is Paul's summary of the gospel. These are the essential points you might share on an elevator ride with an inquiring fellow passenger. If we have to explain the gospel quickly, we can say that Jesus lived, that he claimed to be sent from God, that he was killed, and that his death brings reconciliation to all of creation. Finally, we can share that Jesus was raised from death, ascended to heaven, and will return to bring about the promised reality. To access this gift of God, people need to acknowledge their need for it, turn toward Jesus, and start following him as proof of belief in him.

I long ago abandoned the belief that specific words or religious ideas are required to receive salvation. It is a bit absurd to think that magic words must be said to acquire eternal life. And few people have to rely on an elevator speech as the basis for their relationship to God. Nothing in Scripture says I should be able to tell the entire good news in ten minutes, or twenty minutes, or even ten hours or ten months. I have often suggested a simple elevator gospel message, "Follow Jesus, and he will teach you everything you will ever need to know." Of course, filling in what Jesus teaches will take a lifetime of learning.

People become Christians when they decide to follow Jesus. They may not believe everything the Bible teaches. But if they can get the basic facts and from them reach the point of wanting to be a follower of Jesus, they are on their way. They should know that Christ lived, Christ died, Christ was buried, and Christ was raised and will return to make all things right. But this simple skeleton isn't all that the Bible teaches about following Jesus. Nor does it represent the fullness of the good news we are called to preach.

WHAT GOSPEL ARE WE PREACHING?

Nothing is more insulting to evangelical pastors than the accusation that they are not preaching the gospel. I recall a lunch meeting with a member of the church I was pastoring. We had enjoyed lunch at the restaurant several times before, and I anticipated another delightful experience. It was an Italian establishment that served great spaghetti and meatballs. I poured on the parmesan, wrapped the spaghetti around my fork, and was about to enjoy the first bite when my friend said, "I must share with you my disappointment that you have failed to preach the gospel."

I took a big bite and waited until it found a home in my gullet before I spoke. "I can't believe you said that. I'm preaching through Romans verse by verse. Isn't that the gospel?"

He remained unconvinced. "We're not seeing people getting saved. There are people in our service who need to know how to gain eternal life, and you're not giving them that opportunity." He stood firm with a grim expression on his face. I was finally able to grasp his meaning—I was not laying out the plan of salvation at the end of the service and inviting people to pray the sinner's prayer. I was preaching the truth of Romans, clearly and plainly, but I was not asking for a public response. To this individual the gospel was the plan of salvation. But I was attempting to show how the gospel was the grand sweep of salvation history. We were looking at the story of God's work from Genesis to Revelation, from creation to the fall, and from the promise of Messiah through Israel to his coming in the form of Jesus. We were looking at the life, death, burial, and resurrection of Christ and his promise to return and establish his kingdom.

I could tell that my friend and I were on different pages. We were using the same words, but we were speaking a different language.

Evangelicals expect Christians to have had an experience they can point to—a salvation experience. The more dramatic, the more authentic, and the more powerful one's story is, the more it helps those who hear it. I am no theological curmudgeon. I love a good story, and I've had many a good cry hearing such accounts. But I am convinced that by reducing the complete gospel story of God's work from Genesis to Revelation to a packaged three or four points with a prayer, we have diminished our understanding of salvation and what it means to be a follower of Christ. This shift from gospel culture to salvation culture has weakened the church, diminished the lives of Christians, and made disciple-making difficult. What we should see as the starting line, our conversion to Christ, has become the finish line.

Digging Deeper

MORE THAN THE PLAN OF SALVATION?

In his recent book *The King Jesus Gospel*, Scot McKnight[a] asks the question, "How did the Gospel culture become a salvation culture? How did the gospel become the plan of salvation?" (70). McKnight presents the gospel skeleton of 1 Corinthians 15 and argues that it formed the basis of the early church's gospel message. "First Corinthians 15 led to the development of the Rule of Faith, and the Rule of Faith led to the Apostles' Creed and Nicene Creed. Thus,

1 Corinthians led to the Nicene Creed. Thus, the Nicene Creed is preeminently a gospel statement!" (64).

McKnight explains that the gospel is inherently a story. "The gospel is the Story of Jesus as the completion of the Story of Israel as found in the Scriptures, and the gospel story formed and framed the culture of the earliest Christians" (69). This story is told in all four Gospels: Matthew, Mark, Luke, and John. What we might call "the plan of salvation"—a simplified portion of the gospel story commonly shared on tracts or in preaching—is simply a convenient extract of what is found in Scripture, but *it should not be mistaken for the gospel itself.*

McKnight traces the history of the "plan of salvation" back to the Reformation when "the singular contribution of the Reformation, in all three directions—Lutheran, Reformed, and Anabaptist—was that the gravity of the gospel was shifted toward human response and personal responsibility and the development of the gospel as speaking into that responsibility" (71). McKnight argues that the Reformers reframed the gospel to be primarily about soteriology, or getting saved from the consequences of sin. He points to the Augsburg Confession and its articles on salvation and justification by faith saying, "It is precisely here that a 'gospel culture' was reshaped into a 'salvation culture' or, better yet, 'justification culture'" (72).[b]

Today many teachers speaking about salvation are thinking primarily of justification by faith. But doing so is to make small what God intends to be big. Justification refers to a status; salvation is a whole new life, both now and forever (Rom. 5:8–11). The life of God continues to save us, empower us, and make our experience what John called "abundant" (John 10:10).[c]

After the Reformation, emphasis and discussion of the gospel shifted to narrow focus on people making decisions for Christ. The gospel became a simple collection of facts that speak to an individual: man is lost and in sin; salvation, regeneration, and remission of sin is only in Jesus. In other words, the gospel is about repentance and having your sins forgiven so you can gain entrance into heaven. You've probably seen salvation booklets or tracts used by millions to explain this plan of salvation to others.

[a] Scot McKnight, *The King Jesus Gospel*, revised edition (Grand Rapids: Zondervan, 2011).

[b] To delve deeper into the history, a complete reading of McKnight's book and further reading in church history will be required.

[c] Abundant is such a good word, found in King James and Revised Standard. The Greek word means "in excess."

FROM LUTHER TO BRIGHT

Scot McKnight, in his book *The King Jesus Gospel* (see Digging Deeper section), helpfully summarizes some of the history behind the reduction of the gospel.[13] In the West from the fourth century until the Reformation, it is difficult to find examples of the methods of evangelism known today. Most people came to faith through their families and in cultures dominated by the church and Christian kings. Nearly everyone in the West was baptized into the church at birth.

Prior to the Reformation, Christian theology was structured around the Apostle's Creed or focused more on the nature and holiness of God. With the Reformation came major confessions and other documents crafted with the doctrine of salvation as central. Yet this shift did not immediately affect how the gospel was preached. For example, you would be hard pressed to find a call to salvation or an "invitation" akin to those given by modern speakers in the sermons of Luther or Calvin. Even jumping ahead several generations to the sermons of Jonathan Edwards, George Whitefield, and John Wesley, invitations and calls to accept Christ as savior are still quite rare. Someone once asked George Whitefield how many conversions occurred in a meeting, and he reportedly answered, "I don't know. We should know more in six months."

McKnight marks the beginning of modern evangelism and the plan of salvation gospel with the revivalist preacher Charles Finney. While people tend to blame Finney for *all* of the problems with modern evangelism, in fairness Finney had fairly modest goals. He believed that if you created the right conditions, you could get people to come forward and make decisions. In his famous *Lectures on Revival*, he presented seven principles for how to accomplish this. In his sequel, *Reflections on Revival*, Finney moderated some of his views. But Finney represents the American spirit and our eagerness to get things done and produce results.

Finney was followed by men like D. L. Moody, Billy Sunday, and Billy Graham. My purpose here is not to discount the work of these men nor suggest that their evangelism was not pleasing to God. Yet we must acknowledge that these men greatly influenced how American culture has understood the gospel. Billy Graham, for example, was so persuasive and powerful in American church culture that what he preached literally *became* our gospel. We forget that what Billy Graham preached on television was only one part of what he knew the full gospel to be. He was a champion of discipleship, and his friend Robert Coleman, author of *The Master Plan of Discipleship*, was often responsible for follow-up after Graham's crusades.

However whether intentional or not, Graham's success in preaching had the practical effect of separating evangelism from discipleship by leaving many with the impression that the gospel did not require an ongoing lifestyle of repentance and discipleship. Many thought that the gospel was primarily about forgiveness of sins and entry into heaven, not about ongoing life transformation and the Lordship of Christ.

While Billy Graham was influential in popularizing a forgiveness-only gospel, it was largely *The Four Spiritual Laws* published in 1957 by Bill Bright, founder of Campus Crusade for Christ (now Cru), that made the reduction of the gospel popular in the American church. Please know that I love Bill Bright and spent a good deal of time with him over the years. In fact, my life will be forever changed because of his Christlikeness and passion to reach people for Christ. The fault here does not lie with Bright but in how his simplified gospel became the church's *de facto* gospel presentation. Here is a summary of Bright's four laws:

1. God loves you and offers a wonderful plan for your life.
2. Man is sinful and separated from God. Therefore, he cannot know and experience God's love and plan for his life.
3. Jesus Christ is God's only provision for man's sin. Through him you can know and experience God's love and plan for your life.
4. We must individually receive Jesus Christ as Savior and Lord; then we can know and experience God's love and plan for our lives.

This simple gospel presentation is designed to lead someone to a point of decision. While it says many things that are true and biblical, it is a plan of salvation, not the gospel itself. Certainly it is a tool to get someone started or begin a conversation, but it does not say enough to move a person beyond a decision. It doesn't speak of the expectation of discipleship and in fact makes discipleship optional.

A majority of those who make a decision through a tract or evangelistic meeting and pray the sinner's prayer don't decide to follow Jesus. The reason they don't decide is that discipleship is not connected to the decision they are asked to make. They assent to a statement of facts but do not commit to the costly road of discipleship.

The gospel we preach determines the disciples we produce. For much of the twentieth century, we have been conducting evangelism as a matter of conversion using a plan of salvation that is disconnected from discipleship. But you cannot have one without the other. A plan of salvation does not produce healthy disciples and is no way to build a church. In reality, this kind of preaching is deconstructing the church, and we must start correcting the practice now.

In closing, I want to say that I am not criticizing this practice from the outside. I was a willing participant, as were many in the American church. I was swept up in the river of American evangelistic efforts headed by Billy Graham and Bill Bright. Even with a genuine ambition to reach others, we are all products of our times. Again, my point is not to fix blame. I thank God for these great men and believe that lives were transformed through their work. Yet looking back and evaluating through the lens of Scripture, I must say that our well-intentioned efforts inadvertently reduced the gospel.

Why does it matter that we have "reduced the gospel to salvation and . . . salvation to personal forgiveness"?[14] Because when we make the end-goal of the gospel salvation, everything after conversion becomes optional. People say, "My status with God is settled. I'm his child, and I am going to spend eternity with him. I am loved and accepted unconditionally." They can say this, and yet it has no practical effect on the way they live. This should not be!

I realize that speaking against preaching a simple gospel that addresses our need to get to heaven is not popular. And to be clear, I believe there is a place for this type of presentation. But it should not be the norm for preaching because this reduction of the gospel is lethal to the church and its mission. Since our purpose is to be disciples and to make disciples, nothing matters more than our understanding of what it means to be saved. Jesus is counting disciples, not decisions. If we attempt to grow Christlike disciples with a flawed gospel, we will fail.

The Six Gospels We Preach Today

So what gospel is preached today? Well, actually several different gospels. Remember, the kind of gospel we believe and teach directly determines the kind of disciples produced. If we are not preaching the biblical gospel, we are preaching what Paul would call a different gospel.[15] A different gospel leads to a different Christ, a different church, a different Christian, and a different culture.

I believe that six gospels are prominently taught today, and each creates a different kind of disciple.

For example if you preach a consumer gospel that is focused on the religious goods and services available through Christ, you will create a consumer disciple. This kind of disciple is nearly useless to Christ and his work. Or if you teach a right gospel that is legalistically focused on measured performance, you will create a legalistic disciple.

Most churches *intend* to produce mature, reproducing disciples, but this is generally not happening in reality. The answer is clear. We are attempting

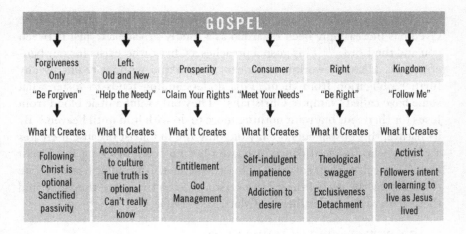

GOSPEL					
Forgiveness Only	Left: Old and New	Prosperity	Consumer	Right	Kingdom
"Be Forgiven"	"Help the Needy"	"Claim Your Rights"	"Meet Your Needs"	"Be Right"	"Follow Me"
What It Creates	What It Creates	What It Creates	What It Creates	What It Creates	What It Creates
Following Christ is optional Sanctified passivity	Accomodation to culture True truth is optional Can't really know	Entitlement God Management	Self-indulgent impatience Addiction to desire	Theological swagger Exclusiveness Detachment	Activist Followers intent on learning to live as Jesus lived

the impossible. We cannot create mature disciples from Christians who believe in a consumer gospel or a legalistic gospel—or any other gospel on the chart except the kingdom gospel. Trying to do so is like pushing a boulder uphill, *because we are trying to get people to act in Christlike ways without correcting what they truly believe.*

THE FORGIVENESS ONLY GOSPEL

The most common gospel preached today focuses almost exclusively on forgiveness. The forgiveness gospel is quite popular because it is simple, explains the basic requirements for getting your sins forgiven and gaining entrance into heaven, and is easy to publish on fliers, brochures, and booklets. The forgiveness gospel tends to equate faith with agreement to a set of religious facts. This decision to agree is typically followed by a prayer or some other protocol, after which a person is proclaimed a Christian forever more. What is wrong with this, you might ask?

The primary weakness of the forgiveness gospel is what it doesn't mention. Often this gospel covers the important topics of forgiveness and grace. But makes no mention of repentance, gives no invitation to follow Jesus, and does not discuss obedience to Jesus that Scripture teaches is required for a life of discipleship. The result in practical terms is what some have called the gospel of sin management. By it you manage your sin rather than having your life transformed. This gospel deals with a specific problem—God's judgment of our sin—by giving a specific solution—Jesus' death on the cross enables you to be forgiven. How do you benefit from this solution? You simply make the right decision, say the right words to make the right confession, and have the right experience.

As Dallas Willard adds, "For some time now the belief required to be saved has increasingly been regarded as a totally private act, 'just between you and the Lord.'"[16] This gospel preaches a Christ who exists for our benefit alone. His only work is to redeem humankind without requiring any further obligation from them. This understanding tends to foster what some have called "vampire Christians." They only want a little blood from Jesus for their sins but want nothing more to do with him until heaven.[17] By its nature, this gospel cuts off any ongoing life in Christ because it creates a person who has confidence in heaven but no stake in living for Christ now. Tragically, when so-called Christians like this stand at heaven's gate declaring by the gospel there is no reason to keep them out, they may find there is no reason to let them in (Matt. 7:22–24ff).

THE LEFT GOSPEL (LIBERALISM)

Listening to the bells of historic Riverside Church next to the Hudson in New York City, you might not know that John D. Rockefeller donated the landmark bell tower in memory of his mother. Over seventy-five years after its construction, the neo-gothic church stands as a bastion of liberalism and progressive thought, and *The New York Times* called it a "stronghold of activism and political debate." The church's first and most famous pastor, Harry Emerson Fosdick, popularized liberalism from the pulpit of Riverside with his marvelous elocution, and he graced the cover of *Time* magazine several times. Union Theological Seminary was once housed in the church, and the seminary and church still maintain a close relationship.

Dietrich Bonhoeffer took classes at Union Theological Seminary on a special fellowship in 1930–31. At the time, the school was too liberal for Bonhoeffer. Reinhold Niebuhr and Union's faculty were leading the way in deconstructing the Bible and forming a theological apologetic for liberalism.

The motive behind the liberal gospel is relevance. The fathers of liberalism were European teachers with names like Bultmann, Brunner, Tillich, and Nietzsche. Their goal was to make Christianity relevant for the scientific age, which meant removing the mystical and miraculous. They also reconceived the entire focus of salvation. No longer would the focus be on saving souls from hell but on the grander goal of transforming society through social justice.

Today we see the fruit of their efforts. In both Europe and the United States, most liberal churches have empty pews. Their once historic congregations have become shells of what they were. Some churches have become museums charging admission. The churches are dying, but sadly, the gospel of the old left that they preach is not.

This left gospel is tied up in liberal politics and ideology. In New York City, Riverside Church, Columbia University, and Union Theological Seminary form a physical and symbolic triangle of church, gown, and collar that reflects this leftist ideology. They stand for justice for all. But their gospel is empty of real hope because they have abandoned the heart of the true gospel: that Jesus is God incarnate, that he is alive and active today, and that his truth is the only thing about Christianity that is truly relevant. Reinhold Niebuhr's brother Richard described liberal Christianity well. "A God without wrath brought men without sin into a kingdom without judgment through the ministrations of a Christ without a cross."[18]

This is the gospel of the old left. The new left has made a different choice. Instead of deconstructing the Scriptures, they have deconstructed the gospel by creating a new hermeneutic. They ask questions of the biblical text and then give creative new interpretations. They reject once foundational teachings such as the exclusivity of Christ, the existence of hell, the sureness of judgment, and the definition of sin, especially as it relates to human sexuality. By the time they finished their reinterpretation, they determined that no one will go to hell except Hitler.

The new left's gospel is a laundry list of accommodations and capitulations to Western culture on the aspects of orthodox Christian teaching that Western culture finds objectionable. Though it lacks a cohesive theology, the new left gospel has been assimilated into traditional liberal groups and even found a home in more liturgical churches. It also hides quite nicely in evangelical groups who lack a strong doctrinal foundation and who don't ask a lot of hard questions. Most of the proponents of the new left are former evangelicals, and they find it comfortable to retain the trappings of evangelicalism, adding some bells and whistles here or there.

But the left gospel lacks the urgency of the biblical gospel. It diagnoses the problem incorrectly and offers the wrong solution. It declares that if no one is going to hell, relax; salvation is not all that urgent. What we must urgently address are not spiritual needs but the real needs of the poor and the hungry, those who suffer and those seeking justice. Liberalism is known for addressing these needs while neglecting the needs of the soul and for wanting people to act like disciples without making new disciples.

What should we make of the left gospel? Well, as George Orwell famously said, "Some ideas are so stupid only an intellectual could believe them."

THE PROSPERITY GOSPEL

While the left gospel falls largely outside the evangelical sphere, the prosperity gospel is the centerpiece of the fastest growing parts of the worldwide church. The prosperity gospel teaches that God guarantees health and financial wealth if we just have enough faith and practice some basic biblical principles. Much of this gospel is based on anecdotal theology, namely that we can expect to see the same miracles today that we read about in the Bible if we just pray for them. This approach tends to ignore the context of biblical passages and does not take into account the unfolding of redemptive history.

Some prosperity teachers emphasize that every Christian should expect physical health because it is part of atonement and essentially guaranteed to us by the blood of Christ. They tell stories of amazing healings and of God granting prosperity to people who have given their last dime to his work.

Many evangelicals have spoken out against the prosperity gospel.[19] What makes this gospel so insidious is that it obscures many of the genuine works of God. He does heal, and he does bless people financially, but when we believe that God is subject to our manipulations or has guaranteed a result if we do X, Y, and Z, we are falling prey to heresy.

The prosperity gospel also creates a spirit of entitlement and that we are empowered to speak a new reality into existence. We can name it and claim it, meaning we can manage God and get him to serve our agenda. Like the forgiveness only gospel, the prosperity gospel is a means of using God for our own ends. But worse, it enables false teachers to exploit the flock. Especially heartbreaking is how this gospel is flourishing in destitute countries. While leaders live in beautiful, luxurious homes, their congregants continue to live in abject poverty.

This false gospel tends to separate the exercise of spiritual power from spiritual maturity, which can be seen in full display when famous proponents fail morally. They face the occupational hazard of receiving more money and power than their character can handle. Being filled with the Holy Spirit does provide spiritual power to cope with the challenges we face. But this filling must also be allowed to nurture the growth of Christ within us and enable us to walk in the Spirit instead of the flesh.[20]

THE CONSUMER GOSPEL

The consumer gospel is also quite popular in the contemporary church. It promises to provide everything a person on the go needs: convenience, speed, sound-bite theology, and instant results. Since impatience is the besetting sin of America, the consumer gospel replaces the slow and difficult path of authentic spiritual maturity with methods and programs that give fast and easy results. As a bonus, our sins are taken off the table and the deeper life of discipleship is optional, something we can pursue if we have the time.

This gospel is easily enfolded into the waiting arms of our self-interest. And another scary thing about this gospel is that few people know they are preaching it. We are naturally attracted to a message of convenience. What is not to like when we can get forgiveness and heaven and still run our own lives? This gospel creates disciples who shop for a church until they find one that meets their needs. When something happens or is taught that they don't agree with or that causes them pain, they move on because they believe that pain, repentance, and difficulty are never God's will. Our enemy does not fear a gospel designed to meet our selfish needs.

But disciples cannot flourish if they have been trained to measure their spirituality by what they thought of the worship service. The real gospel is embodied in Jesus who lived in humility, submission, obedience, and sacrifice. His self-sacrificial love for others is the antithesis of the consumer gospel.

Dallas Willard said it well, "Why Christian faith has failed to transform the masses and to make a more just and peaceful world is because it has failed to transform the human character. The reason is that our gospel most often has not been accompanied by discipleship. Discipleship is not an essential part of Christianity today, in philosophy, program or curriculum."[21] Sadly, this is true of all the gospels presented thus far. But it is especially true for the consumer gospel because its goal is to satisfy the consumer's needs—to keep people happy and pleased. This gospel does not challenge or provoke and offers no prophetic word. It speaks words of comfort and assurance and offers tips and techniques for making the Bible relevant without calling us to die to self and suffer for others.

THE (RELIGIOUS) RIGHT GOSPEL

Just as theological liberalism has a left gospel, the conservative religious right has a right gospel. This gospel tends to prioritize correct doctrine, adherence to a rather narrow moral code, and the exclusiveness of truth. It advocates separation from the culture, although some forms seek to transform culture into having a Christian worldview. In general, the right gospel takes a defensive posture and sees the world as a battle ground where the good and right must take on the forces of evil—most often meaning liberal theology and left-of-center politics. This gospel tends to create disciples who lead a partitioned life that is separated from the people they are called to reach.

While the gospel of the right includes a call to discipleship, it emphasizes holding correct doctrine and staying in the right tribe. What matters in this life is knowing the right doctrines and having the right beliefs.

What you believe matters far more than anything you do. The right gospel's answer to the question of what constitutes saving faith is believing that Jesus and his sacrifice are sufficient to get you into heaven. So being saved is about going to heaven alone. Thus the right gospel narrows understanding of salvation to the next life and does not always show how Jesus and his way of life are relevant to this life.

In his critique of this gospel, Dallas Willard said, "It is left unexplained how it is possible that one can rely on Christ for the next life without doing so for this one, trust him for one's eternal destiny without trusting him for the things that relate to Christian life. Is this really possible? Surely it is not! Not within one life."[22] People are not saved because they are intellectually right. Haven't virtually all Christians found life in Christ before they were doctrinally right about most things? What matters is belief in the right person, Christ. If you have ever been a member of a right-gospel church, you know it's a tough place. There are a lot of dead people at the First Church of the Right because grace there is scarce, and life comes from grace.

THE KINGDOM GOSPEL

What we can call the kingdom gospel best captures the preaching of Jesus and the early church. This is the gospel first announced by John the Baptist: "Repent, for the kingdom of heaven is near" (Matt. 3:2). Jesus preached this gospel as well: "The kingdom of God is near. Repent and believe the good news!" (Mark 1:15). Right up to his ascension, Jesus' disciples expected him to establish the kingdom.[23] The early church also expected this throughout the thirty years after, right up to Paul's last days. "For the next two years, Paul lived in Rome at his own expense. He welcomed all who visited him, boldly proclaiming the Kingdom of God and teaching about the Lord Jesus Christ. And no one tried to stop him" (Acts 28:30–31 NLT). Jesus promised that this gospel of "the Good News about the Kingdom will be preached through the whole world, so that all nations will hear it; and then the end will come" (Matt. 24:14).

What is the kingdom gospel? *It is the proclamation of the rule and reign of Christ over all of life.* This good news began with his deliverance of ancient Israel and his promises to save human kind from the kingdom of darkness, despair, sin, and death through a Messiah. It is the announcement that the promised Messiah has come as Jesus, who is the long-expected king who will sit on God's throne. Through him we have access to eternal life, and we come under his rule by following him and becoming his disciples. From him we learn how to live our lives to the fullest. The good news is that it doesn't matter if we are Jew or Gentile, slave or free, male or female.

Jesus came for us. He lived for us, died for us, was raised from the dead for us, and will return for us and reconcile all things to himself. Those who follow him will live in his presence, under his rule. Those who reject him will eternally exist apart from his loving presence, which is called hell—the best God can do for those who don't like him or desire to be with him.

How do we enter this kingdom of God? Entrance has always been the same. Jesus has invited us to follow him, and he is the entrance to the kingdom. So start walking! We enter by accepting him as our rabbi and our king. We agree to learn from him by following his teaching, submitting to his direction, and praying for his help and provision. As we do, we grow to know him and love him, and through the work of the Holy Spirit, we start to become like him.

Mark Twain once said, "The two most important days in your life are the day you are born and the day you find out why."[24] The kingdom gospel tells us why we were born—for the kingdom of God. The kingdom is the realm of God's effective will, where his will is done, and it has arrived. His will is becoming a reality in the lives of those who follow Jesus and who make up his body, the church.

While the kingdom gospel speaks of forgiveness of sin and eternal life, it is about more than forgiveness, where we will go after we die, or how to get into heaven. It is about more than self-interest, and more than trying to create a better world that fits our political or religious perspectives. Unlike the aforementioned gospels, the kingdom gospel includes a call to self-denial. It is focused on giving ourselves for the sake of others rather than on becoming financially prosperous or satisfied religious consumers.

In short, the kingdom gospel calls us to discipleship. Being a disciple of Jesus, learning from him and submitting to his leading and his teaching, is the norm rather than the exception or the option. It calls us to become apprentices of Christ and learn from him how to live our life as though he were living it. If he were a plumber, what kind of plumber would he be? If he were an accountant, what kind of accountant would he be? This is the gospel for real life.

Dallas Willard speaks of the power of this gospel in his classic work, *The Divine Conspiracy*:

> If [Jesus] were to come today as he did then, he could carry out his mission through most any decent and useful occupation. He could be a clerk or accountant in a hardware store, a computer repairman, a banker, an editor, doctor, waiter, teacher, farmhand, lab technician, or construction worker. He could run a housecleaning service or repair automobiles.

In other words, if he were to come today he could very well do what you do. He could very well live in your apartment or house, hold down your job, have your education and life prospects, and live with your family, surroundings, and time. None of this would be the least hindrance to the eternal kind of life that was by his nature and becomes available to us through him. Our human life, it turns out is not destroyed by God's life but is fulfilled in it and in it alone.[25]

In other words, the kingdom gospel speaks to ordinary people and brings transformation to ordinary lives as people listen to and obey the teachings of Jesus. This is the gospel Jesus preached to ordinary people and related to their everyday experience. Yes, we need to remind people of the background story of Israel and include the apostles' teaching. But the heart of this gospel brings us to knowing, following, and obeying Jesus.

Three Characteristics of the Kingdom Gospel

I'd like to draw out three characteristics of the kingdom gospel to show why it is unique.

First, the kingdom of God grows by investing in a minority population. Jesus describes the kingdom of God through parables and claims that those who have spiritual insight will understand. Those who are not inclined to hear cannot understand. "For they look, but they don't really see. They hear, but they don't really listen or understand" (Matt. 13:13 NLT).

Using a parable of sowing seed, Jesus explained how the word of God receives a variety of responses. His audience was observant Jews who were expecting a political and military revolution but who were not inclined to believe a rural, untrained rabbi. So Jesus told them that around 50 percent of people who hear the message will not accept it. Another 25 percent will respond but be lackluster, nominal, or casual. But the good news is that a quarter of other hearers will respond and produce a harvest of their own, reproducing from a third to a hundred times as much.[26]

Jesus was explaining the nature of his work. The majority will not do anything with the message, but 25 percent will. And 25 percent is a lot; they will be enough to reproduce and grow. He was teaching them that this is where you focus, not on the 75 percent. This is where your work is; this is where you put your energy. He spent his time where it counted. The fact that he spent 90 percent of his time recorded in the gospels with these few men is evidence enough. As disciples of Jesus, we should not fret over the 75 percent; focus on the 25 percent and it will grow. This is how the kingdom works.

Second, the kingdom gospel teaches us to obey God by living intentionally in the middle of diversity and ambiguity. Jesus uses another parable to liken life in the kingdom to a farmer who planted some wheat, but then weeds grew up with the wheat. The wheat and weeds were so intermingled that the farmer couldn't pull the weeds without destroying the wheat. To get any harvest, the two had to be allowed to grow up side-by-side and then separated at harvest time when both were cut down. Jesus explains that the wheat plants are his followers and the weeds are the disciples of the enemy. In the end the angels will separate the two, and off to their respective abodes they will go, wheat to heaven and the weeds to life without God.[27]

Following Jesus requires us to live next to those who do not believe or follow our King. It also means we have an obligation to love them as Christ has modeled for us. We are not charged with determining and declaring who is in the kingdom and who is out. Only an omniscient being is able to do this, and we are clearly not qualified. We are simply to live and love, pray and tell, and some of those weeds will develop ears to hear. The strategy is that if we live among them, we have access. The institutional church does not have the same degree of access or opportunities that its members have every day.

Third, the kingdom gospel reminds us that growth is slow but will ultimately permeate everything. Jesus uses two illustrations to explain how his plan is in all of life, a mustard seed and yeast in bread. A mustard seed is small, but it grows so large that it can provide birds with shade and even a home. This illustration reminds us of many Christians who started with only a helping hand but went on to build orphanages and hospitals. The mustard plant is like the Red Cross, or Christians who help when disaster strikes, or those with a Christian legacy.

Yeast, of course, permeates an entire loaf. Jesus' point is that like yeast, his word spreads in a quiet way, but once it does, it cannot be stopped any more than yeast can be removed from a loaf to keep it from rising. Like yeast, the King's disciples must be worked into the middle of the community to have the greatest contact and impact.

How Do We Participate?

The kingdom gospel proclaims what God has done and is doing. But it also demands a response from us. We must enter the kingdom. How? By repenting, receiving forgiveness of our sin, and following Jesus. Then we are rescued from the domain of darkness and transferred into the *kingdom* of the beloved son (Col. 1:13). But we must become apprentices of Jesus and learn from him how to live our lives. "If you have a Christ without a kingdom, you don't have a Christ. And if you have a kingdom without Christ, you don't have the Kingdom of God."[28]

Jesus describes life in his kingdom as like a treasure that a man discovers.[29] When he realizes what it is worth, there is nothing he won't give up to have it. In a slightly different way, Jesus likens life in his kingdom to a precious pearl.[30] It is so valuable, you would sell everything to own it. The idea of a kingdom is somewhat foreign to our mental template today. Especially for those of us living in the United States, the idea of submitting in obedience to the authority of one sovereign ruler does not sit well with our cultural values. We can accept the idea of a personal relationship with someone. But we may reject the wider social and global implications of the kingdom gospel.

To keep the gospel from being reduced to our personal spiritual experience, we must accept it all. The world will not be shaken by people whose most radical thought is that they will get to heaven someday. Many religions posit some type of afterlife. But the kingdom gospel is unique because it makes global, universal claims. It proclaims that Christ offers all people entry into his kingdom and that all people, everywhere, at all times, must answer to him. Like yeast, his growth strategy is organic, permeating the entire loaf of bread. The kingdom gospel is a call to be a disciple of the King, to learn from him. Jesus' first disciples serve as our example. He asked them, "'Do you understand these things?'

"'Yes,' they said, 'we do.'

"Then he added, 'Every teacher of religious law who becomes a disciple in the Kingdom of Heaven is like a homeowner who brings from his storeroom new gems of truth as well as old'" (Matt. 13:51–52 NLT).

Under the instruction of the Messiah himself, King Jesus, these uneducated men gained new insight into the world, new gems of truth, and understood the old gems given in the Old Testament. They became religious teachers who could explain the whole gospel story from Genesis to Revelation. These disciples were counting on the immediate fulfillment of all the promises of the kingdom.[31] But Jesus told them that the time for the fulfillment was not yet. Then he commanded these trained teachers to be filled with his Spirit, become his witnesses, and take his message to the entire world.

THINK SAINTS, NOT STEEPLES

When we think of a kingdom, most of us think in terms of geography. We envision highways, mountains, deserts, cities, and farms. So when we think of God's kingdom, we tend to think of special spaces or properties set apart by God's people for worship, of buildings with a steeple or cross on the roof. We think that to enter God's kingdom, people must enter one of these spaces, and we believe God is most active and likely to work in this sacred space.

Yet this concept is too limiting and has largely failed us. Jesus' commission to his disciples is not to have people to come to us but for us to go to them. He told us to "Go into all the world and preach the Good News to everyone" (Mark 16:15 NLT). His focus is not buildings—it's people.

When you think of a region, state, or city, picture circular lights representing the disciples of Jesus. We can see these lights everywhere, in every domain of society. They are at city hall and in state capitals and in many homes, malls, and schools. In fact, we would have difficulty finding a place they are not stationed.

Some of these lights are flickering while others burn brightly. The job of our churches is to get those lights to all burn brightly, to activate the Christian population already in place. We do so by reminding, encouraging, and teaching these Christians to believe in and commit to the kingdom gospel. This commitment is best summarized by Jesus in two simple words: follow me.

Jesus' offer comes with the promise that he will teach us how to live the way God made us to live, in obedience to him. Teaching people to obey his commands is not only teaching them what they ought to do. It is also teaching them how to think, feel, and be. The teachings of Jesus speak to the intellect but also to the heart and imagination and give a new vision of reality that changes the way we relate to people, to God, and to the world.

Are Christians and Disciples the Same?

Given that for decades the church has separated discipleship from salvation, we need to ask the question: Are Christians and disciples the same? At first, this question seems to be about the meaning of words, but it is really about expectations. A disciple is a learner, a student of someone. The term implies action and obedience. The term Christian, however, tends to refer to a status or position. Early skeptics used it largely as a term of derision to describe followers of Jesus, and it occurs only three times in the New Testament.[32] For many, the primary requirement for being a Christian is agreement with Christian doctrine.

A Christian is expected to *be* something; a disciple is expected to *do* something. When Jesus invited people to follow him, he asked them to "come and see" (John 1:39 NLT), and then later to "come, follow me" (Matt. 4:19). When Jesus chose the twelve disciples, his invitation was to come and

43

be with him (Mark 3:13). These calls required an active response. The term *disciple* has a built-in expectation that *Christian* does not. Scottish writer George MacDonald explained this difference well: "Instead of asking yourself whether you believe or not, ask yourself whether you have this day done one thing because he said, do it, or once abstained because he said, do not do it. It is simply absurd to say you believe, or even want to believe in him if you do not do anything he tells you."[33]

We can biblically say that all who actively follow Jesus (disciples) also believe in him, and that their belief is sufficient to save them. Therefore I think it is safe to say that every disciple of Jesus is a Christian. But it is not always safe to assume that every person labeled Christian is a disciple, because a professing "Christian" who does not follow Jesus is no Christian at all. Some use the term "nominal Christian," meaning one who is Christian in name only, to describe such people. Let's take a closer look what makes the difference in the teachings of Jesus and Paul.

WHAT DOES JESUS TEACH?

When someone asked Jesus how to receive eternal life, Jesus answered in terms of repentance and discipleship: "Follow me and I will make you to become fishers of men."[34] When Jesus was asked, "What must I do to receive eternal life?" Jesus replied, "What does the law of Moses say? How do you read it?" The man answered, "You must love the Lord your God with all your heart, all your soul, all your strength, and all your mind. And love your neighbor as yourself." "Right!" Jesus told him, "Do this and you will live!"[35]

Jesus called upon people to act, to put away one set of behaviors and turn to another. Jesus linked faith in him with action. At the end of his most famous sermon, Jesus continued to build his case for a righteousness that exceeded that of the Pharisees preoccupation with behavioral markers: "Not everyone who calls out to me, 'Lord! Lord!' will enter the Kingdom of Heaven. Only those who actually do the will of my Father in heaven will enter. On judgment day many will say to me, 'Lord! Lord! We prophesied in your name and cast out demons in your name and performed many miracles in your name.' But I will reply, 'I never knew you, Get away from me, you who break God's laws.'"[36]

The Middle Eastern or Hebraic way of understanding belief always connects it to action. Even John's gospel, which is commonly thought of as a gospel of belief, largely relates the words and works of Jesus.[37] "Jesus said to the people who believed in him, 'You are truly my disciples if you remain faithful to my teachings. And you will know the truth, and the truth will set you free.'" John's gospel presents the verb "believe" more than thirty times, and in each case that belief is connected to eternal life. But again, we need to understand that this belief means more than mere agreement or intellectual assent; it includes an active response. In some cases, it means to abide or to be in fellowship with another: "Yes, I am the vine; you are the branches. Those who remain in me and I in them will produce much fruit. For apart from me you can do nothing. Anyone who does not remain in me is thrown away like a useless branch and withers. Such branches are gathered into a pile to be burned. But if you remain in me and my works remain in you, you may ask for anything you want, and it will be granted!"[38]

In his gospel, John tells us the history of Jesus, and in his epistles, John is a teacher of practical wisdom.

> We can be sure that we know him if we obey his command-ments. If someone claims, "I know God," but doesn't obey God's commandments, that person is a liar and is not living in the truth.
>
> —1 JOHN 2:3–4 NLT

> If anyone claims, "I am living in the light," but hates a fellow believer, that person is still living in darkness.
>
> —1 JOHN 2:9 NLT

> If someone has enough money to live well and sees a brother or sister in need, but shows no compassion—how can God's love be in that person?
>
> —1 JOHN 3:17 NLT

John confirms that being a believer means more than saying a prayer, reciting a creed, or being an expert on the teachings of Jesus. Believers love, serve, and help others, or they are not members of the community of Jesus' followers. Jesus' teachings on belief and actions are also connected to the final judgment. Consider John 5:26–30 for example: "Don't be so surprised! Indeed, the time is coming when all the dead in their graves will hear the voice of God's Son, and they will rise again. Those who have done good will rise to experience eternal life, and those who have continued in evil will rise to experience judgment. I can do nothing on my own. I judge as God tells me. Therefore, my judgment is just, because I carry out the will of the one who sent me, not my own will" (Matt. 7:21–23 NLT).

Both the Synoptic Gospels and the gospel of John teach us that belief embraces discipleship. In the synoptics, Jesus teaches a gospel of repent-ance, a call to follow and do. And John's gospel does the same, just in a different way. In both cases, following Jesus is a demonstration of what faith really is, a belief strong enough to create action.

JESUS AND PAUL

The apostle Paul clearly emphasizes that one becomes a Christian by faith and not by works of the law.[39] There is some discussion about what Paul meant by works of the law, but our immediate question is this: does Paul equate belief with being a disciple of Jesus?

Based on his own account in Galatians, Jesus taught Paul the gospel himself.[40] Paul also met with Jesus' disciples in Jerusalem, so he would have known about Jesus' command to follow him and to make disciples throughout the earth. Paul wrote Romans around the same time that the Synoptics were written. So he would have written Romans and Galatians with the knowledge of their clear call to discipleship. Paul was careful not to alter the gospel he was given to present to the Gentiles. He made it clear that he wasn't going to change his story or his gospel that agreed with what Jesus and the apostles taught, and that everyone should beware of the dangers of other gospels.[41]

Some have tried to drive a wedge between what they call Jesus' discipleship model of the gospel and Paul's transaction model. A helpful discussion on this topic is Robert Picirilli's *Discipleship: The Expression of Saving Faith*.[42] According to Picirilli, Paul's transactional model teaches that if people believe on Christ alone, they are saved. This model has been elevated in modern Christian culture to be the pristine and time-proven way to salvation. Its greatest support are Paul's letters to the Romans and Galatians, and its greatest champions are Protestant churches. The transaction model describes salvation as primarily a judicial decision that is settled for good. It follows the emphasis of the Protestant Reformation in putting justification by faith at the center. Justification is a key aspect of the gospel, but the weakness of the transactional model is that the gospel is preached without calls to discipleship and ongoing transformation.

This aberration is not what Paul taught. He spoke a great deal about the necessity of learning and training in the Christian life.[43] Paul was clear that his work was to teach and exhort everyone to grow up into maturity in Christ.[44] In Romans 12, we see Paul begin to emphasize this point, and what he describes is clearly discipleship: "And so dear brothers and sisters, I plead with you to give your bodies to God because of all he has done for you. Let them be a living and holy sacrifice—the kind he will find acceptable. This is truly the way to worship him. Don't copy the behavior and customs of this world, but let God transform you into a new person by changing the way you think. Then you will learn to know God's will for you, which is good and pleasing and perfect" (Rom. 12:1–2 NLT).

Paul also teaches accountability and covenantal living to help others—the rebellious and unruly, the timid, and the weak—to keep their commitments to God. "Brothers and sisters, we urge you to warn those who are lazy. Encourage those who are timid. Take tender care of those who are weak. Be patient with everyone" (1 Thess. 5:14 NLT). Paul also teaches the importance of teaching others to spread the gospel. "You have heard me teach things that have been confirmed by many reliable witnesses. Now teach these truths to other trustworthy people who will be able to pass them on to others" (2 Tim. 2:2 NLT).

Though they use different words and expressions, Paul teaches what Jesus teaches, that discipleship is essential for believers. When Paul teaches justification by faith alone in Christ alone, he is also teaching that the life of discipleship is the fruit of our salvation in Christ.

Two-Tiered System

What has been the result in our churches of dividing salvation and discipleship?

In recent years, Christians have been divided into two categories. At the core of this division is the idea that salvation has two parts. First, a person receives Christ as savior. Sometime later, they submit to him as Lord. This understanding has led to the existence of a two-tiered Christian population: those who are saved and just waiting for heaven and those who are serious about their faith.

Practically, this two-tiered system has created an expectation that many Christians will languish and never bear any fruit or multiply thirty, sixty, or hundred fold.[45] Because we expect this, we create programs around it. In fact, we may intentionally avoid urging people to study the Bible and act on their faith because these discipleship activities can be interpreted as legalism. We call our church members Christians but refrain from calling them disciples because that term refers to a deeper level of commitment. The biblical terms used to describe believers—followers, disciples, slaves, and servants of Christ—seem much too serious for many church-goers.

We need to reject this two-tiered system. We need to return to biblical labels and speak in biblical ways about the connection between conversion and discipleship and by doing so reclaim this lost understanding of salvation.

2

THE CALL

No one but Christ himself can call us to discipleship.
Discipleship in essence never consists in a decision for
this or that specific action; it is always a decision for
or against Jesus Christ.

—DIETRICH BONHOEFFER, *THE COST OF DISCIPLESHIP*

The call to follow Christ is the call to believe in Christ. When we answer the call and begin to follow, we are reborn and enabled by the Holy Spirit.

Every person longs for a life of purpose. A tax collector was sitting at his booth, and Jesus said to him, "Follow me and be my disciple" (Mark 2:14 NLT). Jesus didn't qualify his statement or try to persuade this tax collector. He gave a simple, unambiguous invitation: if you want to be with me and learn from me, follow me. Jesus didn't require a special or well-informed belief. He only required the tax collector Matthew, also called Levi, to stand up and get his legs moving.

Matthew got up and followed him. He would learn to believe, to obey, to worship, to evangelize, and to pray for others. That is what disciples do—they learn to become like their teacher. If I could say only one thing to a seeker, it would be this: *Follow Jesus, and he will teach you everything you will ever need to know.*

Jesus knew that the disciples he called had had little spiritual knowledge when he called them. The earliest stories of disciples following him are recorded in John.

> The following day John [the Baptist] was again standing with two of his disciples. As Jesus walked by, John looked at him and declared, "Look! There is the Lamb of God!" When John's two disciples heard this, they followed Jesus.

Jesus looked around and saw them following. "What do you want?" he asked them.

They replied, "Rabbi (which means "Teacher"), "where are you staying?"

"*Come and see*," he said. It was about four o'clock in the afternoon when they went with him to the place where he was staying, and they remained with him the rest of the day.

—JOHN 1:35–39 NLT, EMPHASIS ADDED

What began as four days of following this new teacher turned into four months and included several others who chose to follow. We will call this the Come and See period, the first of a fourfold call.[1] After discussions with Jesus, some of these men were convinced that he was indeed the Messiah. Jesus took them to the wedding in Cana, and they went to Jerusalem with him. They likely trembled at his confrontation with the religious leaders when he cleansed the Temple and likely wondered at his various encounters with needy people, particularly the Samaritan women. When she was returning with her fellow villagers, he issued a form of the great commission and sent them home to think it over. After four months together, he left them with this challenge: "My nourishment comes from doing the will of God, who sent me, and from finishing his work. You know the saying, 'Four months between planting and harvest.' But I say, wake up and look around. The fields are already ripe for harvest. The harvesters are paid good wages, and the fruit they harvest is people brought to eternal life. What joy awaits both the planter and the harvester alike! You know the saying, 'One plants and another harvests.' And it's true. I sent you to harvest where you didn't plant; others had already done the work, and now you will get to gather the harvest" (John 4:35–38 NLT).

What can we learn about the relationship between *process* and *belief* from these accounts of Jesus' teaching method? We see that his teaching is more relational than categorical and more process-oriented than transactional. Also, the accounts don't seem to contain a clearly recognizable experience that a modern recorder can point to as the moment of conversion. What is presented is a bit fuzzy and not easily packaged and reproduced. Curiously, Jesus ends this phase of teaching with a semi-formal charge to spread and reproduce the message. We can assume that like John the Baptist, Jesus was teaching his followers about repentance. We don't know exactly what his teaching contained in these early days, but we do know the core: "Follow me."

As Bonhoeffer reminds us, Jesus is the one who makes the call. His call in the Gospels was unconditional and often immediate and came from his inherent authority. Again, Bonhoeffer explains well, "Jesus is the Christ, and he has authority to call and to demand obedience to his word. Jesus calls to discipleship, not as a teacher and a role model, but as the Christ, the Son of God."[2] Bonhoeffer adds what these disciples of the Son of God are called to learn, "It is nothing other than being bound to Jesus Christ alone. This means completely breaking through anything preprogrammed, idealistic or legalistic. No further content is possible because Jesus is the only content. There is no other content besides Jesus. He himself is it."[3] In following Jesus, we learn how to live and what to do from him. All questions are answered not by memorizing content, but by daily experience of life together.

What about those who say no to Jesus? If a yes to Jesus puts someone in a position to learn from him how to believe, then a no means not being able to believe. Believers are called by Jesus to get them moving out of the state where they cannot believe. As long as Matthew stayed in his booth, or James and John in their fishing boat, they could not learn from Jesus in the way that would transform them. Saying no has real consequences.

Jesus Asks for More

What was Jesus asking from his followers? When he said, "Follow me," what did he expect them to do? Once again, the answer is more straight-forward than we might imagine. He asked them to leave their tax booth, drop their nets, and leave their home behind, and he implied that he would handle the rest. Jesus didn't ask for a creedal recital or a formal confession. He asked for a demonstration of just enough faith to begin walking with him.[4] The story of Peter and Andrew provides an illustration. "One day as Jesus was walking along the shore of the Sea of Galilee, he saw two brothers—Simon, also called Peter, and Andrew—throwing a net into the water, for they fished for a living. Jesus called out to them, 'Come, follow me, and I will show you how to fish for people!' And they left their nets at once and followed him" (Matt. 4:18–20 NLT).

Mark's account fills in the rest of the story. "A little farther up the shore Jesus saw Zebedee's sons, James and John, in a boat repairing their nets. He called them at once, and they followed him, leaving their father, Zebedee, in the boat with the hired men" (Mark 1:19–20 NLT). James and John may have already warned their father that this might happen, since they had probably already met Jesus. So Zebedee was left holding the nets, but he probably wasn't surprised. He knew the effect Jesus had on his sons. Yet regardless of what he thought, they left to follow Jesus.

Did leaving behind profession and family qualify as "saving faith"? The truth is that we don't have a nice, neat compartment into which we can place these men. We can't say they were Christians because no church or organization existed at this point. All we can say for sure is that they were followers of Jesus and had much to learn from him at this point.

Researcher Alan P. Stanley points out that making "a distinction between Jesus' call to conversion and His call to discipleship" is popular today. But Stanley argues that conversion and discipleship are essentially the same and that both can be seen as a process of which "conversion is merely one aspect and eternity is the completion."[5]

Disciples Come in All Shapes and Sizes

We should notice that Jesus calls different disciples to different roles, and during his life on earth, disciples followed him in different ways. In the come and see period of his first four months of ministry, Jesus collected more followers than the twelve who became closest to him. Many joined Jesus for a time, even though they may not have been personally invited. Other disciples were marginal or secret, like Nicodemus who came to Jesus under the cover of night and Joseph of Arimathea who was a secret disciple. But they were still considered disciples. Thousands of curious people gathered to hear Jesus teach and pretended to be disciples, but left when the teaching or situation became difficult.[6] True disciples are those who continue into the Come and Follow Me period.

After the Come and See period is the Come and Follow Me period, but this following has different forms for different disciples. While Jesus was on earth, many disciples left their jobs and homes and physically followed him around the countryside. But Jesus would sometimes tell followers to leave him or return home rather than join his band of disciples. For instance after the woman anointed his feet with perfume, he told her, "Your faith has saved you; go in peace" (Luke 7:50 NLT). He instructed a healed leper, "Stand up and go. Your faith has healed you" (Luke 17:19 NLT). When the delivered demoniac begged to go with him, Jesus said, "No, go home to your family, and tell them everything the Lord has done for you and how merciful he has been" (Mark 5:19 NLT).

Jesus left scores of people in small towns and villages behind him and did not invite them to physically follow him. However, they also became his disciples because they believed in him and followed his teachings in the ordinary terrain of life. These differences are helpful for us to remember, because the vast majority of those following Jesus—throughout history and today—is called to work ordinary jobs, raise families, and be lights in their communities rather than being called to leave home to become missionaries, pastors, or international aid workers.

Regardless of how people followed Jesus when he was on earth, walking with him day by day or following him from afar, the goal of their discipleship was the same. Jesus said, "The student who is fully trained will become like the teacher" (Luke 6:40 NLT). The goal of discipleship is to become like Jesus. All of his followers must learn from him how to live like him, and in doing so *become like him*. While the goal is the same, as Paul says being imitators of Christ (1 Cor. 11:1), disciples are called to different roles in the family of God.[7]

The first disciples had the unique historical role of taking over the ministry of Jesus after his ascension. So it was essential for Jesus to establish the paradigm for their training himself for them to use in training others. We should also use the process Jesus established to develop faith in his followers. During the Come and Follow Me stage, Jesus introduced his disciples to what I call the big curriculum. Jesus didn't have lecture notes to hand out, nor did he assign essays for his disciples to write. His classroom was the world, and he used the experiences of daily life to teach, test, and train his followers.

Let's look at some examples. Jesus and his disciples encountered a demon-possessed man who was so violent, everyone feared him. Yet Jesus healed him.[8] The disciples watched Jesus heal a number of people with incurable conditions, and as they journeyed with him from city to city, they observed and learned from his effective teaching in different cultures and to different groups of people. They also saw how Jesus dealt with his popularity and the demands of his ministry, and that even though he often had to hide under the cover of darkness to pray, he prayed continually.

During this time, Jesus had many conflicts with the religious leaders concerning the Sabbath. They took acceptation to his disciples picking grain on the Sabbath and his healing people on that sacred day. But Jesus confronted their legalism and taught, "The Sabbath was made to meet the needs of the people, and not people to meet the requirements of the Sabbath" (Mark 2:27 NLT). His disciples learned much from how Jesus confronted his critics and how he handled these situations. They also saw how these enemies plotted to kill Jesus and how he responded to these threats. They would all need this teaching and this model for their later ministries, as do Jesus' disciples today.

It is easy for us to overlook these contexts and how the disciples learned from Jesus. But we must never forget that the experiences of life shape our faith. The disciples following Jesus from place to place likely had to catch their breath often and were frequently astonished by what Jesus did and said—particularly when he challenged the status quo. The energy of the crowds and the miracles Jesus performed would have created an electric atmosphere that influenced their hearts and minds. Their faith was not the product of theoretical teaching alone. It was built on the craggy, rugged terrain of life where demons possessed people, others were in desperate need of healing, and large crowds pressed them from all sides attempting to just touch their leader. But through it all, Jesus showed his disciples an authority and power that is impossible to deny, and as their experiential knowledge of Father and Son increased, their faith grew stronger.[9]

Keep in mind learning in this relational and experiential way is not necessarily a steady process of increasingly stronger faith because we have moments of doubt. We build faith even as we struggle with doubts. In some ways it is helpful to think of doubt as the "rebar" for our faith. Francis Schaeffer, a great apologist of the last century, wrote that it took several months of living under the dark cloud of doubt to lead him to becoming an evangelist to intellectuals. His faith was tested by his doubts, and when faith survives the travail of doubt, it grows stronger.

However, not everyone will pass these tests. While Schaeffer's faith survived, atheistic theologian Paul Tillich's did not. Tillich spent his entire life trying to argue that God was the "ground of our being." But his gospel was empty of life and power, and it emptied the progressive, liberal churches of his day. After all, who wants to hear a gospel of hope that offers no hope? In the days of Jesus, the Pharisees also preached a message that lacked hope, which was one reason why the people were so desperate to learn from Jesus. He offered something that no one else could.

Constantly Learning

Jesus' teaching led to a variety of responses from his followers.[10] Sometimes they complained, "This is very hard to understand. How can anyone accept it?" (John 6:60 NLT). At other times, they resisted or were anxious about what he was teaching. "They didn't understand what he was saying, however, and they were afraid to ask him what he meant" (Mark 9:32 NLT). Sometimes they had no idea what Jesus was even talking about, and they would just throw up their hands. "Those who heard this said, 'Then who in the world can be saved?'" (Luke 18:26 NLT). Clearly they often lacked faith or insight to grasp the full meaning, causing Jesus to respond, "You faithless and corrupt people! How long must I be with you? How long must I put up with you?" (Matt. 17:17 NLT).

The first disciples didn't always measure up. But far from discouraging us, this is actually good news, because it shows that being a disciple isn't a state of perfection. Disciples are people in process who are still learning, still growing. They make mistakes. The first disciples help explain our own experience, and their stories provide comfort and encouragement because we know in the end, almost all of them produced great fruit. A developing faith is not a flawless faith. Discipleship is realistic, not idealistic.

Alan Stanley further explains the nuance of understanding discipleship as a process: "We must be careful to distinguish between the call to be a disciple and the reality of being a disciple. Since many define discipleship only as the conditions laid down by Jesus in the Gospels, it is not surprising that 'disciple' has become virtually synonymous with 'committed Christian.' Yet as we have seen this was patently not the case with the Twelve and neither is it the case for the rest of the NT."[11]

This leads to another statement we can make about discipleship: *it is the ongoing reality of anyone who desires to follow Christ*. Discipleship is not a one-size-fits-all process, and he doesn't churn out disciples every hour like a widget factory. He calls all of his disciples, and he lays out the same demands and requirements. But he makes allowances for our individual ways of learning and uses our entire lifetime to develop our faith.

We become disciples at conversion, when we answer the call of Christ to follow him. Then we spend the rest of our lives becoming in reality what he called us to be.

The General Call

When he was on earth, how did Jesus call people to follow him? Most often, he spoke a variety of general invitations to the crowds. He told them that following him meant self-denial, taking up a cross, and hating one's father and mother. This self-denial went so far as giving up life itself.[12] Jesus gave these invitations to anyone who would listen. He named no specific task, assignment, location, or time frame for any of this. This general invitation was just to take the first step and follow him.

Distinguishing between Jesus' general callings to the crowds and specific callings to individuals like Matthew and Peter is helpful, and we can learn much from studying each. Let's begin by looking at Jesus' descriptions of his discipleship that are true for all of his followers.

MATTHEW 28:18–20

The first of the general "calling" passages, words that apply to all followers of Jesus, is found near the end of Jesus' earthly ministry as he prepares for his ascension into heaven. The famous words of Matthew 28:18–20, commonly called the Great Commission: "I have been given all authority in heaven and on earth. Therefore, go and make disciples of all the nations, baptizing them in the name of the Father and the Son and the Holy Spirit. Teach these new disciples to obey all the commands I have given you. And be sure of this: I am with you always, even to the end of the age" (Matt. 28:18–20 NLT). Even though this passage was directly addressed to the first disciples, the church worldwide recognizes that it applies to every disciple. These verses are some of the most widely used on discipleship, for good reason. They are a sweeping summons to a worldwide revolution.

Jesus starts the command by informing his disciples, "I have been given all authority in heaven and on earth." Prior to his arrest, Jesus had prayed to the Father, "Glorify your Son so he can give glory back to you. For you have given him all authority over everyone" (John 17:1–2 NLT). This is a helpful reminder of the purpose underlying Jesus' work and teaching. Bringing glory to his Father was the centerpiece of his work since his baptism, and he brought glory to his Father by completing the work his Father had given him to do. In fact, it's fair to say that Jesus' only real concern was completing the task his Father asked him to do.

However in the same prayer recorded in John, Jesus told his Father how dear these men were to him: "I have revealed you to the ones you gave me from this world. They were always yours. You gave them to me, and they have kept your word. Now they know that everything I have is a gift from you, for I have passed on to them the message you gave me. They accepted it and know that I came from you and they believe you sent me. My prayer is not for the world, but for those you have given me. . . . Just as you sent me into the world, I am sending them into the world. . . . *I am praying not only for these disciples but also for all who will ever believe in me through their message*" (John 17:6–9, 18, 20 NLT, emphasis added).

It is clear that Jesus had the Great Commission in mind when he prayed this prayer, because it was not only for the first disciples but for every one of us who follow him. The Great Commission was not an afterthought; laying same charge to bring glory to the Father upon his disciples was the fulfillment of Jesus' prayer and his work. His plan was to pass this responsibility on through his disciples to all future disciples who will believe in him through their message. And with that responsibility he gave the authority to complete the task.

We should feel a special connection to Christ when we read these words, knowing that he prayed for us. His passion and care is so evident in this prayer that when I read it, I feel like I'm part of his team and that he is cheering me on just as he did his first disciples. I'm also reminded of a conversation I had with my friend Robert Coleman, author of *The Masterplan for Evangelism.* I asked him, "If you were to ask one question of the church in America, what would it be?"

He thought a moment and answered, "What is your excuse for not obeying Christ's commission to make disciples?" Coleman's question highlights the sad truth that many neglect this core responsibility that was on the heart of Christ the night before his crucifixion and on the day of his ascension. If you and I want to become serious disciples of Jesus, we cannot read these words and just opt out. We need to reflect and meditate on the driving passion of his heart, the task that motivated his prayers and mission. To be fair, I think many believers ignore their responsibility out of ignorance because leaders do not teach this expectation of following Jesus.

Jesus doesn't just give us a job to do. He gives us the authority to do it. Don't miss this, because it is key. With the call comes authority.[13] And this call is the centerpiece of what God has authorized every one of us to do. While there are many good projects that we can do, they will be judged either valid or void depending on their contribution to making disciples. I'm convinced that our religious activity is a waste of time if it is not obeying Christ's words here. We can start churches, build world mission organizations, lead universities, talk at conferences, and preach to large gatherings. But if we are not making disciples, we are neglecting this call that Jesus gives to each and every disciple. C. S. Lewis said it well, "The church exists for nothing else but to draw men into Christ, to make them little Christs. If they are not doing that, all the cathedrals, clergy, missions, sermons, even the Bible itself, are simply a waste of time. God became man for no other purpose."[14]

Of course, the fact that our churches are not making disciples means that one of the greatest fields for discipleship evangelism is our churches. The first step in a discipleship revolution is persuading church leaders that they must stop what they are doing, repent, and take on this new role. This step begins with a proactive reinterpretation of Scripture and a theological reformulation that is rooted in discipleship.

But some will ask, what about evangelism? When we make disciples, we inevitably engage in evangelism. The entire process of finding converts and baptizing them is part of the central task of making disciples. In fact, by re-evangelizing so-called Christians and nominal Christians and teaching them to choose the life of discipleship, we will set into motion people empowered to evangelize those outside of our churches.

We can and often do make evangelism the centerpiece. But apart from a vibrant culture of discipleship, we get sputtering, inconsistent, non-incarnational, and programmed evangelism. Such evangelism doesn't multiply disciples and sustain itself. We can't break down the cultural barriers to reach the people hidden behind the walls of society's divide because we don't have enough people out in the community. Since Jesus' Great Commission is to *every* nation and people group, we need to penetrate every domain of society with disciples who are trained and motivated.

Perhaps the easiest part of the commission is understanding that converts must be baptized. Much could be said theologically about baptism, but not within the scope of this discussion. Suffice it to say this probably means the generally accepted water baptism testifying that a person has decided to follow Jesus.

The commission tells us to, "Teach these new disciples to obey all the commands I have given you." Jesus' commands provide the curriculum for discipleship. They range from repenting of sin to loving one another. The idea that we should teach people to obey Christ's teachings is not controversial. But what is not as well understood and practiced is how Jesus taught. The majority of teaching today is formal presentation—preaching. But this is just one method Jesus employed to teach his disciples. And the solution is not to just add small groups. Sadly, many small groups lack any form of transformational, experiential learning because *they are simply smaller versions of a sermon experience where people passively learn information but do not change the way they actually live.*

The truth is that we can't teach in ways that change people unless we hold them accountable. We can pass along information, but we can't get at their real issues unless we develop relationships of trust, integrity, and challenging requirements with some teeth in them. If a person can't fail, if there is no risk involved, then it's not discipleship. We know that we can't teach a child to obey directives without structure, accountability, and a supportive relationship. Just saying something may work for a short time, but it is not a sustainable nor effective way of teaching.

The missing element in our discipleship is not a lack of teaching on missions, obedience, evangelism, or any other topic. *The omission is a lack of intentional apprenticeship rooted in a covenantal community*. A covenantal community is a group of like-minded people who want to learn from Jesus and one another how to live as if Jesus were living their life. To put it simply, if Jesus was a plumber, they want to know what kind of plumber he would be and be a plumber as he would. I think Malcolm Gladwell understood this point when he summarized John Wesley's teachings. "If you want to bring fundamental change to people's lives and behavior, a change that will persist and influence others, you will need to create a community around them where those new beliefs could be practiced, expressed, and nurtured."[15]

This dynamic has been the missing component in creating a successful discipleship culture. We'll speak more about the practical side of covenantal communities later. For now, my goal is just to point out that teaching people to obey is the key to discipleship, and doing so involves far more than communicating information. In a sense, we need to create a new monasticism as Dietrich Bonhoeffer advocated. But this new monasticism is not legalistic or moralistic like the old, nor is it a meritocracy. It is a community of grace and discipline.

Jesus finished his charge to his disciples with a solemn promise: "And be sure of this: I am with you always, even to the end of the age" (Matt. 28:20 NLT). These precious words are intended to encourage those who are "all in" with him and his project. Jesus's charge is called the *Great* Commission because its goal is *great*—to meet the deepest needs of the human race. Those needs are to know God, be reconciled to him, and enter eternal life as a follower of Jesus who belongs to him.

What is at stake in all of this? Only the quality of life and the eternal souls of billions of people. And what's the timetable to complete this commission? "The Good News about the Kingdom will be preached throughout the whole world, so that all the nations will hear it; and then the end will come" (Luke 15:17–19 NLT). We don't have unlimited time. That's why we need Jesus with us. It's a great task, and we need a great leader to complete it.

MARK 8:31–37

A second passage that speaks to the general call to discipleship is Mark 8:31–37. At first, Jesus only invited his most serious disciples. But then we are told that he broadened his message to the crowd (Mark 8:34).

What call is Jesus making here? In the preceding verses, Jesus had begun to tell his inner circle that he would soon die. "Then Jesus began to tell [his disciples] that the Son of Man must suffer many terrible things and be rejected by the elders, the leading priests, and the teachers of religious law" (Mark 8:31 NLT). Certainly his disciples had hoped his mission would be accepted by the rich and powerful. But now they were disturbed. Rather than becoming popular among the elite, they understand Jesus is calling them to embrace a life of rejection and hardship. They will never wear the finest robes and be invited to the best parties. Regardless of who we are, this is hard news to hear. But Jesus doesn't hide the truth. He tells his disciples that he will be killed, then in three days, he will rise again. I'm not sure the disciples understood that last part. After all, Jesus had said confusing things before.

Peter doesn't like this at all. He takes Jesus aside and begins to correct him for suggesting that he will suffer and die. "Jesus turned around and looked at his disciples, then reprimanded Peter. 'Get away from me Satan!' he said. 'You are seeing things merely from a human point of view, not from God's'" (Mark 8:33 NLT).

What do we learn about discipleship from this interaction? We learn that the human point of view is normal and understandable, even when it is completely wrong, and that it's our default mode unless we are given an alternative. Peter's response to Jesus should not surprise us. But Jesus would not just excuse Peter's behavior with a shrug. Like Peter, he expresses his convictions with strong emotion. Any close community will inevitably have misunderstandings and arguments, and conflict is often a part of learning.

The tension between desiring worldly acceptance and facing suffering is a fundamental struggle in discipleship. But Jesus makes the necessity of suffering explicit, "If any of you wants to be my follower, you must turn from your selfish ways, take up your cross, and follow me. If you try to hang on to your life, you will lose it. But if you give up your life for my sake and for the sake of the Good News, you will save it" (Mark 8:34–35 NLT). "Your selfish ways" gets to the crux of the matter. The crowd surrounding Jesus was interested in him. But they are primarily interested in what Jesus can do for them. He is a means to an end.

But Jesus' intimate followers are committed. He has taken them through a process, first inviting them to explore who he is when he said "come and see."[16] Then he invited them to "come and follow" and learn to be fishers of people.[17] They are now in the final months of his earthly life, and he breaks this bad news to them.

Though Jesus rebuked Peter, his message of suffering was for the other disciples as well and the crowds who were listening. He addresses everyone because his message is for every person: farmers, teachers, scribes and Pharisees, young and old, sick and well. We are all called to abandon our selfish ways and to embrace the alternative—a life of suffering and sacrifice.

In this context, Peter selfishly wanted the mission to go his way, which was different than what Jesus had just described. Peter, like many of us, had stars in his eyes. He was looking forward to the parades, the respectability, the high position he would attain as a disciple of the Messiah. Like many people, he was expecting a miracle-working Messiah who would reign over Israel and the world. People would bow to this Messiah and worship him, and there would be joy in the streets.

Instead, Jesus warned of death. "Don't hang onto your life," he says. "Give up your dreams and that narrative that warms your heart and charms your soul." Much of what Peter and the others thought would make them happy, solve their problems, and be the pay-off for all their sacrifice was now off the table. Their leader was going the way of shame—to execution on a cross—and they must have wondered what was going to happen to them when Jesus was gone.

Jesus tells his disciples to just release the future. Most of us are driven by selfish desire and as a result are captive to our emotions. Jesus tells us to lay our desires aside and take up the cross. He took up and suffered on his cross for his disciples, but his disciples have one as well. We are to willingly take up this symbol of suffering, shame in the eyes of the world, and death to selfish desires and follow him.

This passage also teaches us that any attempt to prevent Jesus from being the Christ is satanic. We cannot shape Christ the Messiah to fit our agenda. His work is to glorify the Father, not us. Again, Dietrich Bonhoeffer helps us, "When Satan enters the church he tries to pull the church away from the cross."[18] Jesus was only the Christ if he suffered. We show that we are truly his disciples when we are willing to suffer in following him. Taking up the cross means accepting all that accompanies obedience. Most often, taking up the cross means suffering rejection with Christ. We may be rejected for our beliefs and even shunned, despised, and deserted by people we thought loved us.

Taking up the cross also means that we need to do some rejecting, particularly of wrong ideas about discipleship and the values of Western culture. Many of us think that serious discipleship means a life of unpleasant struggle and suffering. We think that growing in holiness requires harsh discipline, long meetings, denial of enjoyment, and forgoing life's little pleasures. Unlike the early Christians, many of us have a fairly rich life with plenty to eat, clean water, and excellent sanitation. Daily life is free from violence, and we have the freedom to say what we want, be with the people we love, and access good medical care. For the most part, we live free of persecution. This good life makes cross bearing difficult for us to even envision.

We also live in a culture that encourages us to develop our entire lives around our selfish desires. Police cars loaded with officials may not be seeking to arrest us, but we must fight the cultural persecution of comfort. It is difficult to live in an opulent, privileged, and self-focused world and maintain holiness, integrity, and faithful service to Christ. We must reject the cultural voices and resist refined temptations designed to destroy our faith. For Satan, there is little strategic difference between killing disciples of Jesus and putting them out of action by encouraging them to feed their selfish desires. Either way he gets what he wants—less people making disciples.

He is happy if we pack out our churches with people who have no intention of following Jesus.

In Mark, Jesus continues his teaching with a question: "What do you benefit if you gain the whole world but lose your own soul? Is anything worth more than your soul?" (Mark 8:36–37 NLT). Our soul is the deepest part of us, and God integrates all parts of our being into our soul. Of all that we possess, it is the most precious, for it houses all that is eternal about us, even the seed of our future resurrection. Jesus tells us that instead of hanging onto our life, we should give it up and embrace our soul, which he can renew and restore.[19]

In other words, we should not sell our soul. Opera composer Johann Wolfgang von Goethe is famous for creating the character Faust who sells his most precious possession, his soul, to the devil in exchange for things that won't last. But Jesus warns us that we should sell our soul to only one person—him. He says, "If you give up your life for my sake and for the sake of the Good News, you will save it" (Mark 8:35 NLT). The truth about discipleship is that if we give up our life for Jesus, he will give it back to us.

Giving up our life is easier said than done because doing so requires powerful motivation. But Jesus offers us this motivation—his love for us. When we realize the value of our personal connection with him, we will willingly reject our own desires and the temptations of this world for him. Love for Jesus frees human beings from slavery to self and to death.

Death is the most serious problem we face. In the end, all religious pursuit and much of what we do is an attempt to escape death. But we can't stop it. Only Jesus has conquered death. In his general call, he offers hope of an eventual reality that is worth putting aside personal goals, ambitions, pleasures, and opportunities to experience. But to receive the eternal life Jesus promises his disciples, we must trust his word by faith, without tangible proof. Taken together, Matthew 28:18–20 and Mark 8:31–37 are good summaries of the general calling Christ gives to all disciples: to obedience and personal sacrifice through faith in his promises for the future and to make other disciples who will do the same. However, other passages add nuance to what Jesus says in Matthew and Mark.

OTHER GENERAL CALLING PASSAGES

In John 6:48–58, Jesus calls himself the "bread of life" and tells his disciples that to receive eternal life, they must eat his flesh and drink his blood (John 6:48, 54). Here he offers not just physical but spiritual nourishment. He offers a new identity and a new family that transcends our physical relationships. In Luke 14:26–33, Jesus requires anyone who follows to put him before self, family, and possessions. As in Mark, he calls his followers to self-sacrifice rooted in personal allegiance and devotion to him. In these and other passages, conversion to Christ is not just a simple agreement or a half-hearted mental assent. Those who truly receive the gospel become new people. And Jesus commissions these new people to spread the message and revolutionize the world.

When he announced the kingdom and in discussion with his critics, Jesus required anyone who followed him to repent.[20] In each case, repentance is the flipside of belief. The Greek word *metanoia*, translated repent, means to change your mind. Thus repentance means to turn around, or to change direction. Those who repent first admit that their life is on the wrong course and then commit to turn around 180 degrees and follow Jesus in obedience to his teaching. John the Baptist also commanded repentance and taught that true repentance should be seen in a person's life. "Prove by the way you live that you have repented of your sins and turned to God," he said (Luke 3:8 NLT). Repentance is more than mental assent or response of regret or sorrow. It is intentional action to obey that is evidenced in behavior.

The most famous illustration of repentance is Jesus' parable of the prodigal son. A son takes his share of the inheritance, leaves home, and squanders his money. After reaching rock bottom, he comes to a point of mental clarity and realizes that he should return to his father. "When he finally came to his senses, he said to himself, 'At home even the hired servants have food enough to spare, and here I am dying of hunger! I will go home to my father and say, "Father, I have sinned against both heaven and you, and I am no longer worthy of being called your son. Please take me on as a hired servant."' So he returned home to his father" (Luke 15:17–20 NLT).

The prodigal's thoughts illustrate repentance and true belief. He had insight into his sin; he saw the consequences of his wrong action and knew sin wasn't just an abstract thing. He acknowledged that he had wounded and disgraced his father, and he felt the guilt and shame of his actions. Then he proved that his repentance was true by his actions. He shows us that repentance involves the whole person. It begins in the heart—usually stimulated by pain caused by a wrong action—and leads to action.

Belief is the positive side of the conversion process. The kingdom gospel requires believing that Jesus is the King, which results in repentance and turning from running our own life to following him.

CALLING AND BELIEF IN JOHN

The importance of belief is evident in all of the Gospels, but in John it is clearly a dominant theme. In fact, John is sometimes referred to as the

Gospel of Belief because he uses the word "believe" more than thirty times.[21] What does John mean by belief? He is referring to faith in Jesus as the condition for acquiring eternal life. "But to all who believed him and accepted him, he gave the right to become children of God. They are reborn—not with a physical birth resulting from human passion or plan, but a birth that comes from God" (John 1:12–13 NLT).

In John 3:14–16, Jesus says that anyone who believes in him will receive eternal life. Of course, the opposite is true as well: "But anyone who does not believe in him has already been judged for not believing in God's one and only son" (John 3:18 NLT). "Anyone who doesn't obey the Son will never experience eternal life but remains under God's angry judgment" (John 3:36 NLT).

A lack of belief is connected with a lack of obedience. We could say, then, that believing *is* obeying, and not believing *is* disobeying. Again contrary to our modern, Western assumptions, belief and non-belief are more than just mental states. Belief and non-belief have corresponding, observable behaviors. Belief is evidenced by the obedience of giving of one's life to Christ. Thus belief is not just initial faith but of ongoing discipleship. Jesus' teaching in John supports this assertion. "Then many who heard him say these things believed in him. Jesus said to the people who believed in him, 'You are truly my disciples if you remain faithful to my teachings. And you will know the truth, and the truth will set you free'" (John 8:30–32 NLT).

What is freedom according to Jesus? People are free when they are faithful to his teachings. Being faithful is also required to know the truth. A glimpse of insight or a eureka moment is only helpful if it sets us on a course of action. We fully receive Jesus' truth when we act upon it, when our entire inner being knows it and is living it out.

Jesus in John employs several organic metaphors to describe the process of discipleship. He speaks of being born again of water and spirit (3:5). He is the bread of life that we can eat and never be hungry (6:35). He is living water that we can drink and have flow from within us (7:38). He is the light of the world, and when we walk by his light, we will not stumble (8:12). Jesus calls his followers his sheep who hear his voice, recognize him, and follow him (10:27). He also speaks directly of keeping his commands as evidence that we love him (14:21; 15:10). All of these passages illustrate the core idea—that belief involves the whole person and cannot be separated from behavior. What we understand (mentally) is organically connected to our response to that understanding, like a vine connected to its fruit. In fact, Jesus speaks of our relationship to him using this same metaphor.

I am the true grapevine and my Father is the gardener. He cuts off every branch of mine that doesn't produce fruit, and he prunes the branches that do bear fruit so they will produce even more. You have already been pruned and purified by the message I have given you. Remain in me and I will remain in you. For a branch cannot produce fruit if it is severed from the vine, and you cannot be fruitful unless you remain in me.

Yes, I am the vine; you are the branches. Those who remain in me, and I in them, will produce much fruit. For apart from me you can do nothing.

—JOHN 15:1–5 NLT

Belief leads to action. True belief described in John eats, drinks, walks, hears, follows, obeys, and bears fruit. If we are not acting on our belief, we do not have true faith.

Specific Callings

To this point, we have looked at how Jesus' call to discipleship is for everyone. In various ways, Jesus invites anyone who hears him to follow him, and he gives no specific time frames or tasks with a general call. The call was often issued to the crowds or groups of people.[22]

But there is another category of calls to follow Jesus that we find throughout the gospels. These are specific calls to particular people. A classic passage of a specific call is Mark 10:17–21. Jesus told a rich man, "Go, sell everything you have and give to the poor, and you will have treasure in heaven. Then come, follow me" (Mark 10:21).

When we read specific calls like this, we can forget that Jesus was speaking to an individual in a particular context. Many readers have assumed that through his command to this man, Jesus was telling all disciples to get rid of their possessions. But I argue that Jesus' purpose wasn't to convince the man to sell his goods but to get him to think about a level of faith and trust in Jesus that would enable him to leave it all behind and become a disciple. Jesus knows people's hearts and their particular idols and strongholds.[23] In this specific calling, he wasn't laying out a rule for all of us to give everything away. He was speaking to this man and his specific struggle. This call was what this man needed to do to follow Jesus wholeheartedly, but not necessarily what everyone else needs to do.

Consider another specific calling in Luke 9:59–60. Jesus invited a man to follow him. "The man agreed, but he said, 'Lord, first let me return home and bury my father'" (Luke 9:59 NLT). Jesus' answer sounds harsh to us: "Let the spiritually dead bury their own dead!" (Luke 9:60 NLT). But we don't hear his tone of voice or the inflection, nor can we see his body posture or facial expression. If 90 percent of communication is non-verbal as some claim, we read this story with a disadvantage. However, Jesus' answer addresses the heart issue. Either by cultural insight or special knowledge, he knew the man's provision was a dutifully sounding excuse. So Jesus told the man that his real duty is to follow him and preach about the kingdom of God. Yes, someday the man would need to bury his father. But this cultural requirement was not a good reason to forgo following Jesus. If his father died while the man was away, someone else could step in and do the service. Jesus was probing this man's commitment and showed that his decision wasn't really serious.

At this point, another person chimes in, "Yes, Lord, I will follow you, but first let me say good-bye to my family" (Luke 9:61 NLT). Jesus' response rings down through the ages: "Anyone who puts a hand to the plow and then looks back is not fit for the Kingdom of God" (Luke 9:62 NLT). This is one that seems aimed directly at me. In this case, Jesus teaches a wonderful general principle from his specific interaction with this man. Looking back and reflecting on past negative experiences can destroy our ability to respond positively in the present and future. Regret can plague our soul. A desire to clean up the past and make everything just right before moving forward can be a powerful barrier to discipleship. Jesus tells us not to look back at things we cannot change but instead look at what is before us and respond to the opportunities God places before us.

However similar to his response to the rich man (Mark 10:17–21), Jesus was not saying here that we must give up our family to follow him. Instead, he was revealing specific pressure points that can be barriers to obediently following him. Our responsibility as readers is to apply the general truths to ourselves. In other words, where are our pressure points? Does our love of comfort, money, or family keep us from obeying Jesus? Alan Stanley sums it up this way. "Where large crowds or the twelve are present, Jesus lays down general conditions for becoming a disciple. Yet when Jesus is addressing an individual, the conditions are specific and varied. In other words, Jesus personalized the cost of discipleship according to what He knew to be the priorities of a person's heart."[24] Jesus gets at the root of our disbelief and disobedience. What keeps us from following him?

Jesus pushes us to confront his radical and exclusive call to himself, a call that necessarily leads to obedience. The etymology of the word "radical" means "to get at the root." To be a radical, one must choose what is most important. Jesus warns those who claim to be disciples but do not obey him: "Not everyone who calls out to me, 'Lord! Lord!' will enter the Kingdom of Heaven. Only those who actually do the will of my Father in heaven will enter. On judgment day many will say to me, 'Lord! Lord! We prophesied in your name and cast out demons in your name and performed many miracles in your name.' But I will reply, 'I never knew you. Get away from me, you who break God's laws'" (Matt. 7:21–23 NLT).

Over the years, people have made many attempts to wiggle out of the implications of this scandalous passage. The works of these exegetical Houdinis are painful to read. Some reserve Jesus' harsh words for the Pharisees. After all, they are the villains, and Jesus uses them as a foil in the Sermon on the Mount. Others argue that the message was really for Jews living then, not for the church now, and that Jesus was speaking to a congregation living under the law, but we live under grace.

A similar interpretation is the most absurd of all. Jesus speaks of people casting out demons and doing miracles in his name, which are greater things than most Christians ever will. But the problem is that they were relying on these acts to save them when salvation is by faith. In other words, these people may have done great things in Jesus' name, but they were trying to earn their salvation by their actions. They were not true believers.

But what is the plain meaning in this story? I think Jesus is saying something that blows up our categories and makes us nervous. If we look back one more time, we will see that he tells us who will get into the kingdom of heaven and why—"not everyone who calls out to me. . . . Only those who actually do the will of my Father in heaven will enter" (Matt. 7:21 NLT).

In other words, not those who merely profess all the right things, nor those who seem to do lots of religious activities give evidence that God is working through their lives. Only those who have done his will produce this fruit and enter heaven. What is required to do God's will? Submission, humility, and learning from Jesus, who says he doesn't know us when we haven't been his follower. Remember when Jesus prayed to his Father, he said, "And this is the way to have eternal life—to know you, the only true God and Jesus Christ, the one you sent to earth" (John 17:3 NLT). Knowing him and being known by him is what matters most. And when we know God, we do his will. Again, this knowing is more than mere mental assent. It is belief made manifest in obedience and the actual behavior of following Jesus.

Today, we have cheapened what it means to know Jesus by linking belief to a formulaic prayer that magically imports us into relationship with him.

But he isn't looking for people who believe by a formula. He is looking for people who trust and obey him. The prayer that pleases Jesus is the living sacrifice of a submitted life.

Passages like Matthew 7:21–23 serve as a definite warning to nominal Christians and remind us that, for all our participation in Christian mission and activity, we cannot neglect the work of the heart and the transformative process of discipleship. These words of Jesus also warn those of us who tend to have a Pharisee's heart, a desire to perform for others and impress them, and who use Jesus for our own personal power and prestige. If we are honest, there is plenty of Pharisee in most of us.

At the same time, Jesus' words are comforting. His "not everyone" implies that many who call out will get in. A nervous tummy before God should not be a problem that keeps us up at night. But it can keep us on our toes, which is not a bad thing. Later in his ministry, Jesus taught that we should never assume that we've got everything figured out. There will be some surprises when we arrive in heaven. "Some who seem least important now will be the greatest then, and some who are the greatest now will be least important then" (Luke 13:30 NLT).

Expectations

A radical approach to reading difficult passages can be simply to understand their plain meaning! A plain meaning of Jesus' words in Matthew 7:21–23 about getting into heaven is merely that claiming to have done God's will is not valid—it is doing God's will that gets you in. Doing is the proof, the visible verification, that you do indeed know God. Consider another example. After telling his disciples he would soon die, Jesus told them that they need to die as well (Mark 8:35–37). Then he adds, "If anyone is ashamed of me and my message in these adulterous and sinful days, the Son of Man will be ashamed of that person when he returns in the glory of his Father with the holy angels. . . . I tell you the truth, some standing here right now will not die before they see the Kingdom of God arrive in great power!" (Mark 8:38–9:1 NLT).

What does Jesus mean here? The good news is that the kingdom of God has arrived in Jesus. It is in the lives of his disciples, and Peter, James, and John will personally experience it on the Mount of Transfiguration. That experience of eternal reality demonstrated that the kingdom was not of this world.

Essentially Jesus is saying to all of his disciples, "If you live for my kingdom in this evil world, as difficult as that proves to be, I will be proud of you when I return. But if you abandon me in disobedience, I will be ashamed of you." Some interpreters have exegeted away from Christians any shame, punishment, or meaningful judgment in the afterlife. I think this is a mistake. True Christians will not face eternal punishment, but Jesus will analyze our actions and evaluate our discipleship.[25] We all long to have Jesus say to us, "Well done, my good and faithful servant" (Matt. 25:21 NLT). I believe that Jesus is saying that if we are ashamed of him, we may not hear the well done we long for.

Jesus is describing a pattern of not behaving as a disciples should—of not speaking up and acting when one should. As Dietrich Bonhoeffer wrote, "Not to speak is to speak, not to act is to act." Paul also proclaimed that there should be no shame in our association with Christ, and he made that clear because shame and embarrassment is a real issue in an adulterous and evil generation.[26]

How does all this connect to our discipleship? We can say that Jesus preached a gospel of expectation. He *expects* us to repent and believe the good news. He *expects* us to be disciples and make disciples. He *expects* us to proudly represent him in this world regardless of the cost. He *expects* us to put aside our selfish ways through the power of the Holy Spirit and the practice of the same spiritual exercises he did. To be saved, to be converted, to have faith, and to believe is to answer his call and learn from him how to live our life as though Jesus were living it. These are Jesus' expectations. Being a disciple doesn't mean we are perfect in our obedience. But it does mean that we take Jesus and his expectations seriously.

3

SALVATION

> *Continue to work out your salvation with fear and trembling.*
>
> —PHILIPPIANS 2:12
>
> *The Consciousness of sin is the "conditio sine qua non" of Christianity.*
>
> —SØREN KIERKEGAARD,
> *THE JOURNALS OF SØREN KIEKEGAARD*
>
> *The only person who can be justified by grace alone is the man who has left all to follow Christ. Such a man knows that the call to discipleship is a gift of grace and that the call is inseparable from grace.*
>
> —DIETRICH BONHOEFFER,
> *THE COST OF DISCIPLESHIP*

Salvation is a big word that covers a great deal of territory. We talk about the need to be saved, or we ask people, are you saved? But what does that mean? What do we need to be saved from? Why do we need to be saved? While we inherently know that humankind is in a complex conundrum of trouble, the great minds of the world have been unable to come up with an answer.

God has provided an answer for us, but our churches also struggle with some of these basic questions. What are we saved from? What are we saved for? The popular understanding of salvation that dominates evangelical churches today has little connection with discipleship or life transformation. Dallas Willard once concluded, "Simply put, as now generally understood, being 'saved'—and hence being a Christian—has no conceptual or practical connection with such a transformation."[1] This is a serious problem. Our understanding of salvation has been divorced from a commitment to following Jesus. Discipleship is relegated to the status of optional, an add-on to the normal Christian life. Many Christians today believe that if we would like to live closer to Christ, we should be more godly people and live a life of peace, joy, and goodness. That's great. But in fact, people believe it is one of *several* options for those who are safe in the security of salvation. It is certainly not something for all Christians.

What is the motivation for becoming like Christ when doing so is no longer seen as a requirement for heaven? People believe that getting into heaven is simply a transaction based on acceptance of a doctrine, irrespective of any behavior change. Being saved is being delivered from the consequences of sin. But all too often being saved does not lead one to become the type of person who actually wants to be in heaven, let alone someone who would enjoy it.[2]

The truth is that if you are saved by acknowledging belief in a specific doctrine, and yet spend most of your life ignoring God's will and using him for your own purposes, you are unlikely to *want* to be in heaven. If a taste of God and a God-centered life is too much for you now, what will you do with a full dose of God forever? If you neither like God nor agree with him in the here and now, why do you think your desires will change with a change of scenery? And if your answer is that God will someday change you so you will like him and want to be with him, you beg the question—isn't loving him now a large part of being a follower of Jesus? And why should you do now what in the end God will do for you in an instant?

God wants willing disciples who love him and are eager to follow him. The notion that we can be saved without loving him is a plain falsehood.[3] Yet this notion is the central problem we face in contemporary Christianity. Many Christians claim to be saved but have no interest in the ways of God.

First Word of the Gospel

As we saw earlier, the gospel is the proclamation of God's good news. The first word of the gospel, which is often overlooked, is repentance. In the New Testament Gospels, the proclamation begins with John the Baptist "preaching a baptism of repentance for the forgiveness of sins" (Mark 1:4). While Jesus had his own nuances, the Gospels indicate that he continued the preaching tradition that John started. "Jesus went into Galilee, where he preached God's Good News. 'The time promised by God has come at last!' he announced. 'The kingdom of God is near! Repent of your sins and believe the Good News!'" (Mark 1:14–15 NLT). The first word of response to the good news that came from Jesus' mouth was repent.

However, the gospel begins as the story of God's relationship to his people Israel and relates the fulfillment of his promises to them to send a Messiah, a savior who would deliver them and through them bring his blessing to the nations. In Acts, we see this historical background in the preaching of the apostles and hear the prominence of the call to repentance in Peter's sermon at Pentecost.[4] Paul summarizes his message in his farewell to the Ephesian elders, "I have had one message for Jews and Greeks alike—the necessity of repenting from sin and turning to God, and of having faith in our Lord Jesus" (Acts 20:21 NLT). The gospel begins with a call to repent from sin and turn to God.

Though we discussed repentance in the last chapter, more on the topic here will be helpful. Wayne Grudem defines it as "heartfelt sorrow for sin, a renouncing of it, and a sincere commitment to forsake it and walk in obedience to Christ."[5] In other words, feeling sorry about an action does not qualify as repentance. Genuine repentance includes both an emotional component and a corresponding decision of the will to make an about-face turn in the right direction and to change behavior. Paul's second letter to the Corinthians speaks of the need for more than sadness over wrong doing. He says that he was not sorry for his first harsh letter because it created a productive sorrow in them: "Now I am glad I sent it, not because it hurt you, but *because the pain caused you to repent and change your ways*. It was the kind of sorrow God wants his people to have, so you were not harmed by us in any way. For the kind of sorrow God wants us *to experience leads us away from sin and results in salvation*. There's no regret for that kind of sorrow. But worldly sorrow, which lacks repentance, results in spiritual death" (2 Cor. 7:9–10 NLT, emphasis added).

As Paul clearly indicates here, repentance involves sorrow that leads us away from sin, and the process of leaving sin results in our salvation. So a necessary aspect of our salvation is real repentance from sin. While this repentance is an ongoing process, we can safely say there is no salvation when sin has not been forsaken.

This is what I mean when I say that the first word of the gospel is repentance. No one can decide to follow Jesus without repenting. Assent to a doctrinal truth is one thing; it is another to forsake sin. Grudem writes, "It is clearly contrary to the New Testament evidence to speak about the possibility of having true saving faith without having any repentance for sin. It is also contrary to the New Testament to speak about the possibility of someone accepting Christ "as Savior" but not "as Lord," if that means simply depending on him for salvation but not committing oneself to forsake sin and to be obedient to Christ from that point on."[6]

73

Yet some have argued that repentance is not required for salvation. Their objection is that repentance in conversion is a form of salvation by works.[7] If the work of actual behavioral change is required for salvation, then by this human effort we somehow contribute to our salvation. In addition, it is a genuine pastoral concern that we are adding a stumbling block or an unnecessary requirement to the gospel. While we may need to address some of this concern, we need to be wary of the alternative—a diluted gospel that promises forgiveness yet demands nothing from us. This diluted gospel preaches grace without calling us out of our willful slavery to sin. It speaks to one issue, not being punished for our sin, yet leaves out God's work with Israel, his law for living on earth, and his greater purposes in redemptive history. It also leaves out the call to discipleship.

I am convinced that the time has come for theologians, pastors, and church leaders to turn this ship around and preach a gospel that calls people to repent. Turning things around begins with the work of scriptural interpretation and theological reformulation that influences preaching in our churches and how we present the gospel to both believers and unbelievers. We should no longer offer invitations to give Jesus a try or make appeals to say a prayer with a promise of eternal life. It would be music to my ears to hear an evangelist say, "If you are not ready to turn away from your sins in your present life, then don't come forward; don't say this prayer. Instead, pray that God will bring you to a point where you realize that your current life is a dead end—then you will be ready to repent and follow Jesus."

On the other hand, when preaching the gospel, we need to avoid adding extra conditions or requiring certain behaviors as conditions for being saved. As soon as we do these things, the gospel ceases to be a gospel of grace. We must preach repentance not as something that earns us favor with God but as a response to the good news that God will reconcile us to himself through faith in Jesus. In this sense, repentance is not works but the obedience that accompanies faith. As Karl Barth says, "Obedience is simple when we do just what we are told—nothing more, nothing less, and nothing different."[8]

This recovery of the gospel will reshape our evangelism. Many of our current evangelistic efforts leave people in a dreamy fog of God's acceptance. They think they are all set for heaven, and until they die or Jesus returns, they are free to do what they want—nothing else is required. Instead of presenting salvation as the end of the road, we need to communicate that it is just the beginning. When Christ calls us, he saves us when we get up on our feet and follow him.

Beyond Justification

One of the key aspects of our salvation is justification, which simply means to be made right with God. It is a status granted to people who have repented of their sins and believed on Christ for salvation.[9] There is some discussion about the timing of justification—is it before repentance or after repentance, before we exercise our faith or after we exercise our faith? I won't try to settle that discussion here. Regardless of the timing, almost everyone agrees that those who place their faith in the work of Jesus and turn from their sin are declared righteous by God. We are given full status as forgiven sinners.

In addition to questions of timing is an ongoing theological debate about the depth and breath of justification. How does being made right with God relate to the ongoing process of sanctification, or actual growth in holiness? Some hold that we are saved by the work of Christ alone and that salvation has no connection to our personal growth in holiness. Our righteousness is imputed to us, or credited to us, apart from works. While this may be true, the practical effect is that we view sanctification as an addition that is separate from our justification.

On the other hand, some feel that we need to recover an understanding of the organic connection between justification and sanctification and have attempted to do this by emphasizing the doctrine of our union with Christ. They argue that being justified by Christ alone so changes our relationship with him that we inevitably bear the fruit of this change in a transformed life. Others hold that justification is both past and future and is less about personal acceptance and more about the acceptance of the covenant community. In this understanding, the final verdict on our life will be determined by the whole life we have lived.

I agree with N. T. Wright's argument about justification: "I am suggesting that the theology of St. Paul, the whole theology of St. Paul rather than the truncated and self-centered readings which have become endemic in Western thought, the towering and majestic theology of St. Paul which, when you even glimpse it, dazzles you like the morning sun rising over the sea, is urgently needed as the church faces the tasks of mission in tomorrow's dangerous world, and is not well served by the inward-looking soteriologies that tangle themselves up in a web of detached texts and secondary theories."[10]

Wright's challenge is that we make the mistake of reading Pauline soteriology back into the Gospels in such a way that we ignore the clear teaching that we will be judged by the life we lived. This is not to negate the theology of salvation by grace alone but does suggest that we need to take more seriously the connection between our acceptance before God and the necessity of living a transformed life.

As a student of Luther and Barth, Dietrich Bonhoeffer had much to say about the relationship of justification to sanctification in his famous book *The Cost of Discipleship.* Bonhoeffer's best friend and most authoritative biographer, Eberhard Bethge, tells what lay behind Bonhoeffer's words.

> He then tried to grasp that Reformed article of faith, justification, and sanctification within the single concept of discipleship. Yet with his key formula, "only the believer is obedient, and only those who are obedient believe," he did not mean to question the complete validity of Luther's *sola fide* and *sola gratia*, but to reassert their validity by restoring to them their concreteness here on earth. He emphatically and explicitly denied that this represented a betrayal or distortion in any way. Justification is an uncontested prerequisite that needs no amplification. On the contrary, the aim was to go beyond mere words, and rediscover and restore its preciousness. Discipleship is an interpretation of justification in which justification applies to the sinner, rather than the sin.[11]

I believe the meaning of justification is broader than just the forgiveness of sin and a special status with God. The narrowing of justification to forgiveness and status alone is to justify the sin rather than the sinner. Justification should also touch behavior and lead to a change in the person, and that is my point.

Rather than delve into complicated theological questions, I simply want to emphasize that wherever we land in this discussion, the church will be better served when our journey in Christ is seen as one seamless and organic conversion. Everything that happens in salvation—from repentance to faith to rebirth to justification and the ongoing process of sanctification—should be understood as a single, unified experience of discipleship. Justification explains how we are accepted by God and is a key part of this process, but it is not the end. When we talk about conversion to Christ, we need to show that the call to follow Jesus is an invitation to a new reality, to a new relationship that pulsates with life. I appreciate the balance in this statement by Donald Bloesch, "Calvin and Luther held that justification, although essentially the verdict of divine acquittal, leads to man's inner renewal by the Spirit of God. For Calvin justification and sanctification are to be distinguished, but they must never be separated. Justification as divine acquittal is extrinsic to man, but the fruits of this justification are then applied to man by the Holy Spirit."[12]

While many agree with Bloesch, this organic connection between justification and sanctification is not always evident in our churches. The language of gospel presentations and the structure of programs often indicate that our concept of salvation is limited to the forgiveness of sins. To be saved means our sins are forgiven and we will be going to heaven. Issue settled. Thus most evangelistic messages focus on the solution to our sin problem. Since justification solves that problem, many don't see their need for God after their sin is dealt with. They think that by believing the right facts and saying the right prayer, they completed the transaction. The success of mission work and evangelistic ministry is measured by how many people make the decision. Once a person is in the fold—saved—the most important work is done. This plan of salvation effectively short-circuits Jesus' call to be his disciple by reducing it to a plan to solve a sin problem.

Once this transaction with God is complete, some believers move on to the optional work of being a Christian. This work includes volunteering at church, going on mission trips, stewarding finances, and attending a Bible study. But this way of being a Christian isn't related to the gospel—it is a grocery list of "to dos" that fill time while we wait for heaven. If our passion begins to wane, we find a couple of Bible verses that assure us we can't lose what we think we have.

How has our understanding of the biblical gospel been reduced to a plan to make a personal transaction with God? One way is by removing our understanding of grace from its relational context. We are rightly taught the foundational truth that salvation is by grace through faith. Unfortunately, in an effort to emphasize that salvation is by unmerited grace, we describe faith in Christ not as something we do—an expression of our dependence and trust in God and his promises—but as something God does for us. But this goes beyond understanding grace as unmerited favor because it sees the entire process of salvation as something exterior—an event that involves God in heaven transferring merit from Christ to our account.[13] This view leads to the pervasive passivity we see among Christians today.

Karl Barth, who believed that justification is accomplished objectively and entirely apart from humans, typifies this view. Barth taught that humanity's conversion had already taken place in Jesus on the cross. Jesus was the representative, and in his death and resurrection, humanity's regeneration and conversion were accomplished. This understanding led Barth to believe that attempting to convert people was superfluous because the work of salvation had already been done. There was nothing a person needed to do, and no response was required. Repentance? Faith? Not needed. Jesus has already done everything necessary.

COMPLETE, JUST NEEDS SERVICING

Though Barth represents the extreme view of cleaving the organic connection between justification and sanctification, the idea of this division plays out in subtle ways. Many churches teach that since we are saved, all we need to do in the remaining days of our Christian life is service our account with God. Some traditions nourish and refresh this account through the sacraments. These practices provide regular maintenance via confession of sin and taking in the flesh and blood of Christ as spiritual food. Some churches require participating in the sacraments as part of ongoing discipleship, but this participation is not generally considered a matter of salvation. Instead, it falls into that mystical, foggy place of spiritual nourishment.

In less liturgical settings, the sacraments are seen as a memorial or a remembrance of Christ. Participating in them isn't essential for continued discipleship and typically happens less frequently. In place of the sacraments are other practices designed to service the account including retreats or seasons of dedication to spiritual disciplines. Other traditions emphasize Bible reading, prayer, and regular participation in a small group.

Some traditions teach that gratitude for forgiveness leads to obedience and transformation, which is at least an attempt to draw a connection between justification and sanctification. The thinking is that because we have been infused with new life, our heart will naturally respond to God's will in a new way. While this may happen at times, actual transformation seems to be no higher in these groups.

My point here is not to point out the flaws of a particular tradition. Every theological camp, from the Reformed to the Wesleyans and cessationists to charismatics, can fall into the error of dividing justification and sanctification. We have all been guilty in various ways of narrowing our understanding of the gospel, salvation, and justification to a limited view. We rightly emphasize the forgiveness of sins, but we divorce conversion to Christ from the biblical call to be his disciple. For this reason, people do not see discipleship as a natural part of salvation. Once again, Dallas Willard sums up the problem well. "Adherence to this view of salvation is what accounts for the transformation of Evangelical Christianity into a version of nominal Christianity over the course of the 20th century, even though, historically, Evangelicalism has strongly opposed nominal Christianity."[14]

In other words, the gospel we have been preaching is having a self-defeating effect on the church. So what is the alternative? Let's look at several texts that speak of salvation and see how the Bible maintains the organic connection between conversion and discipleship.

What Does It Mean to be Saved?

The Greek word σωζω, translated "saved," and its synonyms primarily mean being delivered from something or someone. But salvation is not just a past experience. The Bible speaks of salvation as a present and future reality. While the modern, Western church primarily views salvation as a past event that begins a Christian life, the New Testament speaks of salvation as both an event and a process—a journey. This journey begins with repentance and belief that are followed by a lifetime of discipleship. The ongoing discipleship journey leads to greater sanctification, and in the end, we experience complete transformation in the eternal state. Salvation, then, is much closer to the process of discipleship than our typical gospel presentations depict. The following section breaks down several elements of salvation and sets them into the lifestyle of discipleship.

In Ephesians 2:1–5, Paul speaks of our salvation. "Once you were dead because of your disobedience and your many sins. You used to live in sin, *just like the rest of the world*, obeying the devil—the commander of the powers of the unseen world. He is the spirit at work in the hearts of those who refuse to obey God. *All of us used to live that way*, following the passionate desires and inclinations of our sinful nature. By our very nature we were subject to God's anger, *just like everyone else*" (Eph. 2:1–3 NLT, emphasis added).

I have highlighted three phrases in this passage that show sin is a problem that affects each one of us. Every person begins life in the grip of sin and under the control of the commander of the unseen world, the devil. We are dead because of our sin, and in our spiritual deadness we follow the desires of our sinful nature. For God to rid the world of sin, he must address its presence in each of us. One way to destroy sin is by destroying the world, which God did in the days of Noah. But it did not solve the problem because he saved sinful humans. We are still in the line of fire, or as Paul writes, "By our very nature we were subject to God's anger." Not only do we need to be forgiven of our evil deeds and cleansed from our desire to do evil, we must also face the consequences of our sin. Humanity is currently slated for destruction, along with all that is evil.

In the midst of this depressing situation, Paul explains how God saves us. "But God is so rich in mercy, and he loved us so much, that even though we were dead because of our sins, he gave us life when he raised Christ from the dead" (Eph. 2:4–5 NLT). Paul introduces alternatives to death, anger, wrath, and sin—a life of mercy, love, grace, and salvation. That God shows mercy means that saving us and forgiving our sin are not something we should expect and certainly not what we deserve. By all rights, God should punish us for violating his house rules. Instead, he shows us mercy. Though all people are sinners who deserve punishment, God has offered an alternative to punishment—an act of mercy whereby sin is paid for by another. Christ paid the price, and God raised him from the dead as Exhibit A, proof of his ability to solve the death problem. And he extends his offer of forgiveness and salvation to everyone.

In addition, Paul explains, "It is only by God's grace that you have been saved!" (Eph. 2:5 NLT). The fact that our salvation is by grace means that we are incapable of saving ourselves. What we need to remedy our sin problem is more than better conduct or trying harder. Given the right motive, we know that people can improve their behavior. Rehab clinics and peer pressure tell us that behavior modification is within the range of human capabilities. But it is one thing to change outward behavior and another thing to transform motives so they are no longer selfish and self-centered. The Bible is clear that we do not have the resources to change ourselves in this way and require someone greater than ourselves to do it.

At this point, some will protest that none of us chose to live, and being sinful is not a choice we have willingly made. It is the result of our ancestors, Adam and Eve. Some say, "I never asked for this! And now you tell me I should be grateful that you are going to save me from a fate that I am responsible for but never freely chose?" But this response reveals our tendency to think of ourselves as individuals, apart from relationship to others. The reality is that our accountability for sin is like being born into a family. We may not like our family, but it's our family. We didn't get to choose the context into which we would enter this world. That's just not something we get to control or decide.

We can protest. But in the end, we must admit that Paul's description of the problem is an accurate reflection of human experience. Though we may not understand why and how, we are accountable for the actions of our sinful nature and stand in need of God's mercy and grace. We need to be saved from both our sinful nature and the consequences of the sins we commit, and from both the sinful world we live in and our personal slavery to the devil. These are what we must be saved *from*. But *how* are we saved?

How Are We Saved?

In Ephesians 2:8–9, Paul continues his discussion of salvation. "God saved you by his grace when you believed. And you can't take credit for this; it is a gift from God. Salvation is not a reward for the good things we have done, so none of us can boast about it" (NLT).

In the Greek, Ephesians 2:8 is, Τη γαρ χαριτι εστε σεσωσμενοι δια πιστεως. "For by grace you are saved through faith" is a close rendering. What stands out in this verse are three key words: grace, saved, and faith. Grace, as we saw earlier, speaks of the motive behind God's work of salvation. Some call it his unmerited favor. The Greek word means *gift* in this context. Where mercy is not giving us what we deserve—punishment for our sin—grace is granting us something that we don't deserve and that cannot be earned.

So, we find ourselves in a real predicament, in a place of death, deserving God's wrath and condemnation. We can only be saved from this situation by God's mercy. But we have nothing to offer God in return. So how does God respond? He offers us a gift—his grace, which accounts us as righteous in his sight, adopted us into his family, and granted promises for the future on the basis of Christ's work. Grace is God doing for us what we cannot do for ourselves.[15] All of God's blessing are ours, freely given to us through Christ. They cannot be earned. They can only be received by faith.

Grace is more than just a transaction with God, like making a withdrawal from his ATM. It is a change in the status of our relationship with him. When we limit grace to the salvation act, a one-time-moment when a person "makes a decision," we limit our understanding of grace. Why do we do this?

One reason is our response to liberal teachings that devalue salvation as a gift of God's grace. When we forget that salvation is not something we deserve or earn, we can easily fall into the trap of trying to justify ourselves through good works or efforts in social justice. In the twentieth century, liberal theologians hollowed out the gospel by denying the deity of Christ and questioning the validity of the Gospels. Then they bowed to the goddess of relevance and redefined the Great Commission as a call to social justice. In response, fundamentalists and eventually evangelicals tried to downplay any human effort in salvation. Churches and preachers began to emphasize making a decision and having an experience. But this response was based on a narrow view of justification and was often divorced from any ongoing discipleship.

Another reason we limit grace is our tendency to be pragmatic in ministry. Evangelical culture wanted a yardstick for measuring evangelistic efforts and validating the effectiveness of methods. When we are seeking large numbers, we naturally want to close the door on a process and count noses, because it is easier to count decisions than evidence of character transformation. So churches have tended to prioritize measurable responses over messy issues of character. Also, people want assurance that they are in the fold. So pastors have a tendency to downplay tough calls to discipleship in favor of easy assurance.

I also believe that some of the Greek verb tenses and syntax in New Testament passages like Ephesians 2 have been overemphasized. In several contexts, the Greek word translated "saved" is a perfect passive participle, which means that salvation was an action completed in the past with results that continue on indefinitely into the future. Though these ongoing results should be emphasized, the practical impact of this understanding of salvation as a past event has been to forget that it is an ongoing reality in our lives. In summary, the thinking is generally that if grace is God doing for us what we cannot do for ourselves, what more is left for us to do?

Faith: Salvation's Instrument

If grace is God's motive in saving us, faith is the instrument by which we are saved. Secularists see faith in opposition to reason, so they consider it an irrational alternative for weak minds. Christians rightly reject this simplistic and unbiblical view and describe faith as rational, relational, and active. Faith is trusting in a person. That it is based on someone who is unseen does not make it irrational. In fact, faith is related to hope and can be quite rational.[16]

Also far from being passive, faith requires an active choice to make a commitment as well as ongoing actions. Faith that does not lead to activity, decisions and behaviors based on our commitment, is not a living faith. James refers to this type of faith as "dead"—merely intellectual assent (James 2:14–24). The ability to have faith is a gift, but it is a gift that must be used. We must exercise this gift by acting on it and with it, not let it sit passively on the shelf.

Consider Jesus' call of Matthew.[17] It was a gift to be called by Jesus— Matthew had done nothing to deserve it. Yet he had to trust Jesus and respond by standing on his feet and leaving his tax booth. Matthew showed that his commitment to Jesus was real by inviting Jesus to his house and introducing him to his friends. We can say that Matthew had faith in Jesus *because* we saw Matthew do something in response. His response was more than a tip of the hat; he fed Jesus' followers and gathered others who needed him.

However we need to remember that without this gift of faith from God, human beings do not have the ability to believe in God nor act in faith.[18] This is made clear throughout the New Testament, especially in Paul's letter to the Romans.[19] Faith is the ability and the desire to believe what God has said. It is the ability to see the world in God's way and to act upon this new perspective.

Therefore, faith cannot be reduced to an intellectual assent, as is common today. You may hear a person say, "Yes, I believe in Christ and his teachings. I just don't practice them." But such a statement reveals that the speaker does not understand or have faith. Hebrews 11 destroys this false construct. It begins with a definition: "Faith is the confidence that what we hope for will actually happen; it gives us assurance about things we cannot see" (Heb. 11:1 NLT). While this verse is commonly quoted and referenced, it is the next statement that I find most interesting. "Through their faith, the people in days of old earned a good reputation" (Heb. 11:2 NLT). The writer then launches into a long account of heroic acts that demonstrate the living, active nature of faith. He begins with Abel and includes Noah, Abraham, and other luminaries and even several unnamed people of Israel. He describes the suffering, humiliation, and executions of those who believed so strongly, they were willing to die for their faith. The writer calls them as "too good for this world" (Heb. 11:38 NLT). Notice that no non-practicing believer is among their number, because there is simply no such thing as an inactive faith. Faith always leads to action.

Tucked away in this chapter is a short but penetrating statement. Speaking of Enoch, the writer says: "For before he was taken up, he was known as a person who pleased God. And *it is impossible to please God without faith*. Anyone who wants to come to him must believe that God exists and that he rewards those who sincerely seek him" (Heb. 11:5–6 NLT, emphasis added). As Dietrich Bonhoeffer once said, "Faith is only real in obedience."[20] It is not a mystical experience residing in the soul. Faith is a force, alive and vibrant that is revealed in action.

All of this leads us to a frightening question. What do people have that they think is faith if it is not? To explore this question, we must consider a text in Martin Luther's least favorite letter, the epistle of James.

Having a Saving Faith

In his short letter, James addresses the topic of faith and its relationship to works. At one point, he asks a question that is quite relevant to our discussion: "What good is it, dear brothers and sisters if you say you have faith but don't show it by your actions? *Can that kind of faith save anyone?*" (James 2:14 NLT, emphasis added). The obvious answer to his question is no. Faith that never does anything is not a saving faith. James continues to illustrate his point by employing the example of helping those who are cold, hungry, and in need. A so-called faith that does not help the needy is "dead and useless" (James 2:15–17). True faith is made visible by the works it does. "I will show you my faith by my good deeds" (James 2:18 NLT). Faith is only real when it manifests itself in obedience to God and love toward others. James even ridicules an inactive, dead faith by comparing it to what demons believe. "You say you have faith, for you believe that there is one God. Good for you! Even the demons believe this, and they tremble in terror. How foolish! Can't you see that faith without good deeds is useless?" (James 2:19–20 NLT).

Martin Luther once said, "Christians are saved by faith alone but not by faith that is alone." He meant that true faith would necessarily produce works and joked that while people were arguing whether faith produced works, those with true faith were in the streets doing good works. In this Luther followed the consensus of the Patristic Fathers.[21] Augustine made sure to link faith to works in his commentary on Jesus' words in John 15:5, "Apart from me you can do nothing."[22] Augustine's point was that real faith is not passive but active. Real faith moves people; action is faith's primary property.

In his letter, James concludes by explaining *how* faith works, using Abraham as his example. Abraham confirmed he had faith when he was willing to sacrifice Isaac on the altar. James writes: "You see, his faith and his actions worked together. His actions made his faith complete" (James 2:22 NLT).

So we can conclude with James and the church founders that a faith that saves is a faith that acts. Yet we must understand this truth in light of Paul's words, "Salvation is not a reward for the good things we have done, so none of us can boast about it" (Eph. 2:9 NLT). Recall that the essence of the good news of salvation is that it is a gift. Grace cannot be earned; salvation cannot be attained without God's mercy. "For the wages of sin is death, but the *free gift* of God is eternal life through Christ Jesus our Lord" (Rom. 6:23 NLT, emphasis added).

So whatever we conclude about the relationship between faith and works, we know that works even done in faith will not earn our salvation nor earn us merit before God. I believe that the best way to reconcile faith and works is to say that we are saved by faith, but this faith must be one that acts—a living, active faith that expresses itself in love. If it does not, we are not saved. As James reminds us, we cannot be saved by a dead faith.

Here is where we run into problems in our churches. Because faith has been taught as agreement to a set of beliefs or praying a specific prayer one time rather than obedience to Jesus, our churches are crowded with confused people. Many think they are Christians and wonder why they have little interest in what their pastor or priest is telling them. Conversion for these individuals has never included Jesus' call to follow him, and they have never been taught what it means to be a disciple. If discipleship is not taught as the normal calling of every follower of Christ, then we have a mess of people who see themselves with a ticket to heaven but view the Christian life as a collection of optional activities. Their faith is weak, if not altogether dead. If we think we will make Christlike disciples from a flawed gospel, we are wrong.

What Are We Saved For?

The gift of salvation is not just something nice that God does for us, a good deed to help us out. God doesn't want to earn a merit badge. No, he has a purpose for what he does. The words of Paul are both descriptive and prescriptive, "For we are God's masterpiece. He has created us anew in Christ Jesus, so we can do the good things he planned for us long ago" (Eph. 2:10 NLT). We are saved to participate in God's plan for the world. Through this plan, God will bless his creation, and to the degree that we join in this plan, we will experience the blessing.

People often ask, what is God's plan for my life? Or to go a step further, what is God's purpose in creating us, and why do we even exist? Most of the time, we don't ask this question at the deep, existential level. We simply want to know where we will live, what kind of work we will do, possibly who we are going to marry. But in Paul's mind, these are the secondary details. What matters most is knowing our core purpose and the reason God saved us; everything else comes later.

We are saved to participate in God's plan for the world. Through this plan, God will bless his creation, and to the degree we join in this plan, we experience that blessing. God doesn't reveal the specific details for each of our lives. But he does reveal that we can all be involved in his activities. We can do the things he planned before the creation of the world for us to do, and through which he will guide us.

Once we make a decision to believe on and follow Christ, we should be walking, doing, learning, and becoming something new, for the purpose of our salvation includes becoming something we weren't before. This journey or process is what we commonly refer to as conversion. It is more than an event. We are saved and are being saved, which should involve some significant changes in how we live.

Let's consider a few examples. Something like a machine or a computer that is undergoing a "conversion" is generally taken off line and put someplace where it will be out of commission for a while. Buildings that are being converted are covered with tarpaulins, automobiles put into garages, and computer systems placed off-line. In other words, the conversion process is a major project that takes time. Similarly, the Bible uses the idea of conversion to describe a major change, yet with a key difference. When humans undergo a biblical conversion, they aren't taken out of commission. They're still on the road or on-line, available for use.

Donald Bloesch helpfully defines conversion by looking at root words in the Old and New Testaments: "The English word 'conversion' is associated with the Hebrew word *shuv*, which means to turn back or return, and the Greek words *epistrepho* and *metanoeo*, both of which indicate to turn towards God. The key term in the New Testament is the latter, together with its noun form *metanoia*. This term signifies not simply a change in mind [as in classical Greek], but a change of heart. *Metanoia* can also be translated as 'repentance.' John Wesley was certainly true to the basic witness of Scripture when he defined conversion in his dictionary as "a thorough change of heart and life from sin to holiness, a turning."[23]

Again, conversion is an event, but it is also a process. John Calvin believed that we are to distinguish justification and sanctification but must never separate them. According to Calvin, justification as a divine acquittal is extrinsic to humans, but the fruits of this justification are then applied to humans by the Holy Spirit.[24] Because the biblical concept of conversion captures the sense of a process, I think it is a helpful corrective to our event-oriented notions of salvation. Again, Donald Bloesch is helpful in summarizing the process of conversion: "The drama of conversion can be said to unfold in various stages. . . . Conversion continues throughout life as our relationship to God is deepened by the cleansing power of His Spirit. Conversion is therefore both an event and a process in that it entails an initial surrender to Jesus Christ as well as constant fidelity to Him throughout life. It signifies both taking up the cross in the decision of faith and bearing the cross in a life of obedience."[25]

Salvation through Conversion

But where do we find biblical evidence that conversion is a process? The most comprehensive description is found in Paul's letter to Titus. "For the grace of God has been revealed, bringing salvation to all people. And we are instructed to turn from godless living and sinful pleasures. We should live in this evil world with wisdom, righteousness and devotion to God, while we look forward with hope to that wonderful day when the glory of our great God and Savior, Jesus Christ, will be revealed. He gave his life to free us from every kind of sin, to cleanse us, and to make us his very own people, totally committed to doing good deeds" (Titus 2:11–14 NLT).

Again, Paul points out that we are saved by the grace that God has revealed in Jesus Christ. Yet notice how that grace operates in our lives: it instructs us in how to live. God's grace teaches us to repent, to turn from sin and godless living, and to follow his purpose for our lives. Where is this instruction, and how do we receive it? It is in the teachings of Jesus and learned by following him as his disciple throughout life. In Ephesians 2:20, Paul states that the result of this way of life is "to make us his very own people, totally committed to doing good deeds."

This passage also connects discipleship to conversion by showing us that conversion relies upon the teaching of Jesus and that conversion is connected to salvation as the fruit of God's grace. In other words, we can't have conversion without the practice of discipleship. Our conversion is rooted in learning how to repent and change the way we live. The purpose of the discipleship process is to create loving, Christlike people who live for others. Disciples are not trophies to be admired; we are servants who are to love people like Christ does.

In college I read a book titled *Grace Is Not a Blue-Eyed Blonde* by R. Lofton Hudson. The book was a helpful reminder that our assumptions about grace may not be correct. Here Paul teaches that "the grace of God has been revealed, bringing salvation to all people" (Titus 2:11 NLT). Grace has always been an attribute of God, but until he revealed it to us in a way we could understand and experience, we knew nothing of it. One of the key reasons we are saved is to be messengers of the good news of God's grace. We are converted and become disciples to make other disciples.

When we teach a form of discipleship that does not result in reproduction, we miss the mark. Here is an example of what I mean. It's popular in some small groups to ask the question, "How are you doing?" That's a perfectly reasonable question to ask. But the kind of discipleship that God desires doesn't end with the disciples' own lives. It extends into how they are living for others. So we should be asking, "How are you doing loving the people God has put in your life?" We don't need to go looking for new people to love. We just need to start really loving the ones God has already given us. If we start with them, we will soon be inundated with people God will draw into our lives.

Paul goes on: "And we are *instructed* to turn from godless living and sinful pleasures" (Titus 2:12 NLT). As I mentioned earlier, the genesis of conversion is the turning, the repentance that is basic to daily life in Christ. However the word employed here for turning is not the familiar μετανοια, it is αρνησαμενοι, which means "to say no." This is a helpful reminder that grace is not simply a matter of God overlooking our sin and accepting us for who we are. No, it necessarily involves denying ourselves and turning our life over to Christ. It means that we now answer to a higher authority, renounce all our rights to self-promotion and self-direction, and are ready to report for duty.

In this passage is the word *instructed*. The word (Greek: παιδευουσα) means someone in authority training another through discipline. As Walter Lock suggests, "The thought is akin to the Greek conception of redemption from ignorance."[26] And the purpose of this training is to teach us to say no. This is similar to what Paul modeled for the wild and wooly Corinthians, "All athletes are disciplined in their training. . . . I discipline my body like an athlete, training it to do what it should" (1 Cor. 9:25, 27 NLT).

This kind of discipline causes us to think of a teacher or a guide who teaches us how to turn from one way of life to another. While grace gives us the opportunity to learn, the means is submitting to the teaching of Jesus through others. But exchanging one pleasure for another is not easy because it requires a new way of thinking. For example, exchanging the pleasure of drugs for the pleasure of serving requires a complete change of taste, desire, and purpose, as does living with one spouse rather than an assortment of others. We'll cover the details of the transformation process later, but for now the point is that *conversion is discipleship, and discipleship is conversion*. They are two sides to the same coin.

As we saw earlier, grace is God doing for us what we cannot do for ourselves. We can think of grace as a force, God's power that gets things done and changes us. Grace is the work of God's Spirit in us transforming us into the likeness of Jesus. But don't miss this key point: *the desire to be disciplined is one of grace's greatest gifts*. Unless we desire to be disciplined, the conversion process will not go forward. Clearly Paul has this in mind when he tells Timothy to "be strong through the grace that God gives you in Christ Jesus" (2 Tim. 2:1 NLT). Paul then tutors Timothy on the rigors of teaching, training, and multiplying. He instructs him to teach only faithful people and that doing so will require the dedication of a soldier, the discipline of an athlete, and the patience of a farmer (2 Tim. 2:2–7). It is hard to miss the obvious necessity of discipline or training here. Paul exhorts everyone when he says, "Train yourself to be godly" (1 Tim. 4:7). Training for godliness has benefits in this life and the next, and Paul adds a signature statement, "Teach these things and insist that everyone learn them" (1 Tim. 4:11 NLT).

Returning to the Titus text, we see that grace's instruction is not just academic. It leads to a destination that is God's idea. "We should live in this evil world with wisdom, righteousness, and devotion to God" (Titus 2:12 NLT). This is not an insulated monasticism; it is living fully in the world. In a letter from prison, Bonhoeffer speaks on this topic quite powerfully. "I discovered later, and I'm still discovering right up to this moment, that it is only by living completely in this world that one learns to have faith."[27] Many Christians have not yet learned what Bonhoeffer understood, how to exercise right living and thinking in the midst of the surrounding culture.

While we acknowledge that the world is evil, as Christians we must learn to love the world completely and sacrificially just as Jesus did. The world rejected Jesus and crucified him. Yet it is also attracted to him, his teaching, and his way of life, and many love him and follow his philosophy. Like Jesus, we must not run *from* the world—we should fully live in it, diving headfirst into what God is doing. And what is God doing? He is converting us so we can help convert others. He has strategically placed us in every domain of society as little Christs. "While we look forward with hope to that wonderful day when the glory of our great God and Savior, Jesus Christ, will be revealed" (Titus 2:13 NLT), we are integrated into every nook and cranny of society where we illuminate, preserve, and speak of the good news.

As Paul makes clear, our salvation has a future dimension as well as a past and present dimension. When we think of "being saved," we should think of all the dimensions involved. God's grace was revealed; we now live in this world as repentant followers of Jesus; and in the future Christ will return. This future hope is what pulls us forward. Salvation viewed as a process of conversion is a journey, and every journey has a destination. Some of our journey is behind us, and we look with anticipation and longing toward the day we are completely united with our God in the eternal state.

So why is it that many so-called Christians do not think about the future? I'm reminded of Dallas Willard's words here: "Wouldn't heaven be hell for a person stuck forever in the company of someone as magnificent as Jesus and the Trinity that they did not admire or even like enough to stay as close to them as possible?"[28] Perhaps one reason some do not look forward to heaven is because they don't really know the One who is at the center of it all.

But those who are seeking God will receive a payoff. It begins in earnest when we experience the grace of God, continues with joy and purpose in our lives right now, and will be astounding in the next realm. Paul reminds Titus and us that our future hope should cause us to live rightly now. "He gave his life to free us from every kind of sin to cleanse us, and to make us his very own people, totally committed to doing good deeds" (Titus 2:14 NLT). Freed from the bondage of sin, we are free through disciplined discipleship to Christ to live the kind of life he created us for.

Regeneration

To this point, we have looked at the biblical and theological concepts of salvation and conversion. Now we move to the question, What actually happens to us when we decide to follow Jesus? The answer is summarized in two words: new life. God gives us a new life, and this reality leads to our transformation. In John's Gospel we read, "But to all who believed him and accepted him, he gave the right to become children of God. They are reborn—not with a physical birth resulting from human passion or plan, but a birth that comes from God" (John 1:12–13 NLT).

The concept of being reborn or born again is summed up in regeneration, a word that describes the changes inside people who choose to follow Christ. To regenerate something or someone means to give it a new life. Spiritual regeneration means putting new capacity into a person's immaterial nature. This is what Jesus was talking about when he told Nicodemus that he needed to be born from above, of the Spirit. "Humans can reproduce only human life, but the Holy Spirit gives birth to spiritual life. So don't be surprised when I say, 'You must be born again'" (John 3:6 NLT).

In contemporary Christian culture, the phrase "born again" has been reduced to a slogan, and the amazing reality behind these words has been lost. Being born again involves more than just saying the magic-formula prayer that evangelists have people say. As Jesus makes clear, we cannot manipulate the work of God's Spirit in this way. Being born again means infusing a person with new life. It does not mean an automatic transformation but a life that is new and full of potential that must be developed through obedient discipleship.

Regeneration is being awakened from spiritual death to spiritual life.[29] So while the spiritual pilgrimage requires plenty of dying to the self, it involves much more living than dying. Regeneration is a transfer from the kingdom of death and darkness to the kingdom of life and light ruled by God's Son, Jesus. Paul describes this transfer well, "For he has rescued us from the kingdom of darkness and transferred us into the Kingdom of his dear Son, who purchased our freedom and forgave our sins" (Col. 1:13 NLT).

This new life is "a gift from God" (Eph. 2:8). It is a new psychological reality that includes a new knowledge of God, the ability to know the character of the One who now dwells within us and to experience him acting in us and through us. Jesus said, "And this is eternal life, that they know thee the only true God, and Jesus Christ whom thou hast sent" (John 17:3 RSV). Knowing God and Jesus is eternal life. Therefore, it is wrong for us to think of eternal life as something that will begin when we physically die. Eternal life begins when we decide to follow Jesus, when we are born again and God gives us the ability to truly know him. Consider Paul's careful words to the Corinthians who were struggling with knowing God. "No one can know a person's thoughts except that person's own spirit, and no one can know God's thoughts except God's own Spirit. And we have received God's Spirit (not the world's spirit), so we can know the wonderful things God has freely given us" (1 Cor. 2:11–12 NLT).

Knowledge of God is reserved for those in whom his Spirit resides. The living God imparts his own thoughts to those who are living in obedience to him and through whom he is living on this earth. This new life has a mind of its own, what the Scriptures call the mind of Christ. It is "self-initiating, self-directing, and self-sustaining."[30] Paul explains, "For God is working in you giving you the desire and the power to do what pleases him" (Phil. 2:13 NLT). The reason we think new and strange thoughts about our attitudes and conduct is because God gives us new desires and new thoughts.

This new life within us transforms the way we perceive our environment. An attorney friend who began to believe in Christ described how he began to interact with work quite differently. He entered the courtroom where he worked and scanned it like he had so often before. But when he saw the judge, for the first time he thought, "I could pray for the judge." He had the same thought when he saw the prosecutor, the defendant, the jury, and the families involved. As a believer, this attorney had new life in him which put new thoughts in his mind and changed the way he perceived reality.

We don't live at the cross; we die there. Paul makes it clear that we need more than the death of Christ; we must be saved by his resurrection life. "But God showed his great love for us by sending Christ to die for us while we were still sinners. And since we have been made right in God's sight by the blood of Christ, he will certainly save us from God's condemnation. For since our friendship with God was restored by the death of his Son while we were still his enemies, *we will certainly be saved through the life of his Son.* So now we can rejoice in our wonderful new relationship with God because our Lord Jesus Christ has made us friends of God" (Rom. 5:8–11 NLT, emphasis added).

The cross of Christ is rightly emphasized as the means of our forgiveness and restored relationship with God. But we should not preach forgiveness without also speaking of the new life God offers through the resurrection. Paul is clear here: we are saved by Christ's life. In other words, our salvation can be described as "being caught up in the life that Jesus is now living on the earth."[31] Because Christ is alive, we can live a new life in the power and strength he provides through the Holy Spirit.

New life makes being saved attractive. People are drawn to beauty. Even as Paul was stuck in an ugly prison, he encouraged others to focus on beauty: "Fix your thoughts on what is true, and honorable, and right, and pure, and lovely, and admirable. Think about things that are excellent and worthy of praise" (Phil. 4:8 NLT). But what comes to mind when you think of what is true and right, or pure and admirable? These things are more than just abstract concepts. They are also attitudes and concrete actions like "love, joy, peace, patience, goodness, faithfulness, gentleness, and self-control" (Gal. 5:22–23). When reborn people encounter long lines at the grocery store or traffic jams, patience is manifested in their attitude, facial expression, and words. Others are drawn to these expressions of beauty and other concrete manifestations of God's grace transforming our lives.

Forgiveness

"Each of you must repent of your sins and turn to God, and be baptized in the name of Jesus Christ for the forgiveness of your sins" (Acts 2:38 NLT). Again, we come to the big-ticket item in our salvation—forgiveness of sin. Everyone is quick to talk about forgiveness and thank God for it. But to see ourselves as forgiven implies that we see the need for God's forgiveness. Unfortunately, the truth that sin is an offense against God for which we are accountable is not commonly accepted today. Mark Johnson describes current ideas about sin by saying that "some have a primitive need for some kind of order in our world in order to make sense of it all."[32]

Most people understand that the concept of forgiveness implies that something has been broken in a relationship. Some argue that God owes humankind an explanation and apology for the terrible job he has done, and it is he who needs to be forgiven. The renowned atheist Christopher Hitchens used to rail that God had everyone under constant surveillance and would never allow his creatures to grow up. He thought that Israel's tribal God was guilty of genocide and bloodletting and was an immoral SOB. But even in his railing, Hitchens was assuming a relationship between God and humans that had been broken.

The Bible offers us a clear reason for the world's problems: human sin, which is a reality that we cannot deny. The good news is that God is willing to forgive all our sin that separates us from him and release us from the guilt of our sinful state. Paul says clearly, "So now there is no condemnation for those who belong to Christ Jesus" (Rom. 8:1 NLT). Paul also gives us the reason, "God made Christ, who never sinned, to be the offering for our sin, so that we could be made right with God through Christ" (2 Cor. 5:21 NLT). Everyone who says yes to Christ and follows him is restored to a relationship to him. We are, as Paul says, reconciled to God.[33] Yet despite being forgiven, sin continues to be present in our lives. This ongoing sin is motivated by what the Bible calls the flesh. Paul spends a good deal of time talking about this battle in his letters.[34] Even as disciples, our need for forgiveness is ongoing because we continue to sin.

The apostle John wrote three short letters that are hard hitting and pragmatic, and he was quite honest about the reality of sin and continual need for forgiveness. His teaching helps us understand the practical benefits of living a forgiven life. "But if we are living in the light, as God is in the light, then we have fellowship with each other, and the blood of Jesus, his Son, cleanses us from all sin" (1 John 1:7 NLT). What does John mean by this? He is speaking of not hiding our sin but being open and honest. This honesty requires an awareness of sin that is more than a vague, general sense of wrongdoing. I've met many church people who are willing to admit they are sinners, but if pressed, they can't name a sin they have committed. This situation illustrates that sin can be a great theory, but when we have to admit one, it becomes a threat. John's description could faithfully be translated, "the blood of Jesus keeps on cleansing us from sin." In other words, this forgiveness is ongoing. As we live in the light, open and honest about our sin, we constantly repent and receive forgiveness.

Dietrich Bonhoeffer has much to say about the value of living in the light. "Your sin wants to be alone with you. Those who remain alone with their evil are left utterly alone."[35] The enemy wants to empower our sin by keeping it hidden from others. As fallen human beings, we are programmed to hide our faults and protect ourselves. But as soon as the light of God's grace shines on it, our sin is disempowered. John goes on to explain the benefits of an open and cleansed life. "If we claim we have no sin, we are only fooling ourselves and not living in the truth. But if we confess our sins to him, he is faithful and just to forgive us our sins and to cleanse us from all wickedness" (1 John 1:8–9 NLT).

Forgiveness is the benefit we receive if we confess our sin, acknowledge our fault, and receive this blessing from God. People living a forgiven life experience God's favor or grace every day. Forgiveness puts joy in the heart, a bounce in the spirit, and health in the bones, and gives us a positive outlook on the future. But receiving this gift requires honesty, humility, and submission. A secretive life filled with hidden sin is an awful life, but a forgiven life is filled with joy.[36]

Not many prayers always have a predictable outcome. But one prayer will always be answered as promised—when we admit to God that we have sinned and come to him in a spirit of repentance, he promises to forgive us. If we continually confess our sin as the Holy Spirit brings it to our attention, we will continue to be in fellowship with God and others. The joy will continue; the communication lines will remain open; and the Spirit will continue to flow freely through our spiritual veins.

John says that we should live forgiven lives so we will not continue in sin. Some degree of sinning is inevitable because we are imperfect. But we are not powerless to stop sinning. We are engaged in battle, but just as great soldiers cannot be heroic if they are frozen in fear, soldiers of Christ cannot be afraid of sin. John assures us that our Savior helps us in this battle. "But if anyone does sin, we have an advocate who pleads our case before the Father. He is Jesus Christ, the one who is truly righteous. He himself is the sacrifice that atones for our sins—and not only our sins but the sins of all the world" (1 John 2:1–2 NLT).

Jesus himself is the foundation of the forgiven life. He not only provides the means for our forgiveness, his death on the cross, he continues to be our advocate in the heavenly courtroom. This knowledge is far from being a license to continue in sin. Instead, it gives us liberty to soar above the debilitating sins of daily life by giving us hope that we can complete the work God calls us to do.

Unfortunately, many in the church today do not see sin as something we must fight against in an ongoing battle. Divorcing the process of discipleship from salvation has required people to create other solutions to the problem of sin in the Christian life. One of these creations is a secondary category that some call carnal Christians.

Three Kinds of People

The founder of Dallas Theological Seminary, Lewis Sperry Chafer, wrote an influential book in which he presented a theory, based on 1 Corinthians 2–3, that there are three kinds of people: natural people, carnal people, and spiritual people.[37]

Natural people are unbelievers who are unable to sense or discern the things of God. "The natural person does not accept the things of the Spirit of God, for they are folly to him and he is not able to understand them because they are spiritually discerned" (1 Cor. 2:14 ESV). In contrast to natural people are spiritual people who we would consider believers in Christ. "The spiritual person judges all things, but is himself to be judged by no one. 'For who has understood the mind of the Lord so as to instruct him?' But we have the mind of Christ" (1 Cor. 2:15–16 ESV).

The third type of people are what Chafer refers to as the carnal. "But I, brothers, could not address you as spiritual people, but as people of the flesh, as infants in Christ. I fed you with milk, not solid food, for you were not ready for it. And even now you are not yet ready, for you are still of the flesh. For while there is jealousy and strife among you, are you not of the flesh and behaving only in a human way?" (1 Cor. 3:1–3 ESV).

To be clear, Paul refers to these people as "infants in Christ." Yet he also says that he cannot distinguish them from non-Christians. Is Paul creating a secondary class of Christians here, or are these just bad Christians behaving badly? Or perhaps these are professing Christians who are not born again and are simply acting like what they truly are, non-Christians? It could be that Paul was giving these Christians the benefit of the doubt. But outwardly there seems to be no distinction between the behavior of carnal Christians and natural people. Both appear to be deaf to the things of God.

In arguing for the existence of this secondary class of Christians, Chafer presented the following argument.

> The difference between the spiritual man and the carnal man is as follows: the spiritual man has "no limitation on him in the realm of the things of God. He can 'freely' receive the divine revelation, and he glories in it. . . . The 'spiritual' man is the divine ideal of life and ministry in power with God and man, in unbroken fellowship and blessing." The carnal Christian on the other hand "is born again and possesses the indwelling Spirit; but his carnality hinders the full ministry of the Spirit." He is characterized by a walk that is on the same plane as that of the "natural" man. In short the carnal Christian is controlled by the flesh whereas he that is spiritual is controlled by the Spirit. From this it follows that there are "two great spiritual changes which are possible to human experience." The natural man must become saved, and the saved man—if he is fleshly—must become spiritual."[38]

The problem with Chafer's argument is that it ignores the reality that every true Christian has carnality inside that is potentially debilitating. All believers struggle with the flesh, but all have the capacity to overcome it.

In fact, true believers do overcome their sin and produce fruit in a consistent way. Chafer's classification of carnal Christian, one who has a ticket to heaven yet is fruitless and comfortable with sin, opens the door for confusion because, simply put, such a person does not exist.

What then is Paul saying in 1 Corinthians 3:1–3? In effect, he is telling the Corinthian Christians to stop acting like unbelievers. This is a pastoral response to sinful behavior that is similar to the rebuke we find in Hebrews 5:11–13, where the author calls these Christians "spiritually dull" and hard of hearing. He says they are "like babies who need milk and cannot eat solid food" (Heb. 5:12 NLT). This immaturity is a very real problem in our churches. The question is not whether such people exist but whether we should establish a separate category for them and make allowances for real believers who no longer repent of their sin. If we accept that the category of carnal Christian exists, we slit the throat of the gospel, and in accommodating their sinful behavior, we drive a stake through the call to discipleship.

Carnal Christianity fits nicely with the alternative vision of the Christian life. Carnal Christians can assume they are forgiven and that discipleship is optional. This is a form of cheap grace, or as Bonhoeffer put it, the death of discipleship.

Carnal Christians make much of the forgiveness of sin. In fact, they love to hear that their sins are forgiven and see this as the defining reality of being a Christian. But forgiveness detached from repentance and the call to follow Christ is not the gospel. A real Christian responds to discipline and changes to live and behave differently, according to a different standard. This is why we must include the call to discipleship in our proclamation of the gospel.

Not everyone agrees with this idea. For example, Joseph Dillow writes, "When Jesus calls a man to become a disciple, he is in no instance asking him to accept the free gift of eternal life. Instead, he is asking those who have already believed to accept the stringent commands of discipleship and find true life."[39] Dillow holds that the call to discipleship is not the same as the call to conversion. In other words, the gospel is not about following Jesus. It is about the free gift of having your sins forgiven and gaining admission into heaven. Everything else is optional. In the end, it doesn't matter if one Christian's life and conduct are pleasing to God and another's is not. Dillow goes on to say, "Only when one confuses the demands for discipleship with the demands for simple salvation does one distort and introduce heresy into Jesus' soteriology."[40]

Another writer argues even more plainly, "*Whoever* once truly believes that Jesus was raised from the dead, and confesses that Jesus is Lord, will go to heaven when he dies. . . . *Such a person will go to heaven when he dies no matter what work (or lack of work) may accompany such faith.*[41] This school doesn't expect or require any fruit or change as proof of new life in Christ. They are quite comfortable allowing that carnal Christians, who believe that Jesus died for their sins but do nothing to change or repent, are legitimately Christian.

In response to this, we return to the words of James, "So you see, faith by itself isn't enough. Unless it produces good deeds, it is dead and useless" (James 2:17 NLT). Biblically, there is no such thing as a believer who doesn't bear fruit. All who are saved will be disciples of Christ and by their works will demonstrate that they are indeed saved.

Contrary to those who argue that the demands of discipleship are contradictory to the message of the gospel,[42] Alan Stanley argues that there is no distinction between the call to be a disciple and the call to believe the gospel and gives five reasons why.

1. In order to become a disciple, Jesus declares that one must renounce all one's possessions [Luke 14:33]. Zacchaeus was an example of one who was willing to renounce all his possessions and also received salvation in the same act and moment [Luke 19:9].

2. Jesus' reply to the would-be disciple wanting to bury his father—"let the dead bury their own dead" [Matt. 8:21–22; Luke 9:59–60]—indicates the man had a choice. The choice was between eternal life or eternal death, not whether to be a disciple or simply settle for being a Christian.

3. Jesus calls his disciples "little ones" [Matt. 10:42]. Jesus said you must become like a little child to enter the kingdom of heaven [Matt. 18:6]. In other words, one must become a disciple.

4. In John 12:4 Jesus states, "Everyone who believes in me does not remain in darkness." John 8:12 is very similar except instead of "believe," John uses the verb ακολουθω. Hence "follow" and "believe" mean the same thing—at least for John.

5. The disciples understand the Rich Young Ruler's refusal to sell all he had and follow Jesus as a failure to be saved. This is confirmed by the fact that the disciples have done what the rich man failed to do. They have followed Jesus [Matt. 19:27 pars.] and so are promised eternal life [Matt. 19:29 pars.]. It is quite clear from these passages that to become a follower or disciple of Jesus is at the same time to become a believer in Jesus.[43]

What Then Can We Say Is Reasonably True about Being a "Saved" Person?

So then, what does it mean to be saved? To this point we have surveyed the rich and broad vocabulary of salvation: repentance, grace, regeneration, faith, and forgiveness. In later chapters, we will also look at concepts like reconciliation and redemption. What we have seen is that there is an essential connection between salvation and conversion, between the call to follow Jesus and responding to the gospel. The gospel is not just a promise of forgiveness of sins but includes a call to repentance. And the gospel promises the grace to change. But in the end, no one is saved without repenting.

Those who are saved should know they are on a lifelong journey. Salvation is not something we get done at a Saturday night meeting by saying a short prayer. There is no magical prayer or secret formula that some church holds. We must understand that the work of salvation actually began long before we were born, when God knew and planned the process. It continues as the Holy Spirit makes us aware of our need, and we choose to follow Jesus. The new life that God implants in us grows, and we are reborn as forgiven people of faith. We now must respond to the grace of God's discipline and learn how to live our lives as though Jesus were living through us.

This is our salvation. We are saved from the consequences of our sin, being separated from God and others, and from a life of vanity and triviality. We enter into the pleasures and joy of relationship with God which will continue as we are converted, day after day growing until we are ready for the pure presence of God.

When I think of this joyous end, I'm reminded of the great Romantic poet William Blake.

According to Malcolm Muggeridge, on his deathbed Blake was singing so beautifully that his wife moved closer to listen to his words, "and then he turned to her and said, 'They're not mine you know' and repeated it more emphatically, 'They're not mine.' Then he went on to tell her that they would never be parted, and that after he was dead, he would continue to watch over her just as he had during the years of their long companionship. Blake had said before that to him death would be no more than moving from one room to another, and so it proved to be. He went on singing in his bed in the same divine way until about six in the evening, and then—as he said in one of his poems—silently, invisibly, the human spirit left him, becoming part of the eternity on which his eyes has been so faithfully set during his mortal years."[44] As he wrote in one of his poems:

He who binds himself a joy
Does the winged life destroy;
But he who kisses the joy as it flies
Lives in Eternity's sun rise.[45]

4

THE HOLY SPIRIT AND HOW
PEOPLE CHANGE

Part 1

> *In the long run, only disciples are converts.*
> —GORDON FEE, *PAUL, THE SPIRIT,*
> *AND THE PEOPLE OF GOD*

When George Whitefield was asked how many people were saved in a meeting where he had preached, he answered, "I don't know. We should know more in six months." Whenever the gospel is preached, we know that God works to convert people. But even Jesus indicated in the parable of the sower that we cannot judge if a person is converted by an immediate response.[1] Outward appearances can be deceiving. Like in the seed in the parable, some people grow at first, but in the end they bear no fruit. Jesus teaches that we will know if people are true disciples if they bear fruit over time.

In the previous chapter, we looked at how salvation is both an event and a process. We are saved, yet we are also being saved. But what actually happens within people to effect transformation? How do we change? How does the inward transformation we experience manifest in our decisions and conduct? The answer to all of these questions is the Holy Spirit. This process of change can't possibly happen without the presence and work of the Holy Spirit.

The Holy Spirit is in the business of making us new people by transforming our mind and changing our character. The transformed mind informs the will, and from the will, we act. We all know this by experience.

However, we don't change by just wishing or praying it to happen. A simple exhortation to stop doing something will rarely make a dent in overcoming habitual sin. Some excuse their lack of progress by claiming they need more time to come up with a more profound insight or plan. But the brutal truth is that they use up this time in the same unproductive ways. We need the work of the Holy Spirit to change us.

The Necessity of the Spirit

Thomas Aquinas described the work of the Holy Spirit in this way, "God causes and moves our will, and yet without the will ceasing to be free."[2] What could be worse than being told to love God when we didn't have the inclination or ability to love him? Yet that is exactly where we find ourselves. The situation is even worse when we consider that God told us to become like him. This is where the Holy Spirit comes in. Jesus promised to send all of his disciples a helper. "I will ask the Father, and he will give you another advocate to help you and be with you forever—the Spirit of truth. The world cannot accept him, because it neither sees him nor knows him. But you know him, for he lives with you and will be in you. I will not leave you as orphans" (John 14:16–18).

Soon after Jesus spoke these words, his eleven remaining disciples scattered in fear. But they still had Jesus' promise that God would be with each of them. He was with them as they hid behind closed doors. He was with Peter as he cursed his way through the streets of Jerusalem and into the courtyard of the High Priest. Though the first disciples didn't understand the amazing power of this promise, in just three days, everything would change, and over time, the promises became clearer. Resurrection has a way of lifting one's spirit! Meeting the resurrected Jesus led even a skeptical Thomas to confess, "My Lord and my God" (John 20:28).

The Holy Spirit was introduced to Jesus' first followers in several phases over time. Jesus first spoke of the Spirit as a counselor, guide, teacher, and comforter. He told his disciples that it was good he was going away so the counselor could come (John 16:7–10). Of course, they didn't understand what he meant. They had experienced God's delicious presence in Jesus, and they didn't want to give him up.

Jesus promised that he would come back and that in the meantime, they would not be alone but experience his presence in the Holy Spirit. Keep in mind that Jesus was not hosting an academic seminar on the Holy Spirit; this was real life. His words here have the purpose of comforting and convincing his disciples that they will be ok without his physical presence. He was also making it clear that they needed the Holy Spirit and could not go it alone. In fact, the Holy Spirit will have the broader work of convicting the entire world of sin, righteousness, and judgment (John 16:8).

After his death and resurrection, Jesus spent forty days with his followers. Then he returned to their need for the Holy Spirit. "So when the apostles were with Jesus, they kept asking him, 'Lord, has the time come for you to free Israel and restore our kingdom?' He replied, 'The Father alone has the authority to set those dates and times, and they are not for you to know. But you will receive power when the Holy Spirit comes upon you. And you will be my witnesses, telling people about me everywhere—in Jerusalem, throughout Judea, in Samaria, and to the ends of the earth'" (Acts 1:6–8 NLT).

After promising that the Holy Spirit would come, Jesus ascended into heaven. The disciples waited just as Jesus had commanded, and ten days later, the Holy Spirit came upon them. The disciples became his witnesses by spilling into the streets, preaching the gospel, and the church was born.[3] Though Jesus was gone, they had a new helper and guide in the person of the Holy Spirit who gave them the ability to do with others what Jesus had done with them. These first followers of Jesus went on to experience the work and the power of the Holy Spirit in many different ways. In this chapter, we will look at some of these ways the Spirit works, beginning with the broadest category—sanctification.

Sanctification

A variety of words have been used to describe how a person becomes more like Christ, but all are under the broad theological category sanctification. This English word is derived from the Greek word αγιαζω, which means holy or set apart. In the Bible, the central idea of holiness is that God is different, set apart, unlike anyone or anything else, which is what "God is holy" means. And because God is holy, Christians should be holy, which means we must learn to be different, set apart from the ways of this world and from sin. The Bible calls every Christian a saint, meaning each follower of Jesus is set apart by God for a special life of service. Christians spend their lives growing into this different way of life and adopting the habits of godly character.[4]

In the Scriptures, becoming holy, or sanctified, is connected to being washed and justified, and all of these activities are associated with the Holy Spirit. For example, "But you were washed, you were sanctified, you were justified in the name of the Lord Jesus Christ and in the Spirit of our God" (1 Cor. 6:11 RSV). Paul describes sanctification as common to all believers. "And now I commend you to God and to the word of his grace, which is able to build you up and to give you the inheritance among all those who are sanctified" (Acts 20:32 RSV).

Sanctification is generally understood to be a progressive process that does not end until the eternal state. Over fifty times in Paul's writing alone, Christians are described as being sanctified in various ways.[5] Robert Picirilli gives a good summary of these ways:

1. Initial sanctification, referred to as "past tense," is the setting apart of the believer at conversion. This is the most common and clearly established use of both the noun and verb.

2. Less clear, but probable, is the use of the word to describe what is called progressive sanctification. This is the "present tense" of sanctification. But this is so infrequent that one must build an understanding of what this involves from other passages of Scripture. We must consider other key phrases such as growing in grace, the pursuit of God, and references to discipline.

3. Also infrequent are references to final sanctification, our sanctification in the "future tense."

4. The Bible does not speak of sanctification as a second level experience or as a goal that we aspire. The Scriptures do not teach that we are to live sinless lives; rather we acknowledge the reality of ongoing spiritual conflict and the existence of sin and confess it. We see this in passages like Galatians 5:16–24 and 1 John 1:7–2:2.[6]

SANCTIFICATION AND DISCIPLESHIP

So how is growth in holiness, sanctification, related to discipleship? Dallas Willard offers a helpful, organic description of sanctification that is similar to the biblical definition of discipleship we have been discussing. "It is a consciously chosen and sustained relationship of interaction between the Lord and his apprentice, in which the apprentice is able to do, and routinely does, what he or she knows to be right before God."[7]

Discipleship occurs when we answer Jesus' call to learn how to live by his perspective and standards and become the people who naturally act like him. Discipleship describes our existential daily status as learners and refers to our identity. As discussed in the last chapter, Dietrich Bonhoeffer advocated that we unify the theological categories of justification and sanctification into the concept of discipleship because he believed that discipleship is a more concrete concept of life in Christ. Bonhoeffer's best friend and biographer Eberhard Bethge, speaking of Bonhoeffer's efforts to do this, writes, "[Bonhoeffer] tried to grasp the Reformed articles of faith, justification, and sanctification within the single concept of discipleship. Yet with his key formula, 'only the believer is obedient, and only those who are obedient believe,' he did not mean to question the complete validity of Luther's *sola fide* and *sola gratia*, but to reassert their validity by restoring to them their concreteness here on earth." Bonhoeffer later stated, "Justification is the new creation of the new person, and sanctification is the preservation and protection of that person until the day of Jesus Christ."[8]

Along with Bonhoeffer, I advocate that we recover a functional way of describing salvation that incorporates the Great Commission and the call of the gospel to follow Jesus. If we begin with a proper understanding of discipleship, we can then explain sanctification as living out discipleship.

SANCTIFICATION AND SPIRITUAL FORMATION

Closely related to discipleship is spiritual formation, the Holy Spirit's direct acting on a person's immaterial nature that eventually results in the whole being worshiping God, as Paul urges when he says we should present our entire being, including our bodies, as a living sacrifice (Rom. 12:1–2). Another key passage on spiritual formation is 2 Corinthians 3:17–18. "For the Lord is the Spirit, and wherever the Spirit of the Lord is, there is freedom. So all of us who have had that veil removed can see and reflect the glory of the Lord. And the Lord—who is the Spirit—makes us more and more like him as we are changed into his glorious image" (NLT).

Galatians 4:19 is also helpful to consider. "Oh, my dear children! I feel as if I'm going through labor pains for you again, and they will continue until Christ is *fully developed* in your lives" (NLT, emphasis added). The two English words "fully developed" are the translation of a single Greek word, μορφωθη *(morphothe)*. You may recognize the root "morph," meaning to change or transformation. These three concepts—sanctification, discipleship, and spiritual formation—are intimately related and essentially describe the process of spiritual growth. I like Michael Wilkins' attempt to relate them. "Spiritual formation and discipleship are different sides to the same coin, and that coin is sanctification."

Growth and Reproduction

Discipleship and spiritual formation express slightly different aspects of the sanctification process, but they also reflect the common expectations that every Christian will grow *and* reproduce. At the start of this chapter, I quoted Gordon Fee, "In the long run, only disciples are converts."[9] What Fee means is that followers of Christ prove by their actions that they have been converted into a new way of life. Proof of authentic faith is not simply a creedal affirmation but living the life. As Jesus said, "Not everyone who calls out to me, 'Lord! Lord!' will enter the Kingdom of Heaven. Only those who actually do the will of my Father in heaven will enter" (Matt. 7:21 NLT).[10]

Yet today, it is rare to find pastors or churches who expect much from their members. Even rarer are people who speak of God evaluating us on the basis of what we have done. Instead in our efforts to emphasize grace, we fail to talk about standards and expectations. Some feel that these things smack of rigidity or legalism, or they find them to be unfriendly to seekers or uncomfortable for regulars. Not many churches expect their members to be knowledgeable of the Scriptures, nor do they honestly expect members to witness, bring others to the Christian faith, and discipline new converts to reproduce as well. Again, we have set the bar quite low. We do not expect growth, and we certainly don't expect reproduction.

These two aspects of sanctification are not the only important matters in the Christian life, but I mention them because they are commonly neglected. Again, much of this neglect is due to the effort to extend grace under the guise of love and acceptance. *Yet it is not love to expect less of people because we don't want to put them under any pressure to perform.* It is not grace to set a low standard that anyone can meet if doing so leaves people trapped in their sin and unable to grow. Real love takes action for the benefit of another, and it is not loving to expect less of people than God does.

We've already discussed Jesus' basic expectation of his followers to "make disciples of all the nations" and "teach these new disciples to obey all the commands I have given you" (Matt. 28:19–20 NLT). The problem is not necessarily that pastors fail to preach about this. The problem is our expectations. We do not build expectations of serious growth and reproduction into our church infrastructures, and no accountability accompanies our teaching. This neglect violates the clear purpose at the heart of pastoral work. Consider how Paul summarized his own teaching ministry, "So we tell others about Christ, warning everyone and teaching everyone with all the wisdom God has given us. We want to present them to God, perfect in their relationship to Christ. That's why I work and struggle so hard, depending on Christ's mighty power that works within me" (Col. 1:28–29 NLT).

What is striking is Paul's goal of one day presenting people to God who are spiritually mature in their relationship to Christ. For this Paul worked hard—as they say in German, it is his *kirchenkampf*.[11] Paul also saw this rough and tumble work as spiritual warfare that requires the Holy Spirit to do. Contrary to our contemporary preoccupation with all things convenient, fast, and popular, Dallas Willard challenged us to focus on the difficult and time-consuming work of discipling our regular members rather than trying to attract a crowd: "Ministers pay far too much attention to people who do not come to services. Those people should, generally, be given exactly that disregard by the pastor that they give to Christ. The Christian leader has something much more important to do than pursue the godless. The leader's task is to equip saints until they are like Christ, and history and the God of history waits for him to do this job."[12]

In some ways, Willard's argument is counter-intuitive. He suggests that our best hope of reaching those who don't know Jesus is not attracting them to our church services. It is teaching those who already know Jesus how to follow him as mature disciples. I recognize the tension here and that the pendulum of discipleship and evangelism swings back and forth. But in light of recent history, I argue that our American churches need to recover the work of discipleship before we can be effective in the work of evangelism. In other words, we must start by growing people we already have.

Regardless, the biblical expectation is clear; disciples are to make other disciples.[13] This expectation of Christ applies to every follower of Christ. Paul worked to bring every one of his disciples to maturity.[14] Additionally, Paul expected Timothy to pass on what Paul had taught him to other trustworthy people, and he expected those trustworthy people to "be able to pass them on to others" (2 Tim. 2:2 NLT). A mature disciple both makes disciples and teaches their students how to teach others.

But how do we do this? We must first acknowledge that this is the work of the Holy Spirit. However before we dive into the specifics of how the Holy Spirit transforms us, I think it necessary to sail into the treacherous waters of how different traditions and schools of thought have understood the Holy Spirit's work. I begin by clarifying that almost everyone agrees on the basic fact that, like Paul, we need "Christ's mighty power that works within" (Col. 1:29 NLT) to bring others to maturity. We cannot do this apart from him. But there are differences of opinion on how the Holy Spirit's power, gifts, teaching, advocacy, strength, and counsel operate in the lives of believers.

Digging Deeper

MYSTICAL AND EVANGELICAL SPIRITUALITY

While there are many different ways of looking at the means of transformation, the forms of spirituality can be roughly divided into two
camps: the mystical and the evangelical.[a] Generally speaking, mystical spirituality is rooted in Catholicism and Eastern Orthodoxy
and sometimes incorporates Eastern mysticism and Neo-Platonism.[b]
The works of Thomas Merton and Richard Rohr give a contemporary taste of this way of thinking. Evangelical spirituality, broadly
speaking, developed from roots in the Protestant Reformation and
can be read in the works of Rick Warren, John Ortberg, and others
who emphasize reading Scripture, prayer, and other practices over
mystical experience.

We can compare and contrast the different ways these two forms
of spirituality approach the process of sanctification by looking at
various ways of understanding God and our relationship to him. We
begin with the idea that God is separate and distinct from us, his
creation. What is the goal of seeking God? And how do we know if
we have reached it? Does a Christian mystic who chants or meditates
have a different goal than a Methodist reading the Bible at lunch?
The answer is yes. These two individuals mean different things when
they speak of *experiencing* God. In mystical spirituality, the seeker
and God are understood to merge into one. But evangelical spirituality maintains a proper distance between God as a holy other and
the seeker as God's subject. Whereas mysticism emphasizes God's
immanence (presence in creation), evangelicalism emphasizes God's
transcendence (separateness from creation).

This difference of understanding explains why some in the
monastic movement slip into the thinking and practices of Eastern
mysticism. For example by the time of his death, Catholic Trappist
monk Thomas Merton was considered the leading Western expert
on Buddhist thought. Often, those searching for an experience of
God end up leaving behind a transcendent view of God. Catherine
of Genoa, a noted mystic, went as far as to say, "My being is God, not
simple participation but by a true transformation of my being."[c]

We can see practical differences in the methods of prayer. The
mystical tradition points to Jesus as an example of meditative and

contemplative prayer. Their goal is to be at one with God, not to move him or change his mind but to merge their identity into his and to come into alignment with his person. Christian mystics tend to avoid petitionary prayers in favor of simple prayers that express abandonment to the will of God. The evangelical tradition of prayer is well-described by Karl Barth, "Prayer is wrestling with God, not meditating upon God. It is an attempt to change God's will, not simply a passive resignation to God's will."[d] Evangelicals seek to engage with God as an object to which their prayer is addressed.

However, both the mystical and the evangelical streams of spirituality capture elements of the biblical witness. For example, consider the anguish of Jesus' Gethsemane petition. Jesus alternates between requests, yet his prayer is also mixed with resignation. It is an immense struggle, back and forth, between submission and petition. This prayer helps us understand why both schools of thought exist.

Yet in the end, I believe evangelical spirituality better captures the priorities of the biblical witness. In Jesus' prayer in John 17, we clearly see him speaking to God about his work and making many requests on behalf of his disciples. While the prayers of Jesus contain elements of meditation and resignation to the will of God, they consistently emphasize the importance of making requests and expressing our own desires to the Lord. In fact if we take a close look at Jesus' prayer life, we find that the majority of his prayers were petitionary and intercessory. In both Mark and Luke, he prays about strategy and selecting the twelve disciples. Jesus prayed about his work, asked for the things he needed, and made sure his Father knew what he was doing.

I appreciate what Nathan Soderbloom says in this regard: "So much we may know with absolute certainty from all the Gospel tells of Jesus, that his prayer never was merely a state of soul attained by some sure method, or *oratio mentalis*, a Prayer of Quiet, a mediation, but an intercourse and conversation with the heavenly Father, an outlet for anguish and uncertainty and for questions that needed answer; the bursting forth of a tone of jubilation, a trembling yet confident intimacy longing for undisturbed intercourse with the Father in Heaven, although the feeling of nearness and fellowship with him was wont never to cease during the duties and occupation of the day."[e] In other words, Jesus was not a mystic. He was clear headed and direct in his communication in prayer and with others.

At the same time, we cannot completely discount the mystical element in our faith. Some things Jesus taught using metaphors aren't easy to grasp. They have a bit of mystery to them. For example, Jesus uses the image of a vine and branches to explain his continuing relationship to his disciples (John 15:1–16). He told us to eat of his flesh and drink of his blood in Holy Communion (Luke 22:19–20; John 6:53–58). Identity doctrine in Scripture speaks of being crucified, buried, and raised with Christ and that we who follow Christ no longer live, but Christ now lives within us (Rom. 6:6–10; Gal. 2:20). There is great mystery in these things. But when we approach God, we must maintain the subject-object difference and remember that God is other than us. Radical mysticism seeks to dissolve this relationship. But God remains the holy other—different and separate from his creation.

[a] I must credit Donald Bloesch for identifying these two kinds of spirituality. Much of my thinking was influenced by chapter 7, "Two Kinds of Spirituality," in *Crisis of Piety* (Grand Rapids: Eerdmans, 1968).

[b] Neo-Platonism links Plato's thought to religion or spiritual life. This philosophical school started not long after Plato's death and was dominant in the Greco-Roman world. Its most important merger was the Greek translation of the Hebrew Scriptures called the Septuagint, named after the seventy scholars who translated it. More on Neo-Platonism can be found at *http://www.iep.utm.edu/neoplato/*.

[c] Quoted in Evelyn Underhill, *The Mystics of the Church* (New York: Schocken, 1964), 165, cited in Bloesch, *Crisis*, 100.

[d] Quoted in Bloesch, *Crisis*, 109.

[e] Nathan Soderbloom, *The Living God* (Boston: Beacon, 1962), 59.

Evangelical Approaches

Among those who hold an evangelical approach to spirituality are several approaches to understanding the work of the Holy Spirit. Here are four of the most common.

THE KESWICK MOVEMENT

The first way of understanding the work of the Holy Spirit in our sanctification is the Keswick or Deeper Life view.[15] It was developed in a small town in northern England in 1875. The Keswick approach to spiritual growth is based on the idea that the majority of Christians are living defeated lives because they are walking in the flesh, but we can lay hold of a victorious life and a deeper walk with Jesus through a crisis of faith.

Similar to the idea of carnal Christians discussed in the last chapter, Keswick theology claims that a distinct category of Christian are saved yet living a defeated life in slavery to sinful behaviors and desires.[16] Rather than accommodate the teaching of Scripture to our experience, it is better to simply admit that people who live like non-Christians are likely non-Christians. In Keswick theology, contrasts drawn between walking according to the flesh verses the Spirit are not between two kinds of Christians, but between the unregenerate and the regenerate.[17]

However instead of speaking of defeated or carnal Christians, we should understand our relationship to sin in terms of struggle and warfare, as Paul describes in Romans 7:14–25. The impulse to split Christians into two camps—carnal and spiritual—stems from a desire to please God and live for him. This distinction, however, misunderstands the basic mechanics of how people change.

What is the solution to the defeated life? Though the Deeper Life movement does not officially teach that a second major work of grace is needed, such experiences are common practice. Teachers in the movement speak of "laying hold" of a deeper life, but I don't think they are clear enough. We don't just lay hold of it; we learn it. We don't just passively pray it or will it or meditate upon it. We actively seek a deeper life, and we learn how to live it through faithful obedience, the road on which the Holy Spirit meets us. As Paul wrote, "*I have learned* how to be content with whatever I have. *I know how* to live on almost nothing or with everything. *I have learned* the secret of living in every situation, whether it is with a full stomach or empty, with plenty or little. *For I can* do everything through Christ, who gives me strength" (Phil. 4:11–13 NLT, emphasis added).[18]

THE HOLINESS MOVEMENT

The Holiness movement took shape during the expansion of nineteenth-century Methodism and is rooted in the teachings of John Wesley, Methodism's founder. Participants include the Nazarene church, Pilgrim Holiness, Wesley Methodists, and African-American Methodists. A few splinter charismatic groups also consider themselves in this movement, but we will address the charismatic movement in the next section.

According to the Holiness movement, what is the role of the Holy Spirit in salvation and sanctification? Getting saved is an event when a person decides to follow Christ, repents, believes, and is admitted into the family of God. At some point afterward comes sanctification, which they refer to as the second major work of grace.

I was personally involved in this movement at the age of nine when I went forward at a spring revival at the Northside Pilgrim Holiness Church. There was much rejoicing in our household when I did, especially by my maternal grandmother. She was the one who made sure we all went to church, including her wayward daughter, my mother. Because my mother was not in attendance at the revival meeting, my grandmother took it upon herself to instruct me and make sure I told my mother what happened that night.

Unfortunately a few days later, my salvation began coming apart. I began cussing again on the playground, and I laughed at a few dirty jokes. Sin still had a hold on me, and I didn't know how I would keep up appearances for much longer. Each day, my grandmother would ask how I was doing. She told me that I would struggle for a while, but I needed to go to church, do my Sunday school lesson, and keep myself pure. She assured me that soon I would be sanctified, and when that happened, I could live on a new and higher plane. She told me that since she had been sanctified, she no longer sinned. As a nine-year-old boy, this seemed entirely plausible, since my grandmother never did anything that remotely looked like sin. However to this day, as far as I know, I have not been sanctified in the way my grandmother promised. I know all too well that I still sin.

The Holiness and Keswick movements have much in common. Both teach that extra amounts of the Holy Spirit, received through a special experience, will lead to a deeper or higher life. But like the Keswick, the Holiness movement tends to discount the subtle nature of sin. In fact, it so minimizes sin that we no longer speak of it as sin but as mistakes. I recognize that changes have been made in recent years from the older approach that claimed believers could reach sinless perfection. Wesley called this state "perfect love," an entire abandonment to the Holy Spirit.[19] He believed that God promised to deliver his people from all willful sin, and Wesley called that state sanctification. He even believed as Christians matured, they could eventually return to the state that Adam and Eve knew before the fall.[20]

Yet the idea that an event or experience can decisively free us from having to fight daily with sin is difficult to support from Scripture. And we can point to at least two obvious differences between the life of Adam and Eve before the fall and the life of believers today. We live in a fallen world under a curse and are born with a sinful nature that we will have until death. Thus any approach to understanding how the Holy Spirit changes us must look beyond events and experiences alone to a process for change that aligns with the testimony of Scripture and reflects our experience of daily struggle.

THE PENTECOSTAL-CHARISMATIC MOVEMENT

Similar to the second experience of grace or the deeper life, a third move-ment that arose in the early twentieth century taught that followers of Jesus need to experience an additional work of God's Spirit known as baptism in the Spirit. While most evangelicals teach that all believers are baptized in the Spirit at spiritual birth,[21] those in the Pentecostal movement (as well as many charismatics) believe that the baptism of the Spirit is a second event separate from and subsequent to conversion. It is this signature experience that makes one an empowered believer.

Those in the Pentecostal movement in particular believe that this fresh experience or filling of the Holy Spirit is necessarily accompanied by speaking in tongues.[22] Other signs and gifts like hearing prophetic revela-tions from God are marks of this stream of evangelical spirituality.[23]

All three of these movements—Keswick, Holiness, and Pentecostal-Charismatic—believe that a second work of the Holy Spirit is needed for a person who is saved to become a deeper, more committed, and empowered follower of Christ. While seeking the deeper life is encouraged in all three movements, discipleship is not seen as necessary for salvation. Thus these theological perspectives tend to undermine the idea that our conversion to Jesus Christ necessarily entails a life of committed discipleship.

REFORMED SPIRITUALITY

A fourth approach to evangelical spirituality has its roots in the Puritans and grew out of their influence upon American spiritual growth and devel-opment. While at times this stream has been widespread, the Reformed movement has lost influence as the Pentecostal-Charismatic movement has grown in popularity. Unlike the previous three movements, Reformed spirituality does not teach the need for a second experience of the Holy Spirit. Instead, it teaches that all believers are born again or baptized in the Holy Spirit upon conversion, and that sanctification is both an event and a process.

Reformed theology teaches that we are uniquely transformed by God's grace when we exercise faith in Jesus Christ. But ongoing transformation is a process of renewing the mind in the truth, identifying idols and sinful hab-its, repenting of them, and following Christ in trust and obedience. Thus sanctification is ongoing, progressive, and lifelong. The Holy Spirit actively guides believers to make choices that are in obedience to God and his will, not primarily through an audible voice or prophetic words, but through the truth of God's Word changing their perspective and thinking.[24] Believers'

CONVERSION & DISCIPLESHIP

relationship to the Holy Spirit is give and take, ebb and flow, gradually progressive and rooted in the realism of life. The evidence of the Holy Spirit's work of transformation is the presence of the fruit of the Spirit.[25]

Churches in the Reformed spirituality movement include Puritans, Reformed denominations, and many Baptists and non-denominational congregations. However in many cases, Reformed spirituality has been simplified down to the practices of praying and reading the Bible each day. This movement also draws from some of the other movements including charismatics and from mystical spirituality.

The Change Process

Now that we have reviewed some of the historically evangelical streams of spirituality, let's take a closer look at what the Bible teaches about the way a person is changed and transformed.

STEP 1: TRANSFORMING OUR DESIRES

The Holy Spirit is in the business of changing people. He primarily does this by affecting the intentions of the heart and implanting a desire to serve and please God. The Spirit does work through events to ready people for the process of ongoing change. But events end and eventually fade into memories. So we need to understand that the Spirit's work is more than dramatic events or one-time experiences. His work that matters most is changing our character, which is an ongoing process.

The Spirit affects change by addressing our motivations and transforming our desires. Motivation needs both a why and a how. We must see the goal and be captured by the vision. But vision alone is not enough. Change also requires our commitment to training and discipline. For example Paul said to the young pastor Timothy, "Train yourself to be godly" (1 Tim. 4:7 NLT). Timothy needed a vision for what it means to be godly, but he also needed a process of training that required discipline and perseverance. Our resolve will weaken and fail, so we need to have the vision to become like Christ. That vision will empower the necessary training.

The Importance of the Body

When speaking of the change process, we should notice how Paul emphasizes the importance of the body, particularly in Romans 12:1 when he pivots from the theological to practical: "And so, dear brothers and sisters, I plead with you to give your bodies to God because of all he has done for you. Let them be a living and holy sacrifice—the kind he will find acceptable. This is truly the way to worship him" (NLT).

Nothing is more personal than our bodies. They affect everything we do and relate deeply to who we are. We experience life and relate to others through them. People may know who we are inside, but they identify us by our appearance and voice. Christians have the hope of one day receiving a new body that will be perfect and won't wear out. But until the resurrection, we must be dedicated to caring for the body we have been given. If we do not wash, nourish, rest, and heal our body, it will make us miserable.

Our bodies are essential to our identity. When people think of me, they first think of my appearance—height, weight, and demeanor—and the sound of my voice or laugh. And the body has its own form of knowledge. For example, we don't have to decide to breath, shiver, or sweat. We do these things automatically. The body also has great power that can be used for good or great evil.

Our body can be either our servant or our master. Paul chose to use discipline to make his body his servant (1 Cor. 9:26–27). The body is not morally neutral. Because of sin, our body requires transformation. Everything from our posture to our facial expressions and tone of voice can become our ally or our enemy.

God knows how dear our bodies are to us, which is why it is important to notice that he asks us to sacrifice them, to put our bodies on the altar (Rom. 12:1). If this image of placing one's body on an altar seems unpleasant or strange, that's because it should. The altars Paul's original readers were familiar with typically were used to sacrifice animals, a process which involved cutting and fire and resulted in the body being killed or consumed, a painful experience of death. Yet this is the image Paul uses to speak to the process of change. We are called to become a "living sacrifice." And we should be prepared: it will not be a comfortable experience.

So why would anyone want to offer up their body as a living sacrifice? We give ourselves to God because of all he has done for us.[26] We love him back with concrete actions, not just a rush of emotion. Placing ourselves on the altar and dying to self leads to our transformation into holiness and living in a way that pleases God. And unlike other sacrifices that end in death, this one, though painful, will result in life and eventually resurrection. Paul knows that despite the pain involved, we will do this if we have the right motivation and if the intention of our heart is good and true. There is nothing more worshipful than a willingness to give God what is most precious to us and to allow his Spirit to lead us into holy living. This is the worship that God seeks.

One of my favorite reasons for gathering for Christian worship once a week is our need to rehearse what we have in common. Worship is where we remember and learn to keep our collective story straight. I love the well-known *Book of Common Prayer.* The title implies that when we worship, we have a common language and a common goal. We share our common need for God, for forgiveness, grace, power, and comfort. We renew our motivation and remind ourselves of who we are and what we are to be doing. We remember that we are servants, pilgrims, disciples, and members of the body of Christ and that we are on mission with God. Throughout each week, we all have times when we are tempted to crawl off the altar. But when we gather together, we are reminded that on the altar is where we belong.

At this point, the history of mass conversion movements is quite interesting. In his study of early Christianity, sociologist Rodney Stark surprisingly found that doctrine was not the major factor in mass conversions and the rapid growth of Christianity. While it is true that people heard the message and found it attractive before they embraced the faith, typically their worldview did not change until after conversion.[27] When studying modern conversions to various religions, Stark found that "conversion to new, deviant religious groups occurs when, other things being equal, people have or develop stronger attachments to members of the group than they have with nonmembers."[28]

What this means is that people will not likely convert to a Christianity until they attach themselves closely to others, which is why disciples making disciples in our church communities is so important. The change process continues as we allow the Holy Spirit to work upon us in the context of a worshiping community because we need others to help us learn to confront our sin and live out the fruits of the Spirit.

How Does the Process Work?

Across the spectrum of our churches is agreement that we all want to become more like Christ and fulfill his Great Commission. But how do we become like Christ? Paul gives us a clue in Romans 12:2: "Don't copy the behavior and customs of this world, but let God transform you into a new person by changing the way you think. Then you will learn to know God's will for you, which is good and pleasing and perfect" (NLT).

Transforming behavior requires transforming the mind because the mind is the seat of the will and desires and directs action. In our mind, we sort out our desires, which are more than just thoughts—they are a force that must be controlled. Again, Paul is helpful for understanding how God transforms our mind, "For God is working in you, giving you the desire and the power to do what pleases him" (Phil. 2:13 NLT).

At the beginning of our discipleship journey with Christ, we become a new creation with a new nature, and God's Spirit comes to live in us.[29] Yet many of the sinful desires we had before remain and are not silent. C. S. Lewis well describes these unwanted desires:

> During my afternoon "meditations"—which I at least *attempt* quite regularly now—I have found out ludicrous and terrible things about my own character. Sitting by, watching the rising thoughts to break their necks as they pop up, one learns to know the sort of thoughts that do come. And, will you believe it, one out of every three is a thought of self-admiration: when everything else fails, having had its neck broken, up comes the thought, "What an admirable fellow I am to have broken their necks!" I catch myself posturing before the mirror, so to speak, all day long. I pretend I am carefully think-ing out what to say to the next pupil (for *his* good, of course) and then suddenly realise I am really thinking how frightfully clever I'm going to be and how he will admire me. . . . And then when you force yourself to stop it, you admire yourself for doing *that*. It is like fighting the hydra. . . . There seems to be no end to it. Depth under depth of self-love and self-admiration.[30]

Lewis is right; there is no end to this battle. And the more sophisticated a disciple becomes in understanding the dynamics of spiritual conflict, the more sophisticated the enemy becomes in his deception. But we must not develop an unhealthy preoccupation with the enemy nor with introspec-tively analyzing our base desires. The key to winning is cultivating godly desires and focusing on the one who gives these desires to us.

That's the good news. Paul tells us that through the Holy Spirit, "God is working" in us to give us his desires (Phil. 2:13 NLT). The Greek word translated "working" is ενεργειν, from which is derived the word energy. The Greek translated "giving you the desire" is θελειν meaning "to will." So in other words, God is a force that is moving our wills. He does more than fill our heads with new ideas. He changes our tastes and desires in such a way that they energize us and align us with his plan and purpose for us.

When someone asks, "How does God work, where does he start with us?" this is the answer. In Romans, Paul tells us to "let God transform you into a new person by changing the way you think. Then you will learn to know God's will for you, which is good and pleasing and perfect" (Rom.

12:2 NLT). After God changes our desires to what he wills, he gives us the ability or power to do what we now want to do. Consider how Paul describes this work of God in Galatians 5: "So I say, let the Holy Spirit guide your lives. Then you won't be doing what your sinful nature craves. The sinful nature wants to do evil, which is just the opposite of what the Spirit wants. And the Spirit gives us desires that are the opposite of what the sinful nature desires. These two forces are constantly fighting each other, so you are not free to carry out your good intentions" (Gal. 5:16–17 NLT).

The "good intentions" Paul speaks of here are things that we want to do. Yet as this passage makes clear, we are not entirely free to simply do what is pleasing to God because of our sinful nature. We are engaged in an internal spiritual battle of desires and wills. In addition, our hearts can still be confused and deceived.[31]

Throughout the Scriptures we learn of the two types of desires: the desires of the sinful nature and the desires of the Holy Spirit. We can determine if a desire is rooted in the sinful nature or is God-honoring by looking at the fruit that desire produces. For example, following the desires of our sinful nature results in attitudes and practices that are not pleasing to God: "sexual immorality, impurity, lustful pleasures, idolatry, sorcery, hostility, quarreling, jealousy, outbursts of anger, selfish ambition, dissension, division, envy, drunkenness, wild parties, and other sins like these" (Gal. 5:19–21a NLT). Clearly, this kind of fruit is not consistent with the Spirit active in a disciple of Jesus. In fact, Paul says quite bluntly that people who follow their sinful nature "will not inherit the Kingdom of God" (Gal. 5:21b NLT).

By contrast, following the desires of the Holy Spirit produces character qualities such as "love, joy, peace, patience, kindness, goodness, faithfulness, gentleness, and self-control" (Gal. 5:22–23 NLT). These qualities are expressed through our actions and both are what God wills and what bring him pleasure.

As Paul explains, part of discipleship is learning to put to death our sinful desires and cultivate desires that align with God's Spirit, "Those who belong to Christ Jesus have nailed the passions and desires of their sinful nature to his cross and crucified them there" (Gal. 5:24 NLT). Notice that disciples are required to act here—destroying our desires is not something done to us. We must take an active part in the process.

A desire is a thought, a temptation, or an urge. To participate in the process of changing our desires, we need to understand what is behind them and to better understand the role of our will in the change process.

What Is the Will?

"If anyone is willing to do His will, he will know of the teaching, whether it is of God or *whether* I speak from Myself" (John 7:17 NASB). Jesus says that understanding God's will is interactive, and he invites any willing person to enter his school and learn God's will through obedience. In other words, we learn God's will not through a process of mystical discernment but by simply obeying what we know of God and his ways. When we obey, God teaches and reveals more of himself.

But we won't be able to understand God's will if we have no true desire to change. Daily life will involve struggle and tension as we try to make decisions from the thousands of thoughts that pass through or rumble about in our brain. These thoughts are usually a combination of perceptions, emotions, and mental images of success or failure. Our body contributes to the conflict as well with its needs, pleasures, and emergencies. We must use our will to decide what to do with this mix of thoughts, emotions, and desires. We must organize them all with discernment, sorting good from bad and right from wrong, and manage the forces of our emotions. Disciples of Jesus do this organizing under the direction of the Holy Spirit, who reforms and strengthens our will.

Dealing with sinful desires in particular is not just a matter of will power—or trying harder. It's a matter of training the will in discernment through obedience to new, godly desires. Dallas Willard says it well, "The condition of our mind is very much a matter of the direction in which our will is set."[32] He goes on to explain how we deal with a sinful desire. "If I do not want my will to match God's will, it will be necessary to change my thoughts and feelings. Just resolving not to do it again will be of little use. Will alone cannot carry us to change. But will implemented through changing my thoughts and feelings can result in my becoming the kind of person who just doesn't do that kind of thing anymore."[33]

Two passages help us see how our thoughts and actions shape our will. Understandably, both also speak of conflict. The first text gives us a mental construct, and the second helps us to see the link between thought, temptation, and sin.

Learning to Wage War

In 2 Corinthians 10:3–5 we read, "We are human, but we don't wage war as humans do. We use God's mighty weapons, not worldly weapons, to knock down the strongholds of human reasoning and to destroy false arguments.

We destroy every proud obstacle that keeps people from knowing God. We capture their rebellious thoughts and teach them to obey Christ" (NLT).

If discipleship is learning from Jesus how to live our lives as though he were living them, it requires learning to be people who naturally will what Jesus wills. Yet this transformation cannot be accomplished with the tools available to fallen, sinful human beings. It is guaranteed to fail. Instead, we need the tools or weapons of God that have the power "to knock down the strongholds of human reasoning and to destroy false arguments." The battle is against these mental constructs that the enemy has created to deceive us and keep us from discerning and obeying the truth. These strongholds or fortresses of thought can control the mind, heart, and spirit, and because they feed desires, they can control the will.

How do we deconstruct a false ideology, or a mental framework? Paul describes the process. "We capture their rebellious thoughts and teach them to obey Christ" (2 Cor. 10:5 NLT). We might be tempted to think of this process as exclusively intellectual or the work of apologetics. Certainly the intellect plays a key role. But human reasoning is not sufficient. God's divine weapons also change our desires and reform our will.

The language in 2 Corinthians 10:3–5 pictures breaking into a prison and liberating the inmates. In this case, people are imprisoned by human ideas. This prison must be torn down with God's special weapons and the prisoners freed to choose to obey Christ.

When God changes the desire, he wins the heart. God won't violate the will, but he will inform the mind, energize the spirit, and appeal to the heart, and these in turn influence the will to choose his way. In the end, we must decide which way we will choose and take action. God won't choose for us, but he will make it possible for us to want what he wants.

Facing Temptation

Let's look at the role of our desires and will when we face temptation. James says, "And remember, when you are being tempted, do not say, 'God is tempting me.' God is never tempted to do wrong, and he never tempts anyone else. Temptation comes *from our own desires*, which entice us and drag us away. These desires give birth to sinful actions. And when sin is allowed to grow, it gives birth to death" (James 1:13–15 NLT, emphasis added).

James makes it clear that sin involves a process or journey that begins with our wrong desires and eventually leads to the act itself. James understands that we all have long-established patterns of sin in our lives and "undesirable desires" that affect our choices. These desires exist because we live in a sinful world and are subject to the weaknesses of our own flesh and the influence of demonic principalities and powers.[34] These reasons are why our will needs to be retrained through the renewing of our mind.[35]

Notice that James clears God of any responsibility for temptation. God is not the source of our temptations, nor does he lead anyone into sin.[36] James is clear that God neither tempts us to sin, nor is God himself tempted by sin. Yet what about Jesus? We know that he was tempted at all points as we are, yet he did not sin.[37] Since he had no sin nature, Jesus could not have sinned, yet we can say that he was tempted more intensely than anyone else. What do I mean? Simply that the power of temptation is felt most keenly in resisting, and those who give in to temptation do not truly understand the power of sin. Only those who resist it to the full know the full extent of its power.

So while we can say that God doesn't tempt anyone, he does lead us into situations where we will be exposed to temptation. This happened to Jesus in the wilderness, where he was led by the Holy Spirit.[38] It happened again in the Garden of Gethsemane, where Jesus faced a crisis of his will, yet ultimately resisted the temptation to change it and submitted to the Father (Luke 22:39–46).

In these situations, the enemy Lucifer and his minions, the principalities and powers, do the tempting. They tempt directly but also use the world system and culture to influence our thoughts and desires. Our enemy lies and deceives in order to achieve his goal, stealing us from God and destroying us.[39] James is clear—we must resist the devil and our own wrong desires that also work against our goal of growing into the likeness of Jesus.

To be tempted or to think of a sin is not to sin. I love to golf, and many times I have considered giving myself a five on a hole when I actually got a six. Typically, I reject and dismiss this temptation because the temporary pleasure of having a lower score isn't worth the cost of compromising my integrity as a disciple of Jesus. So it remains a thought, not even really a temptation. But if I fixate on this idea and allow it to grow into a desire to be a golfer who shoots in the 80s rather than the 90s, it becomes a temptation that has the potential to overtake my desire to be a man of integrity.

At this point, I begin to rationalize. I tell myself things like it's only one shot. No one cares, right? I will feel better if I do it. The desires feed my thoughts, and I justify myself. At this point, I've capitulated to sin. In other words, I sin not at the point when I write a five on my scorecard, but when I inwardly assent to these thoughts and desires because I'm no longer resisting. I've given in, and the action is inevitable.

As James says, "Temptation comes from our own desires, which entice us and drag us away" (James 1:14 NLT). The image of being dragged away may be intended to remind us of fishing; the fish is caught with the hook and reeled in. Others say that it pictures a predator dragging away prey to consume it. Both images convey the same basic idea—once we have been hooked by wrong desire, sin will destroy us. Because desires lead to actions, then the work of renovation must be done at the level of desires. This work requires more than wishful thinking. Changing our desires is a process that takes time and divine intervention at deep levels. It is a work of grace yet requires our involvement and effort.

In his grace, God puts his good desires in us to will and work for his good pleasure. At the same time, the enemy works to exploit the sinful desires that are also present in us. The result is internal warfare and it is why God tells us to use his weapons to wage war. It will take his divinely powerful weapons to destroy the false ideas, images, and desires in our minds and win the battle. What are those weapons? They are the topic of the next chapter where we take a closer look at the second aspect of change, what we refer to as spiritual exercises.

5

THE HOLY SPIRIT AND HOW PEOPLE CHANGE

Part 2

> *Widespread transformation of character through wisely disciplined discipleship to Christ can transform our world. It can disarm the structural evils that have always dominated humankind and now threaten to destroy the world.*
>
> —DALLAS WILLARD, *THE SPIRIT OF THE DISCIPLINES*
>
> *There is no need to despair. Hundreds of these adult converts have been reclaimed after a brief sojourn in the Enemy's camp and are now with us. All habits of the patient, both mental and bodily, are still in our favor.*
>
> —C. S. LEWIS, *THE SCREWTAPE LETTERS*

In the last chapter, we looked at how the Holy Spirit must begin our transformation at the level of our desire. But reading and understanding this is not enough. We must put our understanding into action. Similarly, if an athletic trainer explained the dynamics of human anatomy and how all of the training machines work, then tailored a training regime just for you, you would have useful knowledge to improve your health. But that knowledge alone would not change you. You need to use that knowledge to do the exercises the trainer prescribed for you.

Just as we must exercise our physical body to develop strength and maintain health, we must do specific exercises intended to reform, inform, and train our mind, desires, and will. These are the "must have," required, no-exceptions exercises of spiritual growth. Enabled by divine power, they make our mind and will into the weapons Paul says we need to wage war against the strongholds of thought that control us and our sinful desires, temptations, and spiritual enemies.[1] What are these exercises?

- Worshiping regularly with a covenant community of saints
- Serving others through speaking and working in the name of Christ
- Hearing, reading, and studying Scripture
- Confessing sin and prayerful conversing with God
- Submitting to authority
- Practicing silence and solitude
- Intentionally living a mission that includes helping others become disciples

Most of these exercises are not natural for us. It takes time for us to grow accustomed to them and make them into habits.

STEP 2: SPIRITUAL EXERCISES

Paul instructed his disciple Timothy, "Train yourself to be godly" (1 Tim. 4:7b NLT). Over the years, I've found that people approach the practice of these spiritual exercises or disciplines in two ways: the proactive approach and the reactive approach. The *proactive* approach involves intentionally developing a structure of discipline and accountability. A proactive disciple has a specific plan for growth that includes specific exercises. For example, a person might decide to read, study, and journal through the Gospels in one year. Others may decide to covenant with three other people to meet at a scheduled time once a week to discuss questions, pray, and hold one another accountable.

The *reactive* approach isn't a planned or scheduled one but exercises spiritual disciplines in response to circumstances or to positive or negative events in life that lead to significant changes. If you are diagnosed with a serious disease or your spouse leaves, then you react. Reactive disciples who do not have a proactive plan for spiritual growth need a safety net, which for most is their church community. They need to belong to a group of like-minded Christians in a local church who have committed to live a life that is pleasing to God. This needs to be a real, flesh-and-blood church, not just membership in the universal church. When real troubles and difficulties come, disciples need to be surrounded by real people who can offer real help.

The reactive approach is the bare minimum or survival mode for the disciple of Jesus. At times in our lives, we may find ourselves in this mode, just surviving and being reliant upon the grace of God through his church. But we will only grow into maturity as followers of Christ if we develop and follow a proactive plan that promotes growth. So why is doing this so difficult for many people?

I've found that the idea of having a training plan and exercising self-discipline to follow it puts people off. While they may agree that a self-disciplined life is good, they may have tried and failed or are intimidated by the work involved. Others believe that the disciplined life is for elite Christians, but not for common, everyday followers of Christ. Yet as we have seen, God expects every one of his followers to grow to maturity in Christ. And not only that, but to be a contagious carrier of his message.

I believe the kicker, so to speak, is desire. We can develop plans and put structures into place, but if we don't really want to change—if we lack the desire—we will inevitably fail. In a sense, the very thing that must be transformed is the key to transformation. While the initial desire to be disciplined comes from God, he does not magically empower our change apart from our involvement. We must be actively involved in training our desires. Group discipline is usually required to help disciples develop personal discipline.

We must also allow our desires to be changed by responding to the grace of God's discipline. Paul, who preached powerfully of God's grace, was a champion of discipline. In his letters to Timothy, specifically in 2 Timothy, and to the Corinthians, he spoke of the power of discipline, its necessity for growth in the Christian life, and that it is a work of grace.[2]

Based on the content of Paul's letters, Timothy seemed to be a shy man, intimidated by his youth, who tended to be nervous and lose his way. Paul carefully reminded Timothy of the work he was to do and to avoid being sidetracked (1 Tim. 4:11–16). Paul specifically told Timothy not to fear and reminded him of his calling and gifts (2 Tim. 1:5–11).

Paul knew that Timothy would need grace to accomplish his work, for he wrote, "Timothy, my dear son, be strong through the grace that God gives you in Christ Jesus" (2 Tim. 2:1 NLT). Earlier we defined grace as a gift of God doing for us what we cannot do for ourselves. When God provides what we need when we need it, we can say that we've received his grace "in Christ Jesus," because grace is provided to us through our union with Christ and his church.

This work of multiplication that God called Timothy to do is one of the most difficult ministries in the church. Paul summarized this ministry, "You have heard me teach things that have been confirmed by many reliable witnesses. Now teach these truths to other trustworthy people who will be able to pass them on to others" (2 Tim. 2:2 NLT). To do this work, Timothy needed qualities that were not native to his soul. He needed the dedication of a soldier, the discipline of an athlete, and the patience of a farmer.

So how did Timothy receive the grace to successfully engage in this difficult work of teaching others the truth of God? He learned how to do the work in community, by watching Paul teach others, modeling how to accept and pass on the grace to those who desired to receive it. God's grace was something Timothy needed to receive, and he received it by using his mental abilities to gain knowledge and then using his body to actually teach this knowing and doing to others. *If Timothy had no part to play in accessing God's grace, then there would have been no reason for Paul to exhort him to be strong in it.*

In short, Timothy had to do at least two things. He had to pray and ask God to give him the desire and the resources he needed to do his work. Then he needed to step out in faith and do the work with the expectation that God would provide the trustworthy people for him to train in the gospel. I also add one more thing: Timothy must have a plan or structure for his own learning and for teaching others. We can assume that Timothy was guided in his own spiritual growth by his mentor Paul and at least initially based his teaching upon the example Paul set for him during his years pastoring in Ephesus. In fact, Paul wrote Timothy while Timothy was ministering at the very same church in Ephesus. Timothy's knowledge of how to do this ministry was not from a divine revelation of something hidden and unknown. He learned how from Paul, and God's grace came to Timothy through Paul as he exercised discipline in learning, establishing a structure and a plan and then actually doing the work of training others.

In other words, *discipline is a grace that requires structure, planning, and effort to fully receive.* It requires finding people who desire the same things we do and requires using reasoning and common sense to determine what needs to be done, calendars to create schedules, and the knowledge and skills we have been given to get the work done. We also need the support of others in the body of Christ because *discipline is typically best exercised in a group context.* Even those who are not very self-disciplined can be disciplined in a group. So while self-discipline is good, disciples can still grow if they are simply in a community of other Jesus followers who are growing together.

Discipline of the Mind

So we've established that grace is more than just a passive transformation that God works in us. Discipline is also grace that enables us to learn from others, utilize our knowledge and understanding, plan and set schedules, and exert effort toward growing in godliness. But how does all of this relate to the desires we looked at in Step 1?

We need to remember that all sin is the result of the good desires given to us by God turning bad. In other words, sin is a corruption of good desires. So for example a desire for power or for sex or to succeed can all be good in the right contexts yet devastating in others. When we exercise desires that are in accord with God's purposes, they can honor God. But when we exercise desires for our selfish purposes, they are destructive.

In addition, we need to recognize that many of our desires are set deeply in our bodies and as a result have a visceral power over us that can overcome our mind and the best intentions of our will. For example, a man can determine in his mind and will not to lust, or gamble, or lie, but his primal urges for sex, money, and esteem can override his determination. This is why it takes time, effort, and discipline to overcome our sinful desires and why we must train our bodies, wills, and minds in godliness. Even as we mature in Christ, these visceral drives can remain unpredictable and dangerous. Paul speaks of them as the "sin that dwells in my members" (Rom. 7:23 NRSV), and we must not underestimate the power they have over us.

As we saw in Step 1, the will depends on the mind to provide it with information. So what we put in our mind matters. Our minds are filled with thoughts and feelings, many of them subconscious, and they inform and effect our willingness to obey the will of God.

Let me give you examples of what I am talking about. But first, I'll give you definitions of what I mean by the following terms so we are on the same page.

Ideas: beliefs based on our life experience and worldview

Images: concrete and specific pictures or memories

Feelings: passions and desires.[3]

The goal of disciplining our mind is so that our ideas, images, and feelings consistently match the will of God, because we are seeking to conform our will to his. In his wonderful book the *Renovation of the Heart*, Dallas Willard describes it this way: "spiritual transformation only happens as each essential dimension of the human being is transformed to Christlikeness under the direction of a regenerate will interacting with constant overtures of the grace from God. Such transformation is not the result of mere human effort and cannot be accomplished by putting pressure on the will alone."[4]

Adam, Eve, and the Progression of Sin

The first practical example we will look at is the first temptation and sin of Adam and Eve. Their sin began with a simple idea stated by the serpent that even if we do what God has said not to do, "You won't die!" (Gen. 3:4 NLT). All sin begins with a lie. Christopher Hitchens claimed that God is a misogynistic, genocidal killjoy who planned to keep his entire creation under constant surveillance for eternity. Hitchens believed that God doesn't love us, trust us, or want the best for us, and he probably will stomp us out like ants when he has finished his grand, global experiment. Seen in light of the Scriptures, this is a lie because God does really care about the people he has made. We can trust God because he does have our best interests at heart.

Lies like this are derivatives of that first lie. The serpent goes on to develop his lie in Eve's mind. "God knows that your eyes will be opened as soon as you eat [the fruit], and you will be like God, knowing both good and evil" (Gen. 3:5 NLT). How did Eve respond? She believed the serpent, probably because she badly wanted to experience what God experienced. She believed that God was withholding something good from her, a greater knowledge. Satan's lie is like Hitchens, that God cannot be trusted because he isn't all that good. Eve allows the lie to take hold in her thoughts and to influence her understanding of God, his character, and his motives. But it doesn't end there. The thought impacts a desire for something that can often be depicted as an image of a person or thing.

The image that tempted Eve was an attractive piece of fruit. "She saw that the tree was beautiful and its fruit looked delicious" (Gen. 3:6 NLT). Thus the idea—"You won't die!"—is connected to and empowered by the image. Think about the power of advertising images. A mannequin in a department store is used to show us what clothes will look like if we are wearing them. Yet most of us are not built like the mannequin. The goal is to fire up our desire, to get us to imagine how good we would look if we were wearing the clothes and how we would impress all those important people in our life.

Temptation uses attractive and powerful images, of course, but it can also use fear. Consider the ideas that God is not real and Christians cannot be trusted. These ideas are being empowered by frightening images of priests molesting children, pastors having affairs, and television preachers who have lavish lifestyles. These images of hypocrisy strengthen the idea that Christianity is false and that God is powerless. When combined with a lie, an image can connect deeply with our emotions. If unchecked, these emotions can become our default response to the lies and images.

Let's return to Adam and Eve. What feeling did Eve experience after connecting her ideas about God with the image of the fruit?: "she wanted the wisdom it would give her" (Gen. 3:6 NLT). This situation reminds me of an old adage that I have attempted to follow in my life. "Once you are in bed with a beautiful, naked lady, it is too late to change your mind." In other words, if we want to resist temptation, we keep it from reaching our desires and grabbing us at a visceral level. Once desire is attached to its object and the fruit is within reach, we're a goner. Eve allowed herself to be convinced by the serpent's lie and to doubt God, so after she saw the fruit, she wanted it. From this point on, her feelings—her desires for pleasure and wisdom—are in control. While it is possible to stop at this point, it is unlikely that anyone will pull back their hand. Why not? Because we were designed and created to serve, and as the Bible reminds us, we will either serve God or sin. "Everyone who sins is a slave to sin" (John 8:34).

This is why we can't master our sin by willpower alone. Our slave master won't listen to us if we come at it with mere human willpower. The ideas and the images we have allowed into our mind, created by our culture and environment and fed by our desires, will work against our own moral conscience. The natural tendency of our sinful nature is to seek to satisfy our desires and follow where our feelings lead us. This is why we must learn to train our will to resist temptation to sin. Human willpower alone cannot resist sin, but a will empowered and trained by God's gracious discipline can resist sin. In fact, the grace of God's discipline can also train our emotions to be in line with his emotions and will. This is the goal of growing into maturity in Christ—having both a transformed mind and godly emotions—to think the thoughts of Christ and love the things God loves.

As you probably know already, the example we have been considering does not end well. The people eat the fruit, and we experience the result—the trains don't run on time any more! But let's look at one more example from Scripture, the story of Cain and Abel. These two brothers can help us further by answering the question of how we get to the point where we want the right things.

Am I My Brother's Keeper?

Adam and Eve bore two sons and named them Cain and Abel. Abel was a shepherd, while his brother, Cain, was a farmer. At harvest time, each son presented an offering to the Lord. "Cain presented some of his crops as a gift to the Lord. Abel also brought a gift—the best portions of the first-born lambs from his flock. The Lord accepted Abel and his gift, but he did not accept Cain and his gift. This made Cain very angry, and he looked dejected" (Gen. 4:3–5 NLT).

Contrary to popular opinion, this is not a story about why it is better to give a blood sacrifice instead of crops. The difference between the two offerings is in the intention behind them. God is pleased when we give him a portion of the best we have, our "first fruits." Abel did this. Cain did not. The text tells us that he gave God "some of his crops."

God accepted Abel's gift of his best, but he rejected Cain's offering. And Cain became enraged at this rejection. His facial expression and general demeanor revealed his anger. Again we see that sin began with wrong ideas about God. Though we aren't told this, it seems that Cain was aware of what God required, but he didn't think it necessary to do God's standard. His will and his desire were not inclined to give his best to God. Cain's image of success was different than Abel's. Cain responded to God with feelings of anger, a sour look, and a defensive spirit.

God doesn't just leave Cain to wallow in his misery, thankfully. He offers Cain counsel and direction to remedy his situation. "Why are you so angry?" God asks him (Gen. 4:6 NLT), "Why do you look so dejected?" Counselors everywhere are pleased to see that God himself begins his therapy session with questions. Certainly, God knows the answer to his questions. But he wants to help Cain, so he requires Cain to come up with the answers. However, notice that Cain does not answer. So God continues by showing Cain the way out of his predicament: "You will be accepted if you do what is right. But if you refuse to do what is right, then watch out! Sin is crouching at the door, eager to control you. But you must subdue it and be its master" (Gen. 4:7 NLT).

Here we see it all laid out. God provides the road to recovery and warns Cain against the path that would lead to his doom. Unfortunately, Cain does not listen, and he is mastered by his sin. The result? He kills his brother, Abel. Even though God speaks truth to Cain and provides him with a path to obedience, Cain does not want what God offers. He wants his brother to suffer. He wants to exert his own power and show his own importance.

How does God respond? The sad result of Cain's actions is a special curse on him and his family. Cain is banished, sentenced to a life of failure and sorrow for lying to God and failing to fight his sin. But as a sign of his continued grace, God places a mark upon him for his protection. Notice that throughout the narrative, even after Cain killed his brother, he does not take responsibility for the murder and complains about the punishment. All of this indicates that Cain didn't grasp the depth of his sin nor understand that he had become a slave to it.

We can trace the flow of sin through the ideas, images, and feelings Cain has.

> **Cain's Idea:** I can't really trust God to meet my needs; therefore, I can't afford to give him my best.
>
> **Cain's Image:** Success is competing against my brother and proving that my way is better than his way.
>
> **Cain's Feeling:** I long for superiority and acceptance.

Though Cain desired acceptance, he did not seek it God's way. Instead, he sought to justify himself by following his own way of pleasing God. God graciously sought to discipline Cain by telling him how to respond to these sinful thoughts and emotions. Again, notice that God's grace required a response from Cain. First, God tells Cain to do what is right. As followers of Christ, we have all been enabled by the Spirit to choose to do the right thing. Certainly, doing so might be hard at first because we will be fighting against the false ideas, images, and emotions that have trained our will over a lifetime of sin. Yet as we start acting right, we will begin to experience emotions that align with our obedience. Doing things God's way would have led to the very thing that Cain desired. We must learn to trust God, to take him at his word, rather than believing our own ideas about him.

Second, we notice the warning God provides: "If you refuse to do what is right, watch out!" This is the other side of the equation. God tells us that our decisions are not morally neutral and will not go uncontested. Sin will seek to control us. If we aren't serious about training our will and choosing what is right, we are fair game. Remember that the desire to do right comes from God himself and initiates the change process.[5]

Finally, God tells Cain that he must face his sin and wrestle it to the ground. The process of how to subdue sin and master it is unpacked for us throughout the New Testament. For instance, Paul says what God said to Cain in slightly more detail, "Those who belong to Christ Jesus have nailed the passions and desires of their sinful nature to his cross and crucified them there" (Gal. 5:24 NLT). To do what is right, we must nail to the cross the ideas, images, and feelings that have trained our will in sin. We are the authors of this action and active participants in the process.

To this point, we have taken two steps forward in the change process. First, we have looked at the necessity of focusing on our *desires*, seeing that God puts desires in us to do his will. But God's grace does not end there.

He also gives us the grace of discipline, a grace in which we must participate by taking steps of obedience. This is what we have called *spiritual exercises*. Now we turn to the third step in the process: *developing Christlike habits*.

STEP 3: DEVELOPING CHRISTLIKE HABITS

One of the keys to developing Christlike habits is learning to distinguish between our feelings and our will, which requires self-control. I appreciate Dallas Willard's definition. "Self-control is the steady capacity to direct yourself to accomplish what you have chosen or decided to do and be, even though you don't feel like it."[6] If I had depended on my feelings to get this book written, it would never have happened. Many things get in the way of productivity. I discipline myself by willing to do God's will, and I am sometimes surprised at what doing God's will requires of me. When I use my training to break through inertia created by my laziness, I find a joy that is deep and satisfying. The process of developing self-control is how we form godly habits.

Most Christians have a passing familiarity with the fruit of the Spirit. We typically think of this fruit as character qualities or aspects of our personality developed by the Holy Spirit. Yet I want to suggest that *before joy or gentleness is a characteristic of our personality, it is a habit formed by spiritual exercise*. The fruit of the Spirit is habits. And these habits, given enough time and perseverance, will form character and impact conduct.

You have likely heard the statement, "We judge our behavior based on intention; others judge us by our actions." For example, we might defend hurting someone else by saying that we never intended to hurt that person. But the fact is that we *did* hurt the person. The damage was done. If our intention doesn't match our conduct, there is a mismatch, and the message is not getting through to others. Our intentions and desires do not reflect our character until they are matched by our behavior. And that behavior is developed over time by forming habits that conform to the intention of the heart.

Scores of books and resources teach people how to form good habits. Essentially, they instruct us to put off old habits and replace them with new ones.[7] The best term I have heard for this process is *habitudes*, which I learned from Tim Elmore, an innovator in student training.[8] The idea behind a *habitude* is establishing something that does more than change our actions; it changes our attitude as well.

Several passages in Scripture get at the importance of forming long-term habits, but one of the most helpful is Hebrews 5. We'll first look at 5:11–12: "There is much more we would like to say about this, but it is difficult to explain, especially since you are spiritually dull and don't seem to listen. You have been believers so long now that you ought to be teaching others" (NLT).

Spiritually dull? Not listening? Sadly, this paragraph describes many Christian communities at various times in the checkered history of the church. The author of Hebrews has been speaking about Jesus' role in salvation as Israel's High Priest. In the author's opinion, this teaching is not a simple concept to grasp. It requires some deeper engagement. He felt that learning more provided great benefit, but that his teaching would be wasted on his readers. Why? Because they had not shown any progress in growing as disciples. In fact, they had regressed. The assumption behind his criticism is that they should be teaching others by now. Again, we see the importance of teaching and that becoming teachers, both formally and informally, is considered essential to the Great Commission.[9] You can't make disciples without teaching them to obey everything that Christ commanded.[10]

The ability to teach others is one of the expectations that defines growth for followers of Christ. Yet history has shown that entire churches and Christian groups can depart from this basic expectation. Most scholars see the book of Hebrews as an unknown author's words to the church in Jerusalem just prior to the city's fall in 70 AD. If this is true, it means that even the first church—a good church once led by the apostles—can lose its energy and motivation. Human beings who are not growing will naturally regress. The author of Hebrews understood this, and his warnings are an attempt to rock these Christians out of their lethargic resistance to growth. He continues, "Instead, you need someone to teach you again the basic things about God's word. You are like babies who need milk and cannot eat solid food. For someone who lives on milk is still an infant and doesn't know how to do what is right" (Heb. 5:12–13 NLT).

The image here is intentionally insulting. The Hebrews author likens the saints to whiny, diaper-clad babies who can't care for themselves and should all be in the nursery, not out with the adults in worship. Peter uses kind language to encourage his readers to long for the pure, spiritual milk of the word, "like newborn babies" (1 Peter 2:2 NLT). Peter was speaking to a general audience that was regional; in Hebrews the author is dealing with a specific problem. But the author of Hebrews is blunt. He isn't likening these Christians to babies—he is calling them babies. This is not something commendable but a self-inflicted condition created by neglect and self-indulgence.

There is only one way to grow, and growth won't happen overnight. Developing the habits of the heart, the fruit of the Spirit, isn't a quick process. This fruit doesn't just fall onto our heads from the sky. They are habits we learn by placing ourselves into a covenant relationship with others and submitting to the grace of discipline to form new habits. The Hebrews author says as much. "Solid food is for those who are mature, who through training have the skill to recognize the difference between right and wrong" (Heb. 5:14 NLT). How is maturity defined? Notice it is something developed through training. It includes a level of skill, specifically the ability to exercise moral discernment and wisdom. The New International Version gets at the idea that this training requires constant practice. "Solid food is for the mature, who by constant use have trained themselves to distinguish good from evil" (Heb. 5:14). Without practice, we will not form the habits that train our will to act in accordance with God's will.

There are no shortcuts here. These *habitudes* are only formed in those who submit themselves to training. Over a period of time, they will develop skills in right thinking and behaving, which is where we see the difference between immaturity and maturity. The immature may possess the desire to grow. They may take some initial steps and even begin some spiritual exercises. But when they are away from community accountability or when circumstances change, they quit. Only when people take their training seriously will they make progress.

Discipline Isn't Optional

If you read the Bible, you can't escape its clear teaching on the importance of discipline.[11] Earlier, we looked at the importance of training our desires and will in the context of a community with other believers and that discipline is developed in two ways: personal and corporate. While some people are naturally self-disciplined, we can thank God that self-discipline alone is not the only criteria for spiritual growth. The vast majority of people I have pastored and taught over the years have started their spiritual growth with a form of corporate discipline. This group supports us and provides the structure we need for the discipline to be effective.

Sadly, Christians and Christian leaders in the West have given significant push-back against discipline. They do not outright deny the importance of discipline. Yet they resist creating too much structure for community-based spiritual growth and corporate discipline. Typically, sermons focus on self-discipline, providing individualized plans for people to do on their own. Also, some churches have high expectations for leadership development, but do not pass this expectation down to the average church member.

Why the resistance? Well, discipline takes extra work. In other cases, the resistance may be an attempt to avoid looking like a cult or another religious group that places high expectations on its adherents. Some cults, to be sure, utilize corporate discipline as a means of control, but I don't think it is wise to base our strategy on a reaction to an overreaction. Just because a group crossed the line in training students or church members doesn't mean that we should reject discipline altogether. Our challenge is to find appropriate levels of accountability that create healthy change in people.

On average, it takes at least three to four months to form a new habit. For that habit to take up residence in the heart and form the will may take even longer. Forming these habits requires a great deal of support, which even those outside the church acknowledge. Consider the process of escaping an addiction to alcohol, tobacco, drugs, or other destructive behaviors. The recovery movement understands the need for process. But for some reason when developing positive habits that lead to Christ-like qualities, we tend to downplay the importance of establishing a long-term process for growth. The behaviors we want to change may be less destructive than addiction to alcohol or drugs, or they may just be harder to see, similar to the difference between trying to convince a person with stage-four cancer to see a doctor and trying to persuade someone who feels pretty good to adopt a healthier lifestyle. Our challenge in convincing people of the need for discipline is always harder to reach those who don't see their need for help.

How Spiritual Disciplines Form Habits

When we start to train our mind to look at life differently, a great struggle will ensue.[12] And if this training is not in the context of supportive relationships, we will probably fail. Lack of relational support is also why so many people gain back weight after significant weight loss. If they think it is a terrible loss to not eat chips, cookies, pasta, and ice cream, they look on these unhealthy foods with longing and miss eating them. Eventually, they go back to their old habits because they *want* to go back and think they need to.

So like the goals in weight loss and healthy eating, the goal for spiritual growth is to form the will through the process of transforming desires and then through obedience to exercise good desires until they establish good habits and godly character. As Willard says: "We want to have a will that is fully functional, not at war with itself and capable of directing all of the parts of the self in harmony with one another under the direction of God."[13]

As helpful as spiritual disciplines are, they must not be confused with spirituality itself. They are not the basis for our relationship with God but simply practices that provide a context for him to work to transform us. I find it most helpful to think of spiritual disciplines as like the exercises we do to improve our physical well-being. Some disciplines will work indirectly like running, which changes the physiology of the body. The muscles burn energy, the lungs expand to take in increased oxygen, and the heart pumps harder. Over time (several weeks), the muscles grow stronger, the lungs have more capacity, and the heart's ability to pump blood increases. The runner *did not directly will the muscles, heart, and lungs to become better; this happened indirectly.* The runner willed to run to attain the desired result but also gained greater general health.

The spiritual disciplines work in a similar way. Let's say that you desire to become a more loving person. You can't command your feelings to suddenly change. But you can choose to take the actions that will lead to the desired result. You ask God to change your motives. Then like a runner, you begin a program of regularly praying, taking in God's word, and worship him in a variety of ways. Over time, your heart begins to enjoy pleasing him, like many runners begin to enjoy running. You may choose to fast, transferring the physical desire for food to spiritual longing for a deeper experience of God and the nourishment he provides. Then you may choose to serve others by doing loving things for them. Suddenly one day you realize that you enjoy serving others and that loving others has become natural for you. Like running changes the body, your spiritual discipline exercises, developed into habits, change your character, which is revealed by how you act. You chose to keep at these exercises because God put the desire for change in your heart.

Let me give you another practical, concrete example from real life. One fruit of the Spirit is self-control, the ability to do what we intend to do and not do what we don't intend to do. Many people lack this ability. They cannot pass a pastry tray without having a taste, or pass by an attractive person without flirting. Often the desire for that food or person remains in their heart and mind.

In the Sermon on the Mount, Jesus speaks of the process of spiritual transformation. The religious leaders, scribes, and Pharisees were focused on external behavior, ignoring the heart. But Jesus looks at the *source* of behavior, not just the outward appearance. He teaches that true godliness is driven from the mind, will, and spirit. For example, Jesus teaches that murder is the result of anger. If people are not first angry with others, they are not likely to murder them. So rather than avoiding the act of murder, we should focus on thoughts, attitudes, and feelings. Jesus tells us to deal with our anger, cultivate peace and love in our relationships, and forgive others who wrong us.

Here is an analogy. If you are flying to Houston from Los Angeles, you don't have to fly to Seattle. Flying to Seattle is not something you need to worry about. In the same way, if you learn to forgive others and deal with the root of your anger, you won't need to worry that you will kill them.

Lust provides another concrete example and connects to our earlier discussion about self-control. Suppose you are a man who meets an attractive woman, and you allow the image of her to take up residence in your mind. You can't go through a day without thinking about her, having fantasies about her, and creating an alternative universe where you are together. You realize that something must be done to stop these desires. Our first impulse, trying harder to exert our will power, won't work. You can't command yourself, "DON'T LUST. DON'T EVEN THINK ABOUT HER!" Neither will attempting to obey commands and keep promises. No, the problem is too deep for these solutions. You need to address the source of your thoughts and the reasons behind your desire. *The goal is to get to a state where not thinking about the woman does not seem like a loss.* You need to examine your longing and why you feel deprived when you don't have what you desire. You need to bring the provision of God into that place of longing.

These situations are where the spiritual exercises and disciplines are helpful. The good news is that we have remedies to cure wrong desires! Whether our longing is for a person, food, a house, a job, or some other thing, the remedy is the same. We need to consider some basic things:

- Begin by asking God, "Why am I longing for this person, thing, or situation?" Pray for help in discerning the source. Find another person you trust to talk with about it. Dietrich Bonhoeffer often spoke about how sin wants nothing more than to be alone with you. Sin is empowered when we shut others out.

- Take a close look at your expectations and think about the consequences of satisfying your sinful desire. Often, we fail to think through to the end. So we need to ask what would it be like, honestly, to get what we want? Our dreams are filled with assumptions about the world that are not aligned with reality. Graciously, God will show us the fallacy of our dreams, which may have been fed by the values and idols of the culture in which we live. Also, you may have triggers in your life, unconscious ways of responding in which you've been trained to be dissatisfied with what you are or have. Remember that the enemy's goal is to make us dissatisfied with what God has given us and to doubt that he loves us. The enemy wants us to think that God is withholding good things from us.

- Be patient. Change takes time. You may ask why and then have to wait in trust for God to reveal the answer. In the meantime, practice what he tells you. Avoid the triggers and practice the antidote: remember that everything you have is a gift from God and learn to be thankful for what you do have. Focus on the good news of what Jesus has done for you in the cross and resurrection. Your mind will eventually change and inform your will. Over time, you will begin to want what God has convinced you is good. One day it will dawn on you that you no longer miss thinking about that person, food, house, job, or whatever. Its power is gone, and that is just fine with you.

- Keep exercising the spiritual disciplines such as worship, service, Scripture reading and memorization, prayer, fasting, confession, submission, silence, and solitude. These disciplines expose our motives and bring the flaws in our character to the surface. Negative thoughts that have been buried for a long time and create destructive emotions will be exposed. The disciplines will provide the structure and context that you need for long-term growth and maturity.

Before we conclude this chapter, let's summarize the change process. As we saw in Step 1, change begins with the work of the Holy Spirit and the *desire* that God places in us (Phil. 2:13). But desires alone do not change us. We must *respond in obedience*, and one of the helpful tools that God provides for this response is the grace of discipline. With his enabling power, we must train our will by changing the way we think (our ideas), what we want (our images), and our feelings (our emotions). We do these things by engaging in the spiritual practices that God has prescribed for us (1 Tim. 4:7). Over time, these disciplines *lead to habits* that affect both our attitudes and behavior (Heb. 5:11–13). Now, we will briefly consider the result of all this—a change in our *character*.

The Result: The Character of Christ

Peter blessed the church saying, "May God give you more and more grace and peace as you grow in your knowledge of God and Jesus our Lord" (2 Peter 1:2 NLT). The modern mind typically thinks of knowledge as facts and information. While the knowledge of God does inform the mind, knowledge of him goes much deeper than surface level understanding. The knowledge Peter speaks of is gained by someone who has engaged in spiritual formation.[14] It's the knowledge we gain as we take on the character of

Christ that includes the relational intimacy we have with God because of our constant interactions with him to understand him better. Because of this knowledge, we love him more and enjoy being with him. We trust what he says, and our faith is validated in our experience. This type of knowledge changes our character. *Character is the result of the will acting over and over again until it is consistently manifested through our bodies in behavior.* Growing in our knowledge or intimacy with God requires his ongoing grace to help us, and our interaction with him multiplies our understanding of him and his ways.[15]

Peter continues: "And because of his glory and excellence, he has given us great and precious promises. These are the promises that enable you to share his divine nature and escape the world's corruption caused by human desires. In view of all this, *make every effort* to respond to God's promises" (2 Peter 1:4–5 NLT, emphasis added). Through belief in Christ, we have been enabled to share in God's divine nature. So we are to "make every effort" to cause the qualities of his divine nature to be part of our lives.

Peter's point is clear. We have been given something precious, the promises of God; therefore, we should do all we can to develop and use what we have been given. We exercise faith, trusting in God's promises and his grace that enables us to share in the divine nature through our union with Christ. Peter tells us that we must, "Supplement your faith with a generous provision of moral excellence, and moral excellence with knowledge, and knowledge with self-control, and self-control with patient endurance, and patient endurance with godliness, and godliness with brotherly affection, and brotherly affection with love for everyone" (2 Peter 1:5–7 NLT).

These character qualities are not intended to replace Paul's fruit of the Spirit list but are Peter's way of saying much the same thing.[16] Moral excellence, knowledge, self-control, patient endurance, godliness, brotherly affection, and love for everyone—these seven character qualities must be added to our faith, and doing so requires effort. Some people see a progression in these qualities, but I'm not convinced that the order matters. What matters is that we move forward with these as our goal. Peter continues, "The more you grow like this, the more productive and useful you will be in your knowledge of our Lord Jesus Christ. But those who fail to develop in this way are shortsighted or blind, forgetting that they have been cleansed from their old sins. So, dear brothers and sisters, *work hard* to prove that you really are among those God has called and chosen. *Do these things, and you will never fall away*" (2 Peter 1:8–10 NLT, emphasis added).

Again, we need to pay attention to the way the Bible writers exhort people and seek to motivate them to action. I believe that our contemporary churches have greatly shied away from these exhortations. But Peter is quite clear. He tells us to "work hard" and "make every effort," to "do these things," and we will find that these spiritual qualities will serve us well. For Peter, grace is not opposed to hard work, effort, and getting things done. His words here remind me of Paul's, "Work hard to show the results of your salvation" (Phil. 2:12 NLT).

All of this should remind us of the training and discipline involved in signing up as Christ's disciple that we discussed earlier. Peter is simply referring to the expectations of being a student of Jesus. When we are enrolled in the school of discipleship, we should react to the desires God puts in our heart.[17] We should obey him through spiritual exercise and practice, practice, practice to form godly habits.[18] Eventually we will discover that we have become the person Christ called us to be. We will have a new character.[19] We will be of good cheer and love others as Christ has loved us.[20]

As we have seen, our wild and fragmented will is schooled through this change process. Thus Paul says, "let God transform you into a new person by changing the way you think. Then you will learn to know God's will for you, which is good and pleasing and perfect" (Rom. 12:2 NLT). We begin to think differently because God places new thoughts and desires in our mind. We obey and practice his ways which form good habits and then our character. When our new will is conformed to God's will, the result pleases him. William Law presents these ideas in a beautiful way: "Would you know who is the greatest saint in the world? It is not he who prays most or fasts the most; it is not he who gives the most alms or is most eminent for temperance, chastity, or justice, but it is he who is always thankful to God, who wills everything that God wills, who receives everything as an instance of God's goodness and has a heart always ready to praise God for it."[21]

6

WAYS AND MEANS

> *History isn't only the story of bad people doing bad things. It's quite as much a story of people trying to do good things. But somehow, something goes wrong.*
>
> —C. S. Lewis, BBC Radio Broadcast,
> March 21, 1944

> *The impotence of "systems" is a main reason why Jesus did not send his students out to start governments or even churches as we know them today, which always strongly convey some elements of a human system.*
>
> —Dallas Willard, *Renovation of the Heart*

In the introduction to this book, I quoted Dallas Willard on what needs to be done to recover a biblical understanding of discipleship: "It would primarily be a work of scriptural interpretation and theological reformulation."[1] To this point, we've primarily focused on understanding what the Scriptures teach and how to formulate this theological understanding in a way that accounts for both the past and our context. But Willard continues, "Modification of time-hardened practices will also be required. Radical changes in what we do in the way of 'church' will have to be made."[2] To these practices and changes we now must turn. What needs to change in the methods and structures or the ways and means of ministry?

A local church is simply the result of using the ways and means for disciple-making that Jesus prescribed and modeled. From this perspective, the church is not the *cause* behind making disciples—it is the result. Mike Breen is known for his pithy statement, "If you make disciples, you will always get a church. If you start churches, you may not get disciples."[3] A church of disciples may not have a steeple, bells, or a hip worship team, but it will be a *real* church.

What are the ways and means we must employ to end up with a disciple-making church? It should also be said here that pastors are to create disciple-making movements which find their best application in a church. But it is desperately important to keep repeating that churches follow making disciples; making disciples is the first priority. Are some ways and means better than others, or more biblically sound? What ways and means did Jesus and the apostles give us to follow? To answer these questions, we will begin with how Jesus made disciples.

The Jesus Way

John Wesley once wrote, "Give me one hundred preachers who fear nothing but sin and desire nothing but God, and I care not whether they be clergymen or laymen, they alone will shake the gates of Hell and set up the kingdom of Heaven upon Earth."[4] The people who followed Jesus were his apprentices. They would never have grasped or caught his way of life through a seminar or an hour-long talk once a week. So living in close relationship with them, Jesus taught them his ways not only of living but also of relating—his priorities, his passions, and his fears.[5]

I recognize that duplicating the environment of Jesus and his disciples is difficult in modern life. But the consequences of not using his relational approach have been costly. Instead, our churches have settled for the ways and means of the world and relegated Jesus' method to a special department for radicals.[6] Today, studying Jesus is far more common than saying to others as Paul did, "Follow my example, as I follow the example of Christ" (1 Cor. 11:1).

The ways of Jesus are unique. Eugene Peterson writes: "Jesus is the alternative to the dominant ways of the world, not a supplement to them. We cannot use impersonal means to do or say a personal thing—and the gospel is personal or it is nothing."[7] Jesus famously said, "I am the way, the truth, and the life. No one can come to the Father except through me" (John 14:6 NLT). So can we take the truth about Jesus and present it by any means we like? Or is the message married to the means in some way? In other words, is there a "Jesus way" that is just as important as the "Jesus truth"? What if the way Jesus prepared his followers to live and proclaim the truth is just as important as the truth he taught them? Peterson continues with these convicting words, "Jesus as the way is the most frequently evaded metaphor among the Christians with whom I have worked for fifty years as a North American pastor."[8]

If what Peterson says is true, what are we doing instead of the Jesus way? Again, Peterson helpfully points out where we have gone astray. He especially highlights our tendency to disembody and depersonalize the teachings of Jesus, turning relationships into programs and real-life wisdom into principles for self-improvement: "The ways Jesus goes about loving and saving the world are personal: nothing disembodied, nothing abstract, nothing impersonal. Incarnate, flesh and blood, relational, particular and local. The ways employed in our North American culture are conspicuously impersonal: programs, organizations, techniques, and general guidelines, informational, detached from place. In matters of ways and means, the vocabulary of numbers is preferred over names, ideologies crowd out ideas, the gray fog of abstraction absorbs the sharp particularities of the recognizable face and the familiar street."[9]

Or as E. M. Bounds once said, "Men are looking for better methods, and God is looking for better men."

Instead of following the ways of Jesus, the Western church experience has been designed to meet the needs that the American advertising industry has stirred up in consumers. Our churches seek to cater to needs, to offer services, and to provide an experience that will make people want to return. They are in the business of satisfying fantasies and fulfilling false promises, and so have recast the gospel into consumerism. But Jesus calls us to deny ourselves and to follow him to the cross. So "the cultivation of consumer spirituality is the antithesis of a sacrificial, 'deny yourself' congregation. A consumer church is an antichrist Church."[10]

I know this is a hard word for us, especially those who pastor a church. Why is it so difficult for us to see this in our own church? And if we do see it, why do so few heed this warning? Because we have become pragmatic. We think if something appears to work, don't fix it. For the most part, our programs and seminars seem to accomplish the desired goal—until they don't. When they don't work anymore, we try to use secular wisdom and human methods to fix them. But they still won't work, because as Albert Einstein said, rarely is a problem solved through the same means by which it was created. In other words, *this problem cannot be fixed by improving our consumer Christian culture*. It can only be fixed by learning and doing the Jesus way that is found in the Gospels.

JESUS' SUBMISSION TO THE FATHER

Before the beginning to Jesus' public ministry was the beginning of the beginning. Jesus was baptized by John in the Jordan River. This event was more than just a ritual—it was a demonstration of Jesus' submission to the

Father's plan and showed the Father's loving support of his Son. In all three synoptic Gospel accounts, the Father audibly speaks his approval from heaven (Matt. 3:13–17). To this point in his life, Jesus has done little that we would consider noteworthy. He has worked in construction, engaged in the family business. Hardly the work of someone who plans to change the world.

We know few details of Jesus' life before beginning his ministry, but one thing stands out in the words spoken at his baptism: Jesus pleased his Father. Certainly this shows the love in their relationship, but it also hints at Jesus' faithfulness to his earthly family, his study, his worship, and his work. In other words, in all that he said and did, Jesus pleased his Father by submitting to the Father and doing the Father's will. Almost anything is bearable, no matter how insignificant or tedious, for people who know they are doing God's will. Later, as Jesus faced the cross, his submission would serve him well, especially in the throes of his prayer at Gethsemane. In fact, the preparation for that day began immediately after his baptism as the Spirit of God led him into the wilderness to be tempted by the devil.

THE TEMPTATION OF JESUS

Jesus goes into the wilderness where he fasts for forty days: "After fasting forty days and forty nights, he was hungry. The tempter came to him . . ." (Matt. 4:2–3a). Though we often read this account as story about Jesus and the devil, it is really about Jesus and his Father because it describes Jesus' submission to and trust in his Father. Satan is smart enough to know that tempting a hungry man should begin with what his flesh craves. Jesus is hungry, so Satan tells him, "If you are the Son of God, tell these stones to become bread" (Matt. 4:3b). The temptation here is for Jesus to use his power and authority as a vending machine. Satan wants Jesus to turn something useless into a commodity that will meet his need of the moment, to live for himself, to abandon the Father's plan, and take the easy way—the consumeristic path of self-satisfaction.

Isn't this a temptation we all face? We want our needs met, immediate satisfaction, and are all too willing to sacrifice the long-term goal of faithfulness to God to get what we need. And in our churches, how often have we made this same request of the Lord? We pray for him to meet our needs the way we think he should and forget that he often has a different way and goal in mind.

Satan's second temptation is rather spectacular in nature: "Then the devil took him to the holy city and had him stand on the highest point of the temple. 'If you are the Son of God,' he said, 'throw yourself down. For it is written: He will command his angels concerning you, and they will lift you up in their hands, so that you will not strike your foot against a stone'" (Matt. 4:5–6).

Here, Satan takes a different approach and encourages Jesus to dazzle the people, give them something to ooh and ah about and break them out of their boredom. He challenges Jesus to rely upon the spectacular miracle to prove himself.

We are similarly tempted in this way as well—to take something people think is boring and make it exciting and addictive, like drugs, alcohol, and sex. We ask how we can entertain and wow the crowds, leaving them with big chills and big spills. I think this temptation is particularly attractive for those who have exceptional skills or talents. It's the shortcut mentality that we can entertain people with the spectacular.

But Jesus rejects this path because this is not the way to build a ministry and start a movement. Today, it is common to find bankrupt churches, once filled with "miracles," being sold on the open market. Do miracles happen today? Certainly. My point is not to minimize miracles. But miracles alone will not make people into disciples because miracles don't sustain everyday life, and lasting movements require more than a few talented people. They are sustained by a reproducible infrastructure.

Instead of relying on the miraculous and seeking out the talented, Jesus spent 90 percent of his time with just a few ordinary people. Jesus knew the rhythms of ordinary life, for he lived in obscurity for thirty years before his public ministry, and he values the ordinary, the common, and the every day. As Peterson says, "The way of Jesus is not a sequence of exceptions to the ordinary, but a way of living deeply and fully with the people here and now, in the place we find ourselves."[11]

Satan's third temptation offers a way for Jesus to rule the world without having to suffer the agony of the cross. "Again, the devil took him to a very high mountain and showed him all the kingdoms of the world and their splendor. 'All this I will give you,' he said, 'if you will bow down and worship me'" (Matt. 4:8–9). The devil is cunning, but he underestimates Jesus, thinking he has him over a barrel. He is certain that this human will accept another, easier way to accomplish his goal. You see, Satan thinks Jesus' goal is world domination, but Jesus knows that his real goal is world rescue.

Satan offers a world Jesus can run, subject to demonic permission. Perhaps the devil shows something similar to the society Gandhi dreamed of with "systems so perfect that no one would need to be good."[12] But bringing change through external rule and authority is not the Jesus way because it doesn't address the problem of human rebellion. Jesus fixes what is wrong with us—our sin—by giving himself for us. The Jesus way addresses our

145

true need and saves us, bringing us into a personal relationship and the blessings of God.

Consistently, Jesus refuses to do good things in the wrong way. Each of the temptations Satan offers has something good in it: meeting a real need for food, attracting followers by a miraculous sign, and bringing just rule to the world. But Satan is asking Jesus to take a different way than the one he agreed upon with his Father. The devil was also tempting Jesus to depersonalize his work. The way of Jesus is relational, personal, and suited to our need for inner transformation. Jesus did not seek to meet his own needs. He poured his life out for the sake of others. He did not rely upon miracles to win followers. He led by his example, attracting people by his love. And he did not take the easy path to victory but embraced and submitted to the Father's plan. Jesus' call was simple: "Follow Me."

How Did Jesus Relate to His Followers?

The purpose of the Gospels is to tell the story of Jesus. Some calculate that Jesus spent 90 percent of his ministry time with his twelve chosen followers. That is a significant amount of time together! When I was a young teaching pastor studying the life of Jesus and looking at how he interacted with his followers, I found myself wondering, is there any significant difference between the different ways Jesus calls his followers?

So I began to research and found that Jesus asked some to "come and see," others to "come and follow me," a few to "come and be with me," and finally "remain in me." On the surface there seemed to be a few small differences, so I read to find out if anyone had considered what they might mean. I was gratified to learn that A. B. Bruce in his classic book, *The Training of the Twelve*, notes a progression of calls.[13] Upon further study, I found that Robert L. Thomas in *The NIV Harmony of the Gospels* also discusses that the disciples' commitment was a progression.[14] It just so happens that Thomas was my New Testament professor when I attended Talbot School of Theology in the 1970s. My first book, *Jesus Christ, Disciplemaker*, was largely based on my research findings on this question.[15] In that book, I provide the structure for how Jesus trained his followers. In this section, I will summarize what I learned and have taught for the past four decades.

SEQUENTIAL AND SEGMENTED

As I researched, it became clear to me that there were three distinct periods in Jesus' ministry marked by differences in how he related to his followers. We can see these periods through careful study of the Gospels. And as we uncover the sequential development of Jesus' relationship with his followers, a clear structure emerges on how to disciple people through different stages of their growth. While some leaders teach a segmented and sequential process of discipleship, I find that the majority have not taken the process seriously. If anything, over the last twenty years, deeper skepticism or bias against systematic approaches has resulted in teaching designed to meet people's needs or interests. While such teaching "in the moment" is helpful—for instance when you have a flat tire or need to unplug a toilet—learning in a structured manner has greater advantages. Let's be honest. Even those who advocate a "felt need" or "as needed" learning approach start their children in the first and not the fifth grade of school. The majority of formal learning is still done systematically. Though this method is not the only way to learn, it is still effective.

In fact, I advocate both styles of learning for spiritual growth. If you recall from the Step 2, both proactive and reactive approaches to growth have value. We grow when the unexpected happens, when we encounter suffering and conflict, and when life doesn't go as planned. But for this kind of learning, we must rely upon the safety net. We also need to be proactive, establishing a plan and process that is fueled by intention. Because of the nature of life, Jesus taught his disciples using both approaches. He had a plan, though it was probably not written down and carried around in a notebook. He clearly understood the dynamics of his work and how to prepare men and women to take over his work. They needed to understand it well enough to teach others and to believe in him enough to die for the cause.

If you are a pastor or leader, I caution you not to be foolish. Don't wait for the unexpected to provide your curriculum for making disciples. Instead, develop a plan that follows the lead of Jesus and intentionally train willing disciples to become the kind of people who will naturally do what Jesus did and react the way Jesus did. So how did Jesus do this?

Digging Deeper
COUNTER-INTUITIVE LEADERSHIP

If you had only three years to set a plan into motion, a plan to rescue the world, what would you do? Three years is not a very long time. It's a year less than a US presidential term. Jesus answers this question, and let's give him credit—he must have had a plan from the start. If his behavior and relationship to his Father described in the Gospels

CONVERSION & DISCIPLESHIP

is any indication, they were having a conversation about this before he began his public ministry.[a] When he was twelve years old, Jesus already had an understanding of discipleship and how to teach and reproduce from his religious community.[b] Jesus used the values and methods of his culture to accomplish his mission.

Have you ever lain in bed at night wondering how you could make a greater impact for Christ? My thoughts are usually unrealistic. I imagine that something I write will spread virally and lead to revival or global transformation. I remember when President Ronald Reagan held up a copy of Tom Clancy's *The Hunt for Red October* on national television and said it was a good read. Maybe something like that could happen to my book. Why not? Then I come back to reality.

I share this because the first ideas typically reveal how I am a product of my American culture. My first impulse is to launch a large campaign. If I had unlimited funds, I could really get the word out. We need good branding and would use the latest technology. Or I think about ways of expanding my ministry and opening up new opportunities. We'd need to raise funds and get the right endorsements. The more successful the campaign, the more likely people will be to invest. That's how we get the big numbers, right? But are these ideas where we should begin? To be clear, all have their place at times, and there is certainly nothing wrong with using tools or raising funds. The problem is in mistaking a million-dollar donation or a viral video on Facebook for true success.

What did Jesus do? He did what was counter-intuitive. He resisted Satan's temptations in the wilderness, saying no to fame and the shortcuts to success.[c] He told people not to talk about his miracles.[d] At times he avoided the crowds. Just when Jesus was picking up some momentum and gaining popularity, he would withdraw to an isolated place. When his disciples said he should go to Jerusalem, he didn't.

Jesus didn't seem to care how influential or powerful a person might be, even though knowing powerful people who can make things happen is typically seen as an advantage to one's career. Again, to be clear, I believe that fame can be used of God, but it can also detract from or even destroy what God wants done. Far too often, Christian leaders and pastors turn to celebrity influence to accomplish the work that only God's Spirit can do.

Eugene Peterson was once invited to spend time with the world-renowned rock group U2. The band had been reading some of Peterson's work, and they wanted to talk with him about it. But Peterson turned down the band's invitation—for a good reason. He was busy finishing up work on the Old Testament translation of *The Message*. Someone pressed Peterson about declining the invitation, "Come on Eugene, it was Bono," they said.

"No," Peterson answered, "it was Isaiah." At that moment, Peterson knew what he needed to do, what was most important, and he made it a priority over celebrity influence.

It's difficult to resist the powerful pull of fame and success. Again, resisting it is not always necessary, but we need wisdom to discern when and how to use it. The world says that if we want to gain life, we must take control and make it happen. But Jesus said we will gain life by giving it up. If we want joy and happiness, the world says, live in this city, wear these clothes, look this way, and have these friends. But Jesus says we should serve others. He showed us that if we want to change the world, go small, not big. Take the last place, not the first.

Like Jesus, Christian leaders must learn to think in ways that are counter to the ways of the world. When the spirit of the age tells them to substitute numerical growth for spiritual maturity, to be hip rather than holy, disciple-making pastors should follow Jesus.

[a] See Matt. 3:13–17.

[b] See Luke 2:41–52. Jesus amazed the scholars with his knowledge when he spent three days in the Temple talking with the leaders. Add to this his weekly time in his hometown synagogue, and we can assume that Jesus had a wonderful knowledge of the ancient traditions of his faith. I think this knowledge base led to such statements as, "The student who is fully trained will become like the teacher" (Luke 6:40 NLT).

[c] See Matt. 4:8–10.

[d] See Matt. 14:22–23; Mark 1:40–45; Luke 5:15–16; John 6:14–15.

Four phases mark Jesus' discipleship ministry. I think of these as four key invitations.

1. **"Come and See"—An invitation to explore.** This was the period when Jesus introduced a group of disciples to his nature and ministry.

2. **"Come and Follow Me"—An invitation to learn.** In this period, the chosen disciples and other followers left their professions to travel with Jesus.

3. **"Come Be with Me"—An invitation to serve.** During this period, Jesus

kept his twelve called disciples with him and concentrated on training them so they could go out and preach.

4. **"Remain in Me"—An invitation to multiply.** Jesus introduces the new relationship he will have with his disciples and how they will relate to him as they take over the mission of making disciples. He wants them to know they will have a helper, the Holy Spirit. They will not be left alone; they will have special power to fulfill his instructions.

Let's take a closer look at each of these invitations and the corresponding phase of discipleship ministry.

Phase 1: "Come and See"

Text: John 1:35–4:46

Participants: John, Andrew, Nathaniel, Peter, Philip, and a few others

Time Frame: Four months

The first phase of Jesus' disciple-making ministry was a time for them to gather information and investigate. The disciples made a preliminary commitment and learned about the person of Jesus and the nature of his mission. At the conclusion of this phase, Jesus issues a challenge and gives the disciples an opportunity to think about what he is asking of them.

We pick up the story after Jesus was baptized by his cousin John the Baptist and spent forty days in the wilderness resisting the devil's temptation. Soon afterward, Jesus returns to the Jordan and walks by John the Baptist who is standing with his disciples. "John looked at him and declared, 'Look! There is the Lamb of God!'" When John's two disciples heard this, they followed Jesus" (John 1:36–37 NLT).

Following Jesus required a certain amount of faith and getting the feet moving. After the two followed him for a while, Jesus turned around and asked them: "What do you want?" (John 1:38 NLT). Apparently, they were stunned at such a direct question. For a moment they fumble before they ask Jesus a question: "Where are you staying?" Note how Jesus replies. His answer is simple but will change their lives: "Come and see" (John 1:39 NLT).

Notice also that Jesus doesn't answer the question that is most likely on their minds, "Are you the Messiah?" He is not ready to tell them everything they want to know. But he invites them to explore who he is. In fact, he invites them to join him where he is staying.

As the story continues, Jesus meets three others, Peter, Philip, and Nathanael, who are brothers, friends, or neighbors of the first two. What strikes us immediately is that Jesus already has some knowledge of these men. He first shows this knowledge to Peter. "Looking intently at Simon, Jesus said, 'Your name is Simon, son of John—but you will be called Cephas' (which translated means Peter)" (John 1:42 NLT). This is Jesus' first meeting with Simon, yet Jesus knows enough about him to give him a new name, Peter ("the rock"). Put yourself in Simon's shoes for a moment. How would you feel? I imagine Jesus' knowledge of him played with his mind a bit because it likely indicated that Jesus knew something about Simon that Simon didn't know about himself.

Jesus demonstrates a similar form of knowledge of Nathanael. "When Jesus saw Nathanael approaching, he said of him, 'Here truly is an Israelite in whom there is not deceit'" (John 1:47). This statement strikes a chord with Nathanael who is astounded that Jesus knows him. After Jesus speaks of seeing Nathanael prior to meeting him, Nathanael is convinced that Jesus is "the Son of God . . . the King of Israel" (John 1:49).

Nathanael learns, as we all do, that God knows every detail of every person's life. C. S. Lewis speaks of God existing outside of time and encourages us to think about what it would be like to have ten thousand years to review and contemplate every second of each person's life. While God's knowledge seems astounding, the fact remains that he knows us this well. God has the time, space, and the cognitive capacity to know each of us fully.

This truth ministers to our deepest need to be intimately known and loved. Early in his ministry, Jesus demonstrates that he possesses this personal knowledge, and it seems to tip the scales and lead the disciples to trust him in ways they can't explain or fully understand. This is an early form of belief, but the Jesus way of discipleship begins with his personal knowledge and awareness of his disciples.

COME AND SEE WHAT?

Since Jesus already knew these men, this period in his ministry was designed for them to get to know him. This may seem obvious to some, but our churches tend to overlook this simple step. We often invite the public to "come and see" our buildings, listen to our singers, hear our preachers, and watch our liturgy. But this experience can be impersonal and more about showmanship than discipleship. Sometimes this approach is rooted in our doubts, perhaps the belief that what excites seekers is not Christ but the accoutrements surrounding Christ. We want to convince the world that we are not dull.

But in most cases, this approach won't work. People know when they are receiving a sales pitch. While some may gulp down the snake oil, the rest are looking for something authentic, someone who knows them and who sees them. We don't need to water anything down. In fact if anything, we need to be clear that we aren't just messing around and having a good time. I've sometimes wondered what a sign in front of Dietrich Bonhoeffer's church would read. Maybe something like, "Come die with us at 8:00, 9:30, and 11:00." Being clear about the cost, about dying in order to live, is more authentic than talking about having your "best life now." When we choose to lead others the way that Jesus did, we begin by asking people to come and see who Jesus is—his life, his death, and his resurrection. Who he is and what he has done will draw them in, because Jesus himself is the draw.

Simply by being with Jesus for several days then weeks, his first followers grew committed to him. They didn't fully understand everything he was doing or who he was, but they knew enough to follow him. Revealing himself is still his strategy today. People meet Jesus both in the Gospels and as they see him at work. When we love others in humility and serve them, we give evidence that Jesus still cares, still knows people, and still sees them. What does this mean for our evangelism? It means our focus should not be on inviting people to come and see who we are on Sundays and to enjoy the quality of our show. Instead, we must invite seekers into our lives Monday through Saturday and also to our churches on Sunday because in the ordinary parts of our lives, Christ shines the brightest.

We need to rethink where we make the most impact, where we spend most of our time, and where our disciple-making efforts should be focused. If we follow Jesus' example, we will naturally begin with the people closest to us who we have intentionally invited into our lives. When we let them get to know us over time, ministry happens.

Three occasions recorded in the Gospels highlight Jesus' ways and means during this initial stage of his discipleship ministry.

OCCASION 1: THE WEDDING AT CANA

The familiar story of the Cana wedding contains several jewels of truth for us. If you had limited time and had to think about the future of your key leaders, would you begin their training by spending several days at a wedding? But Jesus' plan was to involve his disciples in whatever he was doing. On this occasion, the wedding planner must have miscalculated the amount of wine or the number of guests, for they ran out of wine before the party was over. When Jesus' mother, Mary, asks him to help, Jesus reveals that he is up to something. His response may seem almost cryptic at first: "My time has not yet come" (John 2:4 NLT).

This answer can mean at least two things. First, that Jesus had a plan for revealing his identity, but it was not now. In fact, he does not say his time has come[16] until just a few days before his stating it again in the upper room, when he says to his disciples, "Now the time has come for the Son of Man to enter into his glory" (John 13:31).[17] Clearly, Jesus had a sense of how things were supposed to unfold. Why do I point this out? To remind us of the difference between freewheeling it and just going with the flow and being knowingly and intentionally natural.

Second, Jesus' response to Mary may mean that he was reluctant to use his miraculous abilities. Mary doesn't seem to have any doubt that he can solve this problem. So she instructs the servant to obey her son. Perhaps she had seen Jesus handle similar problems before. Or even more likely, Mary is confident that he will be enterprising and find a solution.

Jesus performed the miracle, and how much wine he made is instructive to note. Six stone jars holding thirty gallons each adds up to 180 gallons or about 907 bottles of wine. That's an extravagant amount. In addition, this is good wine. After tasting it, the master of ceremonies tells the bridegroom that he will get credit for saving the best for last. In most weddings, the best wine was served first, then after the guests had celebrated for a while, the cheaper wine was brought out.

In any case, the effect of this miracle on Jesus' followers was profound. They put their faith in him (John 2:11). In a verse we tend to skip over (John 2:12), we are told that after the wedding, Jesus takes his disciples along with his mother and brothers to Capernaum. This means the disciples were spending time with Jesus 24/7, watching him interact with his family, party guests, and strangers. They saw all of this and later said that Jesus was a man who was without sin. Let's not forget that.

OCCASION 2: CLEANSING THE TEMPLE

Let's look at another instance of Jesus showing us how to make disciples his way. We can say that Jesus created drama but not for drama's sake because he was just being himself. When Jesus told his disciples to "come and see," he wasn't putting on an act.

In this story, Jesus grows angry when he sees the abuse of worshipers in the Jerusalem Temple courts (John 2:14). He was angry because the sellers were taking advantage of the people's need to purchase animals to sacrifice in celebration of the Passover by charging exorbitant prices. Throughout the Old Testament, the prophets thundered against injustices like this and warned that they would bring God's wrath. This injustice and greed was similar to the medieval European church selling indulgences which angered Luther and contributed to the Protestant Reformation.

Jesus was angry but not out of control. Otherwise, he wouldn't have taken the time to make a whip out of cords (John 2:15). We also must remember that Jesus never sinned, so this was not some violent, unjustified rampage. His words make it clear that he felt justified in cleaning house: "Get these out of here! Stop turning my Father's house into a market!" (John 2:16).

I'm sure Jesus' followers were surprised by this display of anger. This is probably the first time they witnessed Jesus confronting people in authority, but he taught them how by his words and actions. When the Jews challenged him by demanding a sign of his authority, "Jesus answered them, 'Destroy this temple, and I will raise it again in three days.'

"They replied, 'It has taken forty-six years to build this temple, and you are going to raise it in three days?'" (John 2:19–20). While we know that Jesus was speaking of his body, his disciples did not understand this at the time and were hard pressed to comprehend what had just happened.

But this is the Jesus way. We don't always immediately understand his ways and means. At the same time, not entirely understanding doesn't mean that the disciples weren't learning. After this event, they knew much more about Jesus than they had before. They understood what made him mad, and they saw who his enemies were. Intense experiences like these tend to set deeply into our memories, and this incident was likely forever burned into the first disciples' minds.

OCCASION 3: THE SAMARITAN WOMAN

At this point, Jesus was becoming well known but not well liked by the Pharisees (John 4:1–4).[18] But Jesus did not abort the plan. He could have increased the confrontation with the religious leaders in Jerusalem and gotten himself killed early, but he needed time to train his disciples.[19] So he dialed back the tension with the authorities and traveled through Samaria.

Samaritans were a mixture of Jew and Gentile blood as a result of Jews intermarrying with people deported into Israel by the Assyrians, and they followed an equally mixed religion. Jesus and his disciples came to a well at Sychar in Samaria at about noon (John 4:5–6). Jesus sent his disciples into town for food, but he stayed behind. It was hot and dry, and Jesus needed a drink. So he spoke to a Samaritan woman, who came to the well at the hottest time of the day, likely trying to avoid meeting others. Note that this was not an artificial event created for teaching purposes. This was an ordinary meeting.

Jesus' conversation with this Samaritan woman is a treasure trove worthy of deeper study, and Jesus must have related these events to his disciples afterward (John 4:7–26). He asks for a drink, and the woman is surprised.

Why? Because most Jewish men (like Jesus' followers) would have ignored her. But had Jesus not gone against the culture, his disciples would have missed an opportunity to see God at work. It is to the degree that Christ is formed in us that we are aware of the opportunities God provides.

Jesus, of course, does not miss this opportunity. He turns the exchange into a somewhat mystical and theological discussion about "living water" that satisfies thirst and never runs dry. The two speak of morality, marriage, and the best place to worship. In the end, the woman ascertains that Jesus is a prophet. How else could he know the secrets of her heart and life? But unlike everyone else, Jesus does not condemn her. Being known like this yet not rejected leads this woman to tell others about Jesus.

When his disciples return they are thinking, *Why is he talking with this woman?* (John 2:27). But what they say is, "Rabbi, eat something" (John 2:31). Again, Jesus' answer is somewhat cryptic, "I have food to eat that you know nothing about" (John 2:32). His statement creates some mumbling about where he got this special food (John 2:33). Jesus spoke of special water that quenches thirst forever, and now he speaks of food that nourishes but can't be seen, chewed, or swallowed. At least he doesn't leave his disciples completely in the dark and explains what he means, "'My food,' said Jesus, 'is to do the will of him who sent me and to finish his work'" (John 2:34).

This explanation also helps us understand why Jesus acted the way he did. Over the years I've noticed a tendency among some to avoid speaking of doing work. Many who are attracted to mystical spirituality don't like to focus on doing work, preferring contemplation. But Jesus did work that nourished his soul. He was fed by God not in silent retreat but in speaking with a woman at a well. Certainly, there is room for both contemplation and work, but we must not think that we are more likely to find God in quiet escapes from the world.

Jesus follows his statement with a challenge. "Don't you have a saying, 'It's still four months until the harvest'? I tell you, open your eyes and look at the fields! They are ripe for harvest. Even now the one who reaps draws a wage and harvests a crop for eternal life, so that the sower and the reaper may be glad together" (John 4:35–36).

Jesus is teaching his disciples the lesson in what he has been doing. They have been out looking for physical food, but he has eaten spiritual food and is satisfied. Then he extends the opportunity to them. They will soon be the ones who will go out and reap the harvest (John 2:37–38).

Over the past few weeks, the disciples have come to see Jesus more clearly. They have seen him with his family and in social settings. They

155

have travelled with him. They've seen him angry, and they've seen him excited. They have heard him say confusing things, but they are learning that both his words and actions have meaning and purpose. They also have a better understanding of what is before them if they choose to continue following Jesus, because he introduced them to himself, to his own ministry, and finally to the mission before them.

Now they need some time to take it all in, to pray and think, and to compare this life with the one they left. They will remember Jesus' words that his food is to do the Father's will and to finish his work and may have prayed, "Can I ever get to the point where I am nourished and satisfied by this work?"

The question is similar for those of us in leadership or teaching roles. We need to ask ourselves, "Can I be patient enough, preserving enough, and committed enough to invest in others? Can I resist the pressure to measure the immediate and to gage my worth by numbers?" The answer comes down to how much we trust Jesus and his ways and means. Is his approval enough? If your answer is, "I'm not sure, but I want it to be a yes," the good news is that you can learn.

Jesus demonstrated that his was an urgent work, but not one burdened by hurry and worry. As the great John Wesley once said, "I am always busy, but never in a hurry." Wesley followed a tight schedule and traveled over 250,000 miles by horse or carriage. He supervised 50,000 Methodists and their progress in Christ in great detail through an elaborate tracking system. He wrote many books, letters, and commentaries. Yet he did not experience any of this as a burden.

Jesus challenged his disciples to enter into his work and mission. But before they did, he wanted them to think about what they had seen. Again, his way is contrary to our culture. Most sales training is based on convincing people to purchase on impulse. Never let the buyer walk away saying they will come back—that's a lost sale. But Jesus isn't interested in selling his product to consumers. He encourages time for reflection. He wants a solid decision based on knowledge, not an emotional surge that fades with time and reality.

What follows may be an interim between Jesus' discipleship phases. The first "come and see" period is over. Jesus' next invitations will be to "come and follow me." During this time, Peter, Andrew, Nathanael, Philip, and the others may have returned to their professions.[20] The fishermen, in particular, had plenty of time in their boats to reflect on their life-changing experience of being with Jesus. When he came next to invite them to come and follow him, they would be ready.

Phase 2: "Come and Follow Me"

Texts: Matthew 4:18–22; Mark 1:16–20; Luke 5:27–28

Participants: Simon, Andrew, James, John, Matthew, and others; 70–120 consistent followers.

Time Frame: 10–11 months

In the second phase of the Jesus way of discipleship, people who responded to Jesus' call on their lives submit themselves for training as apprentices. They learned like most apprenticeships, primarily by being with Jesus, assisting him, and doing ministry beside him. This period was packed full of frontline action and confrontation.

As we saw earlier, Jesus' way of training is on the job. Now he will confront human suffering and need as well as demonic evil. Early in this period, Jesus visits Capernaum and heals everyone from a demoniac to Peter's mother-in-law. Later he calls Matthew, a tax collector, and engages Matthew's ragamuffin, politically-incorrect friends. This period ends with a series of direct confrontations with the religious leaders primarily over the Sabbath. In the end, Jesus must withdraw from this conflict and his growing popularity with the crowds.

Jesus gave his first invitations to discipleship to a select few to come and see, or in other words, to watch and learn by following him. Jesus didn't pressure these men; he invited them into his life and ministry which he showed them. Yet by this point, they were hooked and likely could not envision doing anything else but saying yes to a life with him. They may have even understood that discipleship to Jesus is the greatest opportunity offered to any human.

Matthew records how Jesus walked beside the Sea of Galilee and found Peter and Andrew casting their nets. Later, he encountered two other fishermen, James and John, the sons of Zebedee (Matt. 4:18–22). Mark 1:16–20 tells the same basic story. Luke 5:27–28, however, gives a somewhat different version of the call of Simon, James, and John, and scholars debate whether this passage is accounting the same event or one that happened later.[21] Regardless, Jesus calls four fishermen to follow him and fish for people.

Luke provides the richest details and includes Jesus doing some teaching (Luke 5:1–3). Even though Simon and the others had fished all night and caught nothing, Jesus instructs them to cast the nets again (Luke 5:4–5). Simon protests but complies, and they catch a net-breaking, boat-sinking load of fish. This account seems to indicate that Peter had grown skeptical of Jesus in some way, and perhaps Jesus was dealing with this issue. Simon sees the miraculous catch, is cut to the heart, and says to Jesus, "Go away from me, Lord; I am a sinful man!" (Luke 5:8). But Jesus replied, "Don't be afraid; from now on you will catch men" (Luke 5:10). In response, all the fishermen "pulled their boats up on the shore, left everything and followed him" (Luke 5:11).

What would any rational person do here? Jesus has just shown Simon that he controls the sea. Jesus has given them all a word of promise and envisions a future for them. Who could resist an opportunity like this? The call to be a disciple is a gracious opportunity—an undeserved gift. And this is where our lack of preaching discipleship when we present the gospel robs people of the good gifts of God—the idea that God's purposes and his work through Jesus are things to be desired and longed for. Christ gave himself so we can live to the full. Without Christ, we have nothing of value and are in fact enslaved to our enemy who seeks to destroy, kill, and ruin God's plan. Simon's sense of his own sin and his limitations makes Jesus' offer irresistible.

Matthew's account of the calls of Simon, Andrew, James, and John is also worth studying (Matt. 4:18–22). In Matthew, these fishermen drop everything because they knew Jesus and had likely already been with him for several months. They may have been wondering when they would see him again. Jesus had prepared them to say yes, and when he came for them and invited them to follow him, they responded positively to his greater call. This was not a "come and see" invitation. It was a drop your nets, pull up your boats, leave your family, and start walking kind of invitation. But true belief takes action.

If Jesus had conducted his recruitment and training like many of us, he would have done the following. First, he would have told them how important the mission was and what was at stake. Then he would have challenged them to accept the task. If they didn't respond, he would have used some pressure and guilt until he was able to convince a few to say yes. Then he would have ended up leading a group of people who didn't really want to go on this mission, and more importantly were not ready spiritually to go on it.

How often we make this mistake: We give people a manual or a pep talk and then send them off and hope for the best. Now you may protest, "I'm not doing that!" But let's be honest. This description is at least *close* to how discipleship is generally done. We send people out to do things that we haven't done ourselves and certainly haven't shown them how to do (like reaching our neighborhood for Christ). Remember, "come and follow me" is very different from "go and do that!"

Digging Deeper

JOHN WESLEY, DISCIPLE-MAKER

The industrial revolution in England began in the early 1700s. For those who owned the factories and mines, life was good. But beneath the belching smokestacks, in the shadow of the grimy mills, impoverished workers made up the vast majority of society. The ever-widening gap between rich and poor set into motion a powerful undercurrent, a brewing cauldron set to boil over in a civil war.

One of the worst consequences of the industrial revolution was the horrific working conditions for children. Many began working at five or six years old, and one member of Parliament reported that children as young as three spent eight hours a day working in brickyards and would never see the inside of a school room. Alcoholism among the poor was out of control, even among the youth. In 1736, every sixth house in London was licensed as a pub. This epidemic of drunkenness eroded what little decency was left among the working class. Into this country in 1703, John Wesley was born into a large and highly disciplined family.

Wesley's father, Samuel, was an Anglican clergyman and a great scholar. John could read Greek and Latin by age ten and seemed on his way to a great academic career. His mother, Susanna, bore nineteen children, eight of whom died in infancy, and she is well-remembered for raising her children with great discipline. She called her method "the management of the human will," and she passed onto her children the discipline of strict time management. This upbringing explains John's incredible work ethic that made it possible for him to accomplish so much. Susanna emphasized that the children "methodize" their lives.

John was admitted to Oxford University and graduated at age twenty-one. He applied for holy orders and was admitted into the priesthood of the Church of England. He became a tutor at Lincoln College, Oxford, in 1729 and developed what became known as the Holy Club. Eventually, this Club grew into a movement called Methodism. This movement became the saving grace for the country, transforming a growing resentment in the underclass into striving for "social holiness." The only kind of holiness Wesley would accept was social, meaning holiness that affected all of life—the way a person dressed, spoke, worked, and loved. In many ways, Wesley modeled what it looks like to be fully committed to Jesus' command to make disciples and teach them to obey everything he commanded.[a] And it is important to note that Wesley used Jesus' ways and means in his own ministry and demonstrated their continued effectiveness.

How did Wesley use Jesus' ways and means of discipleship? He developed three modes for growing Christlikeness in his followers.

The Society: The Cognitive Mode

Wesley's first mode for discipleship was the cognitive mode, and to facilitate growth in this mode, he developed the society meeting, primarily times of Bible teaching intended to transform minds and hearts into God's worldview.[b] The aim of these meetings was to arm the general population with knowledge of God and help them understand truth, right and wrong, and the basics of healthy living. The meetings were held once a week at times that did not conflict with the Church of England's worship schedule. Wesley was an Anglican, and he would die an Anglican priest. He never had any plans to begin a new church.

The society was open only to those who agreed to Wesley's covenant. People could visit up to three times and then had to decide if they wanted to commit. If they did, they were interviewed and if accepted would receive a ticket for twelve meetings that promoted cognitive growth. Wesley believed that transformation had to begin in the mind (Rom. 12:1–2). There was no feedback or discussion at the meetings. But the message was clear: people who wanted to live for Christ had to commit to his plan and his ways.

The Class Meeting: The Behavioral Mode

Along with addressing the cognitive, Wesley understood that Jesus called for behavioral change, so we also must confront behavior and provide a path for obedience. So the buy-in to join the society was a commitment to cognitive *and* behavioral change. Members of the society were automatically included in a class meeting. Wesley didn't care much if people had all their beliefs straight at first. He was convinced that if people started behaving right, they would begin to think right.

The class meeting was considered the most influential instructional unit in the Methodist movement. Simple in its design, it was first developed as a fundraising plan for the Bristol Society. People would covenant to meet weekly with ten other people, and each member was required to give a penny a week. They had to attend the meetings, give the penny, and participate in the discussion. Just showing up when they could and speaking if they wanted was not allowed. Those who covenanted were held accountable.

Each class of ten to twelve had an appointed leader whose role was to be sure the group met once a week to ask about the state of their souls. The group would advise, reprove, comfort, and exhort each other. They would also discern how they could help the poor. Each meeting began with a hymn. Then the leader would state the condition of his or her soul and give a short testimony of the previous week, thanking God for progress and honestly sharing any failures, sins, temptations, griefs, and inner battles.

Visitors were allowed to come twice to a class meeting. But if they decided not to join, they were no longer eligible to attend. Also, those who did not join a class meeting could not attend the society meeting. At the end of each quarter, members were interviewed, and if they had not missed more than three meetings, they were issued a ticket for the next quarter. This method was quite labor intensive for the leaders, so to make things easier for them, no spectators were allowed. Everyone was a participant.

For many years, Wesley fought off pressure from his friends to create room for "hearers only." Sadly not many years after his death, his followers made this change, and it sucked the life out of the movement. Wesley understood what Jesus taught and modeled—that we need to set the bar high if we want to grow mature followers. We cannot give the same status to casual followers as we do to committed disciples who are leaders in training.[c]

The Band: The Affective Mode

While the society was open to all, the class meeting required a greater level of commitment. For those who felt called to be more and do more, Wesley developed a third and more intimate mode of discipleship, the band. These were voluntary groups in which participants were matched by gender, age, and marital status. The band was Wesley's favorite level of community, and he expressed remorse later in his life that he had not begun more of them. They were his method for going deeper and training members for leadership who had expressed this as a goal.

I believe the Jesus way is reflected in Wesley's ways, particularly in the band. Wesley sought to provide opportunities to get people learning, talking, and then behaving differently. At the heart of each band meeting were questions that each person would answer:

1. What known sins have you committed since our last meeting?

2. What temptations have you met with?

3. How were you delivered?

4. What have you thought, said, or done which you're not sure was a sin or not?

5. Is there anything you want to keep secret?

Along with honestly answering these questions, a foundational principle of the system was active participation. In fact, this was the only real requirement for membership. The two reasons people could be expelled from the band group were unfaithfulness, meaning lack of attendance or commitment to the group, and dysfunctional behavior, both of which threatened the system. Wesley understood that ongoing discipline and accountability requires solidarity, and casual attendance is a serious threat to that sense of community.

[a] Much of this Wesley story is found in D. Michael Henderson, *John Wesley's Class Meeting—A Model for Making Disciples* (Nappanee, IN: Evangel, 1997).

[b] Ibid., 83–125.

[c] See Mark 3:13–14; Luke 10:1–10; John 6:60.

THE FISHERS OF MEN VISION

Jesus may not have had a better moment to communicate his mission to his disciples than his encounter with Matthew (Levi). "Jesus went out and saw a tax collector by the name of Levi sitting at his tax booth. 'Follow me,' Jesus said to him, and Levi got up, left everything and followed him" (Luke 5:27–28).

This encounter is amazing. We have no record of Jesus spending any previous time with Matthew before he got on his feet and followed, and that alone is worth noting. But what happens next is particularly instructive for the other disciples: "Then Levi held a great banquet for Jesus at his house, and a large crowd of tax collectors and others were eating with them. But the Pharisees and the teachers of the law who belonged to their sect complained to his disciples. "Why do you eat and drink with tax collectors and sinners?" Jesus answered, "It is not the healthy who need a doctor, but the sick. I have not come to call the righteous, but sinners to repentance" (Luke 5:29–32).

In case you don't catch the cultural context here, you should know that the Jews despised men like Matthew (Levi) because he was selling out his own people to the Romans. In an extreme Jewish view, tax collectors represented national treason, and national treason was blasphemous because God was their King. On top of that, Matthew had likely become rich by stealing from the common people.

By this time Jesus had gained a reputation as a miracle worker. Prior to his encounter with Matthew, he healed a paralytic. And the people loved it! "Everyone was amazed and gave praise to God. They were filled with awe and said, 'We have seen remarkable things today'" (Luke 5:26). Now Jesus is heading to a party with this sell-out tax collector. Both the religious leaders and Jesus' own disciples were probably wondering one thing, "Why?"

Matthew likely organized a big feast for Jesus. And we can assume that Jesus and his disciples were at the party eating, drinking, talking, and having a great time. This situation alone would have been a wide-eyed experience for Jesus' observant Jewish fishermen. I can imagine some of them thinking. *So this is what fishing for men is like. This isn't what I expected!* I can also guess what some of Matthew's friends were thinking. *This guy is okay for a rabbi, a religious guy. He's something new, not like those other losers. I like him.* Granted, we don't know what Matthew's friends actually said, but Luke records what the Pharisees said (Luke 5:30). They complained that Jesus was going against their religious culture by eating with sinners. They likely thought that the disciples were spending too much time with unclean men.

In response to this, the disciples see yet another side to Jesus—his sarcastic side. Jesus plays to the spiritual blindness of the religious leaders by letting them assume they are who they think they are—righteous men who don't need God's forgiveness. He tells them, hey, it's not the healthy (like you Pharisees) who need a doctor but the sick. That's why I have come, for the benefit of these "hideous sinners," the people I am having dinner with.

So what did Matthew and his outcast friends, and Jesus' disciples, learn from this encounter? That Jesus was someone special not just to poor, rural Jews. He attracted the attention of the wealthy and "sinners" as well. Not only did he call one of these greatest of sinners to become his disciple, Jesus partied with these people. Thus the disciples learned many ways to reach people.

The disciples had witnessed miracles and healings, as well as some pretty scary confrontations with the religious leaders and demons. They saw that people who were humble and contrite always received good treatment from Jesus. He saved his anger for the arrogant, those who misused their power, and those who made life hard on those they controlled.[22] At Matthew's party, they see that Jesus is willing to accept those who are genuinely interested in what he has to say. Unlike the religious leaders, Matthew and his friends were hungry for Jesus and his words. The disciples also saw Matthew's concern for his friends and his desire to share Jesus with them.

The Pharisees and religious leaders, on the other hand, learned a different lesson—that Jesus was going to be an ongoing threat to their way of life and popularity. But they were unable to learn more because of their pride, which blocks God's grace and makes teaching impossible.[23] By listening carefully, Jesus' disciples would have caught his sarcasm and understood that those who admit they are sinners receive his help—not self-righteous people who won't accept it. Peter and company learned that working with the receptive and the hungry is the goal and that wrangling with the closed-minded and proud is a waste of time.

The first discipleship period we considered, come and see, concludes with an introduction to the Great Commission. This second period, come and follow me, ends with Jesus showing the disciples how to make disciples. This second period is also filled with calling new disciples, new teachings, healings, debates, and questions about Jesus' identity and mission. Jesus had now established his followers in the basics. He had shown them what following him means and had given them a crash course in his teachings.

As the ire and hatred of the religious leaders grew, Jesus ended this period of training by retreating from the threat: "Aware of this [that the Pharisees were plotting to kill him], Jesus withdrew from that place. A large crowd followed him, and he healed all who were ill. He warned them not to tell others about him" (Matt. 12:15–16). This was not a retreat for reflection. It was a move for survival and a delay of the confrontation that would inevitably come. By this time, Jesus' disciples understood that following him was not safe.

In the third phase of discipleship training, Jesus issues a new call to his disciples, "Come and be with me." This period will take them to the final stage of preparation for being leaders of a new movement.

Phase 3: "Come Be with Me"

Text: Mark 3:13–14

Participants: The Twelve Disciples

Time Frame: 20 months

In the third phase of training, Jesus is focused on preparing the twelve to take responsibility for world mission. The revolutionary principle in this phase is that the primary function of spiritual leadership is to equip others to minister, not to perform the ministry itself. This is the account of how Jesus chose the group for leadership training: "One of those days Jesus went out to a mountainside to pray, and spent the night praying to God. When the morning came, he called his disciples to him and chose twelve of them, whom he also designated apostles: Simon (whom he named Peter), his brother Andrew, James, John, Philip, Bartholomew, Matthew, Thomas, James son of Alphaeus, Simon who was called the Zealot, Judas son of James, and Judas Iscariot, who became a traitor" (Luke 6:12–16).

Mark says, "He appointed twelve *that they might be with him and that he might send them out to preach*" (Mark 3:14, emphasis added).

After a night of prayer and contemplation, Jesus chose twelve men out of a crowd. Notice that a number of disciples were gathered at this time. "He went down with them [the twelve] and stood on a level place. *A large crowd of his disciples* was there and a great number of people from all over Judea, from Jerusalem and from the coast of Tyre and Sidon" (Luke 6:17, emphasis added). We notice that none of the twelve are called Pharisees or rabbis or politicians. I am sure some were pleased, and that other disciples who were not chosen were disappointed.

Jesus chose to give a few of his many disciples a special place and a different name. More than just disciples—learners or students—they were now apostles. The Greek word translated "apostle" means "messenger," and suggests that the twelve have a new calling and role. They are going to be sent out to take the lead.

We should also note that Jesus was willing to disappoint hundreds of disciples for the sake of his mission. Likely, he could have chosen them all, and they would all have said yes. But Jesus had a plan because he knew what lay ahead and that he only needed a few to carry the DNA of his movement forward. Most of what we have in the Gospel accounts is covered in this third phase. But rather than cover every story, let's focus specifically on Jesus' ways and means, how he prepared these men for their future mission.

Jesus launched this period with his kingdom manifesto, the Sermon on the Mount. He followed that message with teaching on the nature of the kingdom, much of which he communicated in parables. As Jesus taught, the pressure from the religious establishment grew even more intense and dangerous. Much of his work continued to be field preaching and healing. He traveled from village to village and town to town simply being himself and engaging the people. Notice that although Jesus taught in the synagogues, he didn't sit around waiting for people to show up on the Sabbath. He was out during the week engaging people wherever they were: "Jesus went through all the towns and villages, teaching in their synagogues, proclaiming the good news of the kingdom and healing every disease and sickness. When he saw the crowds, he had compassion on them, because they were harassed and helpless, like sheep without a shepherd. Then he said to his disciples, 'The harvest is plentiful but the workers are few. Ask the Lord of the harvest, therefore, to send out workers into his harvest field'" (Matt. 9:35–38).

These words may have a familiar ring, but well trained ears will hear the difference. Earlier, after his conversation with the Samaritan woman, Jesus talked about the great harvest and need for workers (John 4:34–38). But then the disciples were mere novices; they hadn't seen and done all that Jesus had now showed them. Now that Jesus is a world-class phenomenon and the crowds are huge, he explains the method his disciples need to use to reap this harvest. They need to pray to the Father and ask for more workers, because the Father is in charge of the project. Little did the disciples suspect that they would be the first answer to their own prayers.

COMMISSIONING THE TWELVE

With the new title of apostles came new responsibilities. Matthew, Mark, and Luke all record their formal commissioning for their first mission—without Jesus.[24] They were on their own, travelling two-by-two throughout the Judean countryside. Afterwards they report back and find Jesus very busy. In fact, he is so busy that they have to steal away from the crowds to talk.

So what can we learn from Jesus' calling and sending the apostles? First, I think we need to take seriously Jesus' call to pray for workers, but we should not stop there. We go and find them as he did through the process of making disciples. Notice carefully what Jesus did here. He immediately commissioned the apostles and then sent them out. In other words, the disciples became the answer to their own prayers, and the same is true for us.

Have you ever raised your hand in a meeting to point out a need, only to have the leader assign you the job of solving the problem? In a way, Jesus acted like this leader. The key to his mission's success is expanding the disciples' responsibilities. But Jesus didn't send them out to just find new workers. He sent them out to learn how to minister, to practice all the skills they needed for future ministry. Until now, they had mostly watched and observed. Now they needed to learn by doing.

TIGHTENING THE COLLAR

Training the twelve was a daily affair. But learning to be a leader requires learning on multiple levels, so this was more than just cognitive training. Emotional and psychological dynamics were also part of the learning as the politics and pressure on Jesus increased. The disciples had different opinions about what Messiahship should look like and how everything would unfold. The crowds also made several attempts to take Jesus by the arm and rush him to Jerusalem for a coronation.[25] Jesus had to frequently correct his disciples, and at times they were clearly not on the same page.

For example, when Peter proclaimed Jesus as Messiah, Jesus praises his confession (Matt. 16:15–19). But when Peter objected to Jesus' talking about his death, "Peter took him aside and began to rebuke him" (Mark 8:31–33). Does Jesus offer a gentle word of correction here? No, he rebukes Peter right back using rather harsh language and calling him Satan: "You do not have in mind the concerns of God, but merely human concerns" (Mark 8:33).

This was a moment when the disciples realized that things were not going to end well. Jesus went on to teach what it really means to follow him, "Whoever wants to be my disciple must deny themselves and take up their cross and follow me" (Mark 8:34).[26] During this period, Jesus spoke about putting allegiance to him above all things, including family (Luke 14:25–33). Much of Jesus' public ministry from this point forward was heavily laced with conflict, and he delivered some of his most famous words in the context of debate with those who sought to kill him.

All of this leads to Jesus' triumphal entry into Jerusalem. The disciples were probably thinking that Jesus would enter like a conquering general in his golden chariot adorned with a laurel wreath. Instead they got Jesus plainly dressed and riding on a donkey. Through it all, Jesus was trying to teach his disciples that the path to glory goes through suffering.

THE SCHOOL OF GETHSEMANE

To paraphrase Samuel Johnson, the prospect of one's death has a way of focusing the mind. This was no less true for Jesus. As he entered his last week of earthly life, he was incredibly focused. In his Olivet discourse, he taught his disciples that the key event that will bring the end is preaching the gospel to the ends of the earth (Matt. 24:14). As Jesus and his disciples celebrated the Passover meal together, he added teaching elements, including washing the disciples' feet to show by his example the kind of leaders they needed to be. He also prayed for himself and them at the end of the meal. Commonly called the High Priestly prayer, Jesus talked with his Father about the work he had accomplished and what would happen in the future (John 17:1–26). He spoke of turning the work over to his disciples and asked his Father to protect them and to use them. Jesus showed that he valued them and loved them as much as the Father loved his own Son. We need to take these words seriously, because they may be the greatest affirmation of the worth of human beings in all of Scripture.[27]

Jesus invited three of the disciples—Peter, James, and John—to go with him for his anguished prayer in the garden. Of course, we also have the inglorious record of them falling asleep while he wrestled in prayer.[28] Jesus understood their weakness, of course, saying, "The spirit is willing, but the flesh is weak" (Mark 14:38). He was speaking to them, but perhaps also to himself, affirming that human effort alone would not complete the mission. Jesus cried out three times begging his Father to consider another way to finish the work. We know that this time was physically and psychologically stressful, as Jesus sweat a mixture of blood and water, revealing the genuine anguish in his soul.

Why did the disciples fall asleep? They didn't want to; in their spirits they wanted to complete the assignment Jesus gave them. They gave it their best shot, and Jesus even told them *how* to complete the assignment. "Keep watch and pray, so that you will not give into temptation. For the spirit is willing, but the body is weak!" (Matt. 26:41 NLT). The reason they could not complete this assignment was because they were not yet transformed. Good intentions are not enough; transformation of the entire person, including the body, is essential. And even then, disciples need training. As Jesus said, preparation and prayer are required to complete any project he gives us.

Jesus also warned the disciples that they would flee when trouble came that night, but the disciples emphatically denied they would fail.[29] They did not know themselves as Jesus did. But they were still operating in survival mode, guided by the flesh and living in the fear of death, so they ran. As Dallas Willard remarks, "Our bodies have a life of their own which far outreaches what we know of ourselves."[30] Their bodies could not support their intentions. In other words, how could they die for him if they couldn't even stay awake for him?

We all must learn this basic lesson in discipleship. Here is an illustration of it from physical health. The truth is that many of us have trouble losing just five pounds. If you've ever tried to diet, you know that willpower alone will not do the trick. We can lose the weight, but it goes right back on. No, we must completely change our eating and exercise. Only by changing our desires, our thinking, and our habits can we become the *kind of people* who will be able to resist the temptation.

The same is true in discipleship. We learn to become like Jesus by adopting the practices, disciplines, and exercises he followed, such as solitude and silence, prayer, fasting, worship, study, honest fellowship, and missional work. As his followers, we learn to confess our sin. When we acknowledge that he knows us better than we know ourselves, we admit our failures. Only then will we truly be prepared for the mission he has given us. Even though Jesus' best men failed to stay awake, ran when he was arrested, and hid after he was resurrected, they were learning powerful lessons that would enable them to carry on his mission after he ascended.

Phase 4: "Remain in Me"

Text: John 15:5
Participants: The apostles and all disciples who choose to follow Jesus
Time Frame: From Pentecost till today

This third phase of discipleship training, come and be with me, ended in tragedy. Jesus' disciples—his closest and most trusted followers—fled the scene and abandoned him. Even though he knew they would, we can be certain that their behavior was not easy for him. These men had been his mission, his plan for the future. The next three days were dark indeed for Jesus and his followers. On the human level, his work had been a colossal failure.

But as we know, this was not the end of the story. The cross is not a sign of failure but of the completion of the mission. Within weeks, the disciples would see in a different light, empowered by the Holy Spirit, and begin preaching, teaching, rejoicing, and dying for their resurrected Lord.

However before these things happened, they needed to experience a final phase of discipleship. They needed to learn how to be with Jesus and what it means to remain in him. In another book, I have written about the "remain in me" period when Jesus taught the disciples in the upper room.[31] Here I am speaking more generally of a transitional period from Gethsemane to the Great Commission that is the fourth phase of discipleship training. *Jesus' disciples had proven that they were well-trained failures.* But the resurrection and post-resurrection appearances of Jesus gave new life and confidence, as well as more information on making disciples of all peoples (Matt. 28:18–20). When Jesus promised that he would be with them until the end of the age, they now believed him.

Jesus ascended to heaven, yet the disciples remained. As he commanded, they prayed and waited for the power of the Spirit to come (Acts 1:12–14; 2:1–4). Jesus had charged these newly minted apostles with making of disciples. And what happened? The church was born.

Before we turn to our next subject, the church, I want to close our look at Jesus' ways and means of disciple-making with these words from Elton Trueblood.

> One of the truly shocking passages of the gospel is that in which Jesus indicates that there is absolutely no substitute for a tiny, loving, caring, reconciling society. If it fails, he suggests, all is failure; there is no other way. He told the little bedraggled fellowship that they were actually the salt of the earth and that if this salt should fail there would be no adequate preservative at all. He was staking all on one throw. . . . One of the most powerful ways of turning people's loyalty to Christ is by loving others with the great love of God. . . . If there should emerge in our day such a fellowship, wholly without artificiality and free from the dead hand of the past, it would be an exciting event of momentous importance. A society of genuine loving friends, set free from the self-seeking struggle for personal prestige and from all unreality, would be something unutterably priceless and powerful. A wise person would travel any distance to join it.[32]

Digging Deeper

HOW WESLEY PREPARED LEADERS

We've already looked at several community modes that John Wesley employed to teach and equip disciples. An additional mode is commonly known as the select company, a hand-picked group designed to model what Methodism is all about. This elite corps of enthusiasts had worked their way through the modes of society, class meeting, and bands and were considered the *crème de la crème*. They had no rules, no leader, and no prescribed format, and they met with Wesley every Monday. Today we would call this group the organization's DNA.

Wesley taught this group the ladder of leadership, which was later used in pastoral training in the Methodist Church. Continuing up this ladder shows how Wesley's followers applied his teaching, which was inspired and based upon the ways and means of Jesus.

Each point below is a rung of the ladder. As disciples mature, they ascend the ladder and take on greater responsibilities.

1. **Street Preacher.** When people are converted, they are expected to give their testimony in public. If they prove they are good at it, they can go to the next rung.

2. **Sunday School Teacher.** When teachers can communicate simple Bible truths and hold interest in the class, they may advance.

3. **Preacher.** As preachers, candidates are permitted to lead worship and preach now and then. If the pastor is pleased with their performance, they are promoted.

4. **New Preaching Point.** When candidates are sent out, their success is measured in an objective way—they must produce converts. If they can sustain this success, they go on to the next level.

5. **Christian Worker.** Upon application, candidates are evaluated and accepted as a Christian worker.

6. **Pastor-Deacon.** Candidates are assigned an area in which they are expected to plant a church. If they do not gain converts and form a nucleus of a new church, they go no higher, nor do they receive the title.

7. **Pastor.** This is the last test. In order to be promoted to pastor, candidates must present sufficient evidence to the Annual Conference that they can leave secular work, dedicate themselves to full time to ministry, and be financially supported by the congregation they have gathered together.[a]

Wesley believed that a leader's primary function is to equip others to lead and minister, not to perform the ministry personally. In the eighteenth century, the clergy were a limited number of the cultural elites. Even though he was a member of that elite, Wesley's system was open to common people who could work their way up the ladder. The system based on earned privilege—people had to produce to move forward. What would be the result if our churches were led only by those who had proven themselves effective in discipling and training others?

Our contemporary, Western churches continue to tell people what they should be doing. But the model of Jesus and Wesley is all about people talking about what they are *already* doing. Wesley trained his pastors to measure their success by how *the people they were training* were actually performing the ministry, rather than by how *they personally* were performing the ministry.[b] Can you imagine the revolution that would occur in our churches if this was the standard we used to evaluate ministry?

Our churches are focused on getting people to come and watch a show. Jesus and Wesley trained people to go to the world and introduce others to Jesus who had changed their lives.

[a] D. Michael Henderson, *John Wesley's Class Meeting—A Model for Making Disciples* (Nappanee, IN: Evangel, 1997), 152–53.

[b] See Eph. 4:11–16; 2 Tim. 2:2.

7

THE CHURCH

The promise of our modern churches to attenders has been something like this: We promise that if you practice certain disciplines and do it here in our church, you will become a mature Christian, which will bring glory to God and the church. Who can argue with this?

Well, I do, for one. My dislike of this promise is similar to Karl Bonhoeffer's dislike of the teachings of Sigmund Freud. Bonhoeffer (father of Dietrich Bonhoeffer) characterized Freud's psychotherapy as "the bad fruit of people who like to busy themselves with themselves."[1] My problem with the contemporary approach to discipleship is its teaching that spiritual maturity is largely about the church. It's a grand vision, to be sure, but few ever say that they have reached maturity. Who do you know who has "become mature, attaining the whole measure of the fullness of Christ" (Eph 4:13)?

Part of the problem is that our focus is largely on ourselves. In our gatherings and small groups, we often ask, "How are you doing?" Or we might want accountability and ask others, "How am I doing?" While these questions have their place, they tend to divorce our discipleship from our mission. The real question in spiritual formation is not introspective—it is a concern for the welfare of others. If the well-read words of Philippians 2:5–8 tell us anything, they teach that Jesus lived for the sake of others. He maintained the attitudes of humility, submission, and sacrifice, and his purpose was serving others.

So while "How are you doing?" is not wrong to ask, the question doesn't go far enough. The real question for a disciple is this, "How are you doing loving the people God has put in your life?" The goal of spiritual maturity is not self-improvement. It is transformation into people who live to love others.

This is a necessary corrective to the common way of thinking of spiritual disciplines. We practice spiritual disciplines so we can become the kind of people who love and live for others. We study the Scriptures so we can gain the knowledge, perspective, and guidance to help others. We become Christ to others in all the domains of our life. And in the process of living for others, we end up becoming mature people in Christ.

Maturity is not an end in itself. It is a byproduct of following Jesus. We keep our eyes fixed on him and follow him, and as a result, we grow. This focus rescues spiritual exercises from becoming self-focused, meaningless activities and is consistent with the teachings of Jesus. We never find what we are looking for by grasping at it directly. We find our purpose and joy in giving up our life, and by doing so, we save our life (Luke 9:23–25).

The Blessed Cul De Sac

Christ is not finished with his work on the earth. He has chosen to continue his life through his church. And I'm not just speaking about the universal church. Jesus works through local bodies of believers gathered together in his name to learn from his word.

Around the world, the worst failure of churches has been the alarming disparity between what Christ is like and how his disciples turn out. But churches exist for the primary purpose of making disciples, and those disciples are meant to be a gift to the world. The goal of churches in reproducing disciples of Jesus is to enable those disciples to reenter the world and demonstrate a higher quality of life and a level of skill in presenting Jesus in word and deed that will penetrate the natural resistance of unbelieving souls. The people of God are to love the world like Jesus does, in concrete and sacrificial ways that crush arguments and pretensions of unbelief.[2] Their love should show Jesus, be a love that counts and against which there is no argument.

Part of the problem in making disciples like this, of course, has been a lack of good teaching about who and what we are to do as disciples. Most pastors assume that making disciples refers primarily to making better Christians out of existing believers. As a result, many churches have set low expectations for what being a good disciple means. What is missing is the notion that a disciple *makes other disciples*. We have failed to communicate to believers that they themselves are expected to make disciples who will be able to make disciples.[3] This is the truly revolutionary idea that must inform our understanding of churches and why they exist.[4] A revolution requires a message and a platform for communicating that message. In this case, the delivery system is the disciples themselves. When disciples respond to the call of Jesus and make other disciples, they show the world the church as Jesus created it to be. It is a disciple-making factory.

Who Me?

Jesus' calling of the first disciples was completely unambiguous. "Follow me," he said to Peter, James, John, Andrew, and Matthew, and they dropped everything and followed him. They were not confused about what Jesus was asking.[5] Of course when he was on earth, Jesus did not invite everyone to follow him. He spoke to, healed, and helped others and told them to go to the Temple or to return to their home. In fact, the majority of the people who heard Jesus and received his ministry were not invited to travel with him.[6]

Some take this aspect of Jesus' earthly ministry as support for the idea that churches have a two-tier system of clergy (professional teachers) and laity (regular believers). This idea causes people to say that not everyone is called to the deeper discipleship of being with Jesus every day. That's just for the clergy—the pastors. Again, Dietrich Bonhoeffer helps us respond to this issue.

> There is something wrong with all of these questions. [He refers here to people who are looking for a biblical out for discipleship.] Every time we ask them, we place ourselves outside the living presence of the Christ. All of these questions refuse to take seriously that Jesus Christ is not dead but alive and still speaking to us today through the testimony of Scripture.... It is within the church that Jesus Christ calls through his word and sacrament. The preaching

and the sacrament of the church is the place where Jesus Christ is present. To hear Jesus' call to discipleship, one needs no personal revelation. . . . No one but Christ himself can call us to discipleship. Discipleship in essence never consists in a decision for this or that specific action; it is always a decision for or against Jesus Christ.[7]

In other words, rather than seeing the disciples who travelled with Jesus as the exception, we should see them as the norm for all believers today. The risen Lord who sends the Holy Spirit to indwell believers calls all of them to discipleship with him just as clearly as he called those first disciples. This call is for *everyone*, not just a special few. We don't need a special revelation or experience to receive this call. If we listen to the word preached, if we participate in the sacraments (or their equivalent according to our tradition), God is speaking to us through his word. We are all disciples called to follow Jesus.

Disappointment, Disparity, Distraction

As I mentioned earlier, many are disappointed with the church. They see and feel a disparity between what they hope for and what is actually delivered. And many are critical of our churches and their leaders. Often today pastors find themselves in the role of a defense attorney, apologizing for the faults of churches and trying to explain away the disappointment members feel.

I find our situation to be similar to a man having trouble with his car. He doesn't understand why the car is not running right, so he brings it to the mechanic. The mechanic quickly discovers that the man has been mixing water with the fuel. Since the car was built to run on gas, not water, the mechanic advises the man to stop mixing in water. He should only use the fuel prescribed for the car—nothing else will work. The same is true of spiritual development in Christ. A prescribed fuel is necessary for a person to grow, thrive, and mature. If all people are driving on is watered-down fuel, they will sputter and stall. We cannot disciple people to disciple others if they aren't running on the right fuel. That's why we need to recover and preach the gospel that Jesus and his disciples preached, teaching our members to preach that gospel as well.

The operational words of that gospel are "follow me." The starting point for every person who wants to grow in Christ is adopting the mindset of a learner, an apprentice. Christianity is more than just professing belief. It involves work, change, and ongoing transformation. It involves studying, learning, obeying, and an ongoing willingness to follow Jesus wherever he leads, with no conditions or limits. Yet this set of standards is quite different from what is generally believed and taught in our Western churches. As Dallas Willard writes, "the governing assumption today among professing Christians is that we can be 'Christians' forever and never become disciples."[8]

Because Western churches tend to have great influence over global Christianity, our lack of a call to discipleship and of a robust process of making disciples who make disciples directly threatens the growth of Christianity in the rest of the world. *Yes, we are a threat to global Christianity*. We can greatly harm the vitality of churches around the world if we export our models and infect others with the same diseases we have. This issue is another serious reason why we must correct the ways and means of our churches.

To this end, we now turn to the model of the first church started in the city of Jerusalem. Our question is simple: Did the disciples of Jesus disciple others? If the answer to that question is yes, then we want to know the answer to a second question: How did they do it? What foundation did they build upon to make reproducing disciples?

A Look at the First Church

The first day of the first church was a huge success by today's standards.[9] This church had it all. They preached the gospel in sixteen separate languages. A supernatural energy, an electric vibe, was in the air. The apostle Peter gave an extemporaneous message, and 3,000 people believed the story and were baptized. And the growth didn't end there. Over the next few months, these new believers learned a few practices and were formed into a new community. The book of Acts describes this church as follows.

> All the believers devoted themselves to the apostles' teaching, and to fellowship, and to sharing in meals (including the Lord's Supper), and to prayer.
>
> A deep sense of awe came over them all, and the apostles performed many miraculous signs and wonders. And all the believers met together in one place and shared everything they had. They sold their property and possessions and shared the money with those in need. They worshiped together at the Temple each day, met in homes for the Lord's Supper, and shared their meals with great joy and generosity—all the while praising God and enjoying the goodwill of all the people. And each day the Lord added to their fellowship those who were being saved.
>
> —ACTS 2:42–47 NLT

Did I catch you skimming the words there, or even skipping the passage altogether? Perhaps you've read it before. Maybe you've even preached on it. I know that passing over something familiar is normal. But I want you to focus on this passage for a bit and think with me about the apostles' teaching. It didn't come out of nowhere, right? The apostles' teaching was simply the teaching of Jesus, what they had learned from their teacher. What else could it have been? They hadn't had enough time to screw it all up. So they were simply passing along what they had been taught, and were in this way multiplying Jesus' message.

The phrase "each day" is used twice in this text, which tells us the practices here were routine. But this is a good thing! When activities are routine, they form our habits and become the embedded practices of a community, forming the community's culture and the worldview. Even bad churches are good at forming habits, they just form bad ones and create cultures that reek of moralism, legalism, and shame, not grace, discipline, and loving correction. So what are some of the good habits that the earliest Christians practiced? What shaped and informed their discipleship?

1. DEVOTED TO THE APOSTLES' TEACHING

The Apostles' teaching were the teachings of Jesus. Luke is the author of The Acts of the Apostles, which we commonly shorten to just Acts. Luke wasn't present the first day of the Jerusalem church, but he ended up writing a large chunk of the New Testament by relying on letters, documents, and the oral accounts of eye-witnesses. In the introduction to Acts, Luke refers to his Gospel, "In my first book, I told you, Theophilus, about everything Jesus began to do and teach until the day he was taken up to heaven after giving his disciples further instructions through the Holy Spirit" (Acts 1:1–2 NLT). Luke fully understood what Jesus had done and taught, so it makes sense that when he speaks of the apostles' teaching, he is referring to what Jesus had taught them. How did they communicate this teaching? In lists of rules or propositions to memorize? No, the apostles gave their eye-witness accounts of Jesus' activities and recounted his parables and sermons. The apostles were Jesus' messengers and witnesses, and they were committed to retelling all they had seen and heard.

Six major sermons recorded in Acts give us a good summary of the apostles' teaching. And whenever they gathered, they retold the accounts, which is essential to any foundation.[10] Even when the disciples were warned by the Jewish leaders not to speak in the name of Jesus, they refused saying: "We cannot stop telling about everything we have seen and heard" (Acts

4:20 NLT). Their teaching was not theoretical or abstract. It was their experience, and it was compulsory.

2. SPENT TIME IN FELLOWSHIP

In addition to telling stories about Jesus and sharing what he had taught, the disciples all spent time together. Not many people speak of fellowship anymore. The word has fallen out of use and the idea rebranded with catchier phrases like "community," "body life," "life together," or "doing life together." Some have even gone to the source and use the Greek word *koinonia*. But what is fellowship? Fellowship is the unity of the body of Christ in the Holy Spirit. But at a practical level, we should understand fellowship as a verb, meaning an activity. Fellowship is forming and deepening relationships in such a way that we help each other keep our commitments to God. Some people call this accountability. But whatever term we use, fellowship is what we do and say that hold us together. Without fellowship, the foundation of the apostles' teaching will crumble.

The early church met together in one place, which could have been outdoors or in the Temple area. The Temple area is equal to forty-six football fields; if one walks there today, many groups are praying, studying, and discussing religion. People sold property and shared whatever was necessary to make sure everyone had what they needed to live. They also worshiped together in the Temple daily, and on a regular basis met in homes to share the Lord's Supper.

Many believe that the numbers eventually grew to over 5,000, and administration became a problem the apostles had to address. This is why they appointed deacons to oversee meeting physical needs (Acts 6:1–7). Many believers could have been living in temporary housing, having attended the festival in Jerusalem. So a natural diaspora occurred when these disciples went back to their homes at some point. The overall atmosphere was one of joy and generosity, where all were "praising God and enjoying the goodwill of all the people" (Acts 2:47).

However, it did not take long for this perfect church to begin breaking down. "But as the believers rapidly multiplied, there were rumblings of discontent" (Acts 6:1 NLT). These rumblings in Jerusalem were a prelude to the many corrective letters that Paul would later write to his churches throughout Asia. Disillusionment has always been part of church experience, and one reason is that the claims and promises of Christianity are beyond our own capacity to achieve. Eugene Peterson once said, "The church we want is the enemy of the church we have." Our idealized Christian community is often far from reality, and a fixation on the shortcomings of our churches will only lead to constant disappointment.

Dietrich Bonhoeffer was even more direct in speaking of this disillusionment and the importance of acknowledging it and moving ahead.

> The sooner this moment of disillusionment comes over the individual and the community, the better for both. However, a community that cannot bear and cannot survive such disillusionment, clinging instead to its idealized image, when that should be done away with, loses at the same time the promise of durable Christian community. Sooner or later it will collapse. Every human idealized image that is brought into the Christian community is a hindrance to genuine community and must be broken up so that genuine community can survive. . . . Those who love their dream of Christian community more than Christian community itself become destroyers of that Christian community even though their personal interests may be ever so honest, earnest and sacrificial.[11]

When we have an idealized picture of what Christian life together should look like that doesn't match the reality we see before us, our dreams can be crushed. We will likely run from place to place looking for the "real" church or a better community, not realizing that such a place cannot be found this side of eternity. Our ideal only exists in scattered pieces, in snippets, in moments when we get a taste of what is yet to come. We must value these moments, but durable, sustainable Christian community is not built on these moments. It is built on the truth that the Christian life is a battle. We need to engage the fight, and we need others to help us in it. When we go wrong, when we fail, we need someone to pull us back, prop us up, and keep us marching ahead. The gifts and graces of our fellow followers meet our daily need for grace.[12] So the foundation of a disciple-making church consists of both the apostles' teaching and fellowship—those imperfect but redemptive relationships that glue us together and allow us to practice and live out the teachings of Jesus.

3. EXPERIENCED A SENSE OF AWE

Luke continues describing the first church. "A deep sense of awe came over them all, and the apostles performed many miraculous signs and wonders" (Acts 2:43 NLT). The Greek text translated "awe" here is φοβος, or "fear deep in the soul." What is this fear or sense of sober-minded wonder they experienced? If we think of discipleship as a fight that we must engage, then it is helpful to consider the difference between a soldier training with blank bullets and one training with live ammunition. The soldier training with blanks may be motivated by a desire to succeed or to avoid failing, but he knows that his life is not really on the line. The adrenaline doesn't flow that much when we are not truly in danger. But what these early Christians were seeing, hearing, and doing was real and dangerous—literally a matter of life and death. This awe they felt is an indication of the depth of their emotional engagement. Because their lives were on the line, they were willing to live sacrificially, giving all they had for the sake of the mission.

We might describe our sense of wonder by saying, "It blew me away," but our true feeling is expressed in our actions, what we do to show our awe. The first disciples sold what they had so they could share the money with the others. This is another key difference between the early church and our approach to discipleship. The emphasis today tends to be on getting people "jacked up" and excited by a preacher or during a worship service. The focus is on the subjective experience, how people feel in the moment. But often churches are relying on techniques and technology to give people a holy buzz. I have preached in several churches that used dry ice to create fake smoke. The goal here is to get people to applaud, hoot, and holler in a heartfelt act of praise to God.

Techniques and technology have their place, and there is nothing wrong with a little applause, hooting, and hollering. But these are not signs that people are living in awe of God. When people are living spiritually bland lives and are bloated with materialism, they will always find it difficult to worship. *The right atmosphere, good music, and a charismatic worship leader cannot fix the deep spiritual problems of the heart.* If the focus of worship is meeting our needs as consumers, we will not experience the awe and fear of the Lord that leads to authentic change and true obedience. Sadly, many people determine a church's effectiveness by how they think their needs are met and the way they feel emotionally about the worship service. But these things have nothing to do with discipleship. They are the products of a consumer gospel and a self-centered Christianity.

We cannot make disciples by creating worship environments that cater to people's felt needs. True obedience comes from the heart and is lived out every day. C. S. Lewis explains the connection between life and worship. "I had never noticed that all enjoyment spontaneously overflows into praise.... The world rings with praise-lovers praising their mistresses, readers their favorite poet, walkers praising the countryside, players praising their game.... I think we delight to praise what we enjoy because the praise not merely expresses but completes the enjoyment; it is appointed consummation."[13]

181

As the Psalmist writes, "How good to sing praises to our God! How delightful and fitting!" (Ps. 147:1 NLT). The quality of our worship—our awe of God and what he has done—will be most evident in the life we live. A life of worship is a life of sacrificial discipleship, giving ourselves as a living offering to God.[14]

4. GREW IN NUMBERS

How do you measure success? Do you quantify your results? Albert Einstein once said "Not everything that can be counted counts, and not everything that counts can be counted." With insights like that, I suspect that Einstein would have been a pretty good politician. What happened to the early church as it followed the apostles' teaching, engaged in fellowship, and lived in awe of God through lives of constant worship? "Each day the Lord added to their fellowship those who were being saved" (Acts 2:47 NLT).

We naturally view large churches as success stories. Denominations have special gatherings for pastors of larger congregations. Most of the speakers at church leader conferences are chosen because they pastor a large church. And the First Church in Jerusalem certainly qualified as a megachurch. Within a few weeks, they could boast a membership of "about 5,000, not counting women and children" (Acts 4:4 NLT). So the total number could have been as high as eight to ten thousand. Daily, they were receiving new members through conversion. I think it is fair to say seeing conversions should be the hope of every church. We want to see people coming to Christ and being discipled to make disciples. But we don't see these conversions if we don't have the first three elements.

What we learn here is there is no silver bullet for growth. Rather, growth requires a combination of the elements that make up a healthy, yet imperfect and difficult-to-run, disciple-making church. Even this first church had trouble following through with the mission. Jesus told his followers to be his witnesses in Jerusalem, Judea, Samaria, and the farthest parts the earth (Acts 1:8). So did they pack up their bags and head out? No. It took a persecution to scatter them out to preach the gospel to the nations. While how much time passed between Pentecost and the persecution isn't clear, it was at least one year and maybe as many as five.[15] Giving them the benefit of the doubt, we could say that while they planned to launch their evangelistic church planting strategy, it was stuck in committee.

True Believers

Many years ago a longshoreman named Eric Hoffer wrote about people he called true believers.[16] He was not speaking about religious devotees but fanatics who were totally committed to a person or a cause. While some personalities are predisposed toward fanaticism, someone cannot be forced to be a fan. It comes from within, motivated by passion and love. This is true of those who entered the first church in Jerusalem, and beginning with Stephen, hundreds, then thousands, and now millions have become true believers of Jesus. They are fans in the best sense of the word—fanatic about Jesus and willing to die rather than recant their faith. Even as I write this, the news is filled with Christians who have been beheaded for refusing to deny their faith.[17]

What makes people willing to die for what they believe? Christians in North America sometimes wonder: *Do I have that kind of faith? Would I pass the test?* But the test of a true believer isn't just a matter of confessing Christ when a gun is put to your head. Sometimes confessing Christ involves losing wealth or security and comfort. Persecution may not be a raised fist but a raised eyebrow. Faith that stands fast in life-threatening circumstances is formed in day-to-day choices to follow Christ.

Faith is more than a feeling, and true belief is more than just an emotional response to an experience. The first weeks of Jerusalem's first church were likely an adrenaline rush. But then reality set in. Christians had to live by what they really believed and thought rather than how they felt in the moment. True belief begins with knowledge of God and of ourselves, and this knowledge affects and trains our emotional responses to circumstances. This knowledge is especially important to remember as we are discipling others: "*One of the worst mistakes that can be made in practical ministry is to think that people can choose to believe and feel differently.*"[18] When we attempt by manipulative techniques or environments to move people to action based on emotion, we create disciples who are unstable. They inevitably crumble under pressure.

Instead of trying to believe, disciples act in faith on the knowledge we have and trust God by taking the first steps. We then immerse ourselves in Scripture and allow the knowledge of God to train our will and form our desires for the things that he says will make life better. Our desires may not be good when we begin, but we go on what we have—a hunger for God and a faith in his promises. As we immerse ourselves in Scripture, we begin to command our (changed) will that has been trained and shaped by the knowledge of God to choose what is right.

What is the knowledge of God? Specific truth about God, of course, who he is, what he does, and what he has revealed to us. This includes Jesus' teaching about responding to evil, returning good for evil, and forgiving and praying for our enemies. It also encompasses our relationships, for example being loyal to our spouse, telling the truth even when doing so costs us, and so much more. Knowledge of God means being aware that he is working all elements of life into something good and that happiness comes through service to others and sharing our wealth.

The knowledge of God should be communicated to us through our churches. But this transfer of information is more than just preaching. Yes, preaching is important and necessary, but forming true believers takes more than just a message once a week on Sunday morning. A good friend and pastor Robby Gallaty tells a story about a conversation he had with Avery Willis. Robby was proposing that his PhD thesis be on the role of preaching in making disciples. Willis said to him, "Robby, thinking you can disciple people through sermons is like going into a nursery, spraying the newborn babies with milk, and claiming you have fed them." In other words, preaching is one means of sharing knowledge of God, but it doesn't always address the nuances and particulars of our individual circumstances.

The example of the first Jerusalem church demonstrates a combination of at least four ingredients are required to create true believers. In addition to preaching (the apostles' teaching) is meaningful fellowship and sharing life and material goods with those in need. Third is shared worship that gives both a common sense that God is at work in our midst and an awe at what he has done. Fourth is evidence that God is adding people to our community because we are engaged in conversions with people who are interested in following Christ and joining us. As disciples, we are making other disciples.

Another Disciple-Making Church: Ephesus

While instructive for us today, the first church in Jerusalem was not the only disciple-making church we learn about in Scripture. Today we can travel to Turkey to the ancient city of Ephesus and sit among the ruins of its amphitheater, listening to a symphonic orchestra entertain us while we sip the beverage of our choice. Two thousand years ago, the apostle Paul traveled to Ephesus as well, but his visit ended with a riot in that same amphitheater.[19] Irate citizens protested his message and demanded his expulsion because he and his followers were seen as a threat to the Ephesian way of life. In fact, the local silversmiths incited the riot because the Christians were having such an impact on the community that people were converting to Christ and no longer buying their handmade silver gods. In other words, the Ephesian church was bad for business.

I believe the church at Ephesus is the best example of a disciple-making church that we can find in the New Testament. We can learn a great deal from this church. This new church plant was started from scratch and experienced signs, wonders, and miracles that were sure to attract the charismatically inclined crowds. The Ephesian church had a further social and economic impact by casting out of demons and upsetting the status quo.[20] Last but not least, this church valued training and teaching. Paul trained, debated, and strategized with a steady stream of disciples, new and old, from the city and the surrounding twenty-seven provinces.[21] Scripture's portrayal of the Ephesian church helpfully illustrates how Paul and his followers understood Jesus' words, "Go and make disciples of all nations, baptizing them in the name of the Father and of the Son and of the Holy Spirit and teaching them to obey everything I have commanded" (Matt. 28:19–20).

Paul's visit to the city of Ephesus lasted three years, longer than any other stop on his three missionary journeys. The church was started with twelve men who had never heard the gospel of Jesus—they were only aware of the teaching of John the Baptist. So Paul explained Jesus' gospel. They believed, were filled with the Holy Spirit, and began to speak in tongues.

Next, Paul went to the Ephesian synagogue where he preached and debated for three months. Similar to the field preaching of Wesley, Paul went where people gathered. Eventually, these gatherings became too disruptive, so Paul took the believers and started teaching them five hours a day in the lecture hall of Tyrannus. He did this for the next two years, "so that all the Jews and Greeks who lived in the province of Asia heard the word of the Lord" (Acts 19:10). In my book *The Disciple-Making Church*, I seek to fill in the gaps, unpacking what Paul and those disciples might have done each day for those five hours.[22] Here are several reasonable conclusions we can make.

1. Meeting five hours a day, six days a week, for two years does not mean that Paul was always talking. We know he used the Socratic teaching method, so classes likely included a great deal of debate and discussion rather than just lectures.
2. Classes must have also included practical application, since Paul had been trained in the rabbinic educational model, which Jesus also used. We know this training of disciple-makers bore fruit.
   - These followers started six new churches that are listed in Revelation 2–3: Smyrna, Pergamum, Thyatira, Sardis, Philadelphia, and Laodicea. We can also add to the list Colossae and Hierapolis. Paul's letter to the Ephesians was meant to be circulated and read in all the other churches started during his time in Ephesus.

- The disciples in Ephesians also learned from other teachers and apostles. We know the apostle John lived in Ephesus until his death, writing the Gospel of John and three epistles from the city. Timothy followed Paul as pastor in Ephesus, when Paul wrote his pastoral epistles to him.

3. God worked many miracles among the Ephesians which contributed to creating a large congregation. He worked many through Paul, whom he gave special power for reaching people. Acts tells how the people responded. "The story of what happened spread quickly all through Ephesus, to Jews and Greeks alike. A solemn fear descended on the city, and the name of the Lord Jesus was greatly honored. Many who became believers confessed their sinful practices. A number of them who had been practicing sorcery brought their incantation books and burned them at a public bonfire. The value of the books was several millions dollars. So the message about the Lord spread widely and had a powerful effect" (Acts 19:17–20 NLT).

I share all of this to say that if post-evangelicals are looking for ways to impact others, they need to look no farther than Ephesus. Here we have it all in its embarrassing simplicity. Build a church like the disciple-making church at Ephesus. Paul's plan for making disciples was what Christ himself taught him (Gal. 1:11–12). Paul preached, trained, prayed, sent disciples out, and followed up on them, and then he trained others as they joined him in Ephesus. He planned for his succession by replacing himself with Timothy, and he sent correspondence around the new church world through couriers. Paul even wrote to congregations in places he had never been, such as Rome.

Eugene Peterson once said, "There are no 'successful' congregations in the Scriptures or in the history of the church."[23] I agree with him . . . and disagree. I agree that the early churches had great moments, typically followed by seasons of futility. Church success usually ends up making enemies and creating problems, which happened in Ephesus. After a successful three-year run, Paul's ministry was brought to an abrupt close by a riot and town rebellion. A few months later, Paul met with the Ephesian elders on the island of Miletus to say goodbye.[24]

Peterson's point is that even "successful" churches will experience struggle and disappointment. You might recall that the Ephesian church was not ready to accept Timothy as pastor, and he struggled to follow Paul.[25] In Revelation, Jesus points out that the Ephesian church lost its first love (Rev. 2:4–6). However, Peterson's "successful" is in quotes because he is referring to an inferior, outward definition of success that is not from God.

Peterson goes on to describe the church at Ephesus: "Ephesians is a revelation of the church we never see. It shows us the healthy soil and root system of all the operations of the Trinity out of which the church that we do see grows. It does not describe the various expressions of what grows from that soil into cathedrals and catacombs, storefront missions and revival tents, tabernacles and chapels. Nor does it deal with the various ways in which the church takes form in liturgy and mission and polity. Rather, it is an inside look at what is beneath and behind and within the church that we do see wherever and whenever it becomes visible."[26]

This rings true to me. You see, I have always been more in love with the church I want than the church I have. The problem, of course, is that the church I want does not exist. The church I have is always there, warts and all. As an idea, a dream, the church can seem very attractive. In the opening paragraphs of Paul's letter to the Ephesians, we get a taste of this ideal church:

> Even before he made the world, God loved us and chose us in Christ to be holy and without fault in his eyes. God decided in advance to adopt us into his own family by bringing us to himself through Jesus Christ. This is what he wanted to do, and it gave him great pleasure. . . .
> God has now revealed to us his mysterious plan regarding Christ, a plan to fulfill his own good pleasure. And this is the plan: At the right time he will bring everything together under the authority of Christ—everything in heaven and on earth. Furthermore, because we are united with Christ, we have received an inheritance from God, for he chose us in advance, and he makes everything work out according to his plan.

> —Ephesians 1:4–6, 9–12 NLT

Paul knows he is speaking of something not seen before in human history, and he was thankful to have been a part of this unfolding mystery: "I was chosen to explain to everyone this mysterious plan that God, the Creator of all things, had kept secret from the beginning. *God's purpose in all this was to use the church to display his wisdom in its rich variety to all the unseen rulers and authorities in the heavenly places.* This was his eternal plan, which he carried out through Christ Jesus our Lord" (Eph. 3:9–11 NLT, emphasis added).

Paul is speaking to the unmet needs of the human heart and its deepest questions.[27] These are what drove Nietzsche to the asylum and caused other towering German theologians to construct elaborate and rather silly explanations of the reality plainly before them. Paul described possibilities and a field of knowledge that the intellectual elite could never imagine. "Now all glory to God, who is able, through his mighty power at work within us, to accomplish infinitely more than we might ask or think. Glory to him in the church and in Christ Jesus through all generations forever and ever! Amen" (Eph. 3:20–21 NLT).

Paul introduces us to the God who is the cause behind the creation, who is personal, loving, all knowing, and has a plan for all humans. Paul taught that we can know this God in Christ and talk to him in prayer on a personal basis. He explained that the realm of the knowledge of God is so great, only a submitted and humble will can access it. And this God desires to do more among his people than we can imagine.

Human beings have a new reality because of Christ. When we speak of this reality, hopes for our churches run high and dreams are lifted up. Yet wrongly understood, this ideal can cause great disillusionment and is the enemy of our churches. In Ephesians, Paul keeps the hope for the church and realities of earthly life in tension. He describes the ideal to inspire the church with a lofty, God-sized vision and gives hope through glorious vistas of God's majesty, power, and personal care for every person. In later chapters and with a dose of street-wise reality, Paul teaches the Ephesians how to walk toward these visions.[28]

This tension is at the heart of our churches. Together, we are a community of forgiven sinners, broken people in the process of being made fit for heaven.[29]

Working Together

Paul begins Ephesians 4 by looking at how the body of Christ is one and how its members must work together to make everyone and everything whole. He instructs, "Always be humble and gentle. Be patient with each other, making allowance for each other's faults because of your love. Make every effort to keep yourselves united in the Spirit, binding yourselves together with peace" (Eph. 4:2–3 NLT).

Becoming a mature disciple means refusing to live a "minimalist" spiritual life in isolation (just me and Jesus). The mature also reject shortcuts. There are no steroids for spiritual growth. It is a long-term process that must be done with others, and it is challenging. Paul's instructions to the church are personal, but not individualistic. He gives these instructions to the community, not individuals, because they must learn to intentionally train together.

Our churches should be where we learn to love, both our friends and our enemies. Love is actions taken for the benefit of others. The emphasis here in Paul's letter is on becoming a humble, patient, kind person. We must not put the responsibility on others to treat us well. It is our responsibility to respond with grace and love to others. Of course, we can find ways to avoid these relational challenges. Some people think they belong to a church by slipping into the service on Sunday morning and then slipping out without any meaningful contact. In my mind, they might as well skip the service and read the Sunday paper instead. Either way, they are living a banal life of self-absorption.

At times our churches are beautiful, and at times the ugliness of sin shows through. I have never been loved so well nor hated so deeply than by my fellow followers of Christ. I have spent many sleepless nights dealing with conflict in my church. Yet in the end, most of the ugly stuff has faded from memory. We've worked out our conflicts, and God has turned them into good. Many scream in the middle of the pain of conflict, "I don't need this!" But the Bible is clear that we do need it. God uses pain as fuel for our formation in Christ.[30]

Who was humble, patient, kind, sacrificial, and made allowances for *our* faults? Christ, of course.[31] Our churches should be dedicated to shaping us to become like Christ. We can't get there without taking up our own cross and suffering. Becoming mature takes time and cannot be hurried. So leaders creating the right environment are basic to transformation.

Leaders Create Communal Character

As we continue in Ephesians 4, we see Paul's focus turn to the gifts Christ has given to serve his body, the church. First are leaders: apostles, prophets, evangelists, pastors, and teachers.[32] These gifts are also officers that our churches need to be what God designed churches to be. Apostles lead the way.[33] Prophets encourage, exhort, and comfort God's people.[34] Evangelists break new ground and proclaim the gospel in the world.[35] Pastors guide the congregation,[36] while teachers instruct members in the Scriptures.[37]

Remember if you are looking for a place outside the church to make disciples, forget it! Because outside the church, you will not find these gifts, which are the full complement of resources God provides in each congregation.[38]

About these leaders, Paul writes: "Their responsibility is to equip God's people to do his work and build up the church, the body of Christ" (Eph. 4:12 NLT). The word "responsibility" here is inferred, but it is an appropriate addition. The work is to equip των αγιων, "the saints," people whom God has called and set apart for service. The focus, then, is not on the performance of the gifted leaders. It is on the end result, equipping and preparing the saints for ministry. And this equipping is more than just teaching skills—it also implies growth in character. The language used here is important. The Greek word translated "equip" is also used in reference to mending a frayed fishing net, resetting a broken bone, or preparing an athlete for competition. And the word διακονιας, translated "work," refers to service or ministry. The purpose of this equipping is so that each saint can build up other saints. *So the responsible measurement of a leader's work is this: does he or she produce effective ministers out of common saints?*[39]

This is how we know if a church is truly functioning as God intended: Are the saints being equipped to serve? The church is a luminous community set on a hill. Multitudes are drawn to its light. The lofty goal of serving this world is vital because it draws us out of self-absorption into the liberating purpose of serving others. Still, the process is never clean and neat. In fact, it is quite messy. But the result is worth the effort. "This will continue until we all come to such unity in our faith and knowledge of God's Son that we will be mature in the Lord, measuring up to the full and complete standard of Christ. Then we will no longer be immature like children. We won't be tossed and blown about by every wind of new teaching. We will not be influenced when people try to trick us with lies so clever they sound like the truth" (Eph. 4:13–14 NLT).

How long will this process take? The time required is connected to the need and the goal. In other words, it takes as long as needed until the goal is reached. And the goal is lofty. We are seeking unity in faith and knowledge and maturity in meeting the standards of Christ. If you feel like throwing up your hands and giving up, you are not alone. How can anyone attain to such an ideal?

I believe these goals are attainable, and we are encouraged in several other places in Scripture.[40] The Bible speaks often of growing to maturity and sets it against the stage of immaturity, of being "like children." Paul clearly expects growth that will move his disciples beyond immaturity into maturity. We know children's brains physically develop as they grow to adulthood, even that a pruning process occurs during the teen years when the ability to reason is developing yet still limited. Brains do not fully mature until the later teens and early twenties.[41] Despite these scientific findings, parents have known since the Stone Age that as we grow, our abilities and understanding change. The same is true with our spiritual development.

Of course, we should not fault the young for being immature, for it is natural in children. Yet we should expect them to grow. In moments of exasperation, parents will sometimes say, "When will Bill ever grow up?" But we also need to understand that growth takes time. Some people stall, get stuck in adolescence, and are overdue to "get it." This is a common problem in our culture of narcissism, where the hallmark is obsession with getting and spending instead of *becoming* more. The culture tells us to live better without growing up.[42] To this end, businesses, the entertainment industry, and even government spend billions of dollars every year to fund trickery, craftiness, and deceitful scheming. And most distressingly, so do our churches. And the situation is certainly not getting any better.[43]

Our churches have been led astray in a number of clever ways. We are easily satisfied with superficial success and judge this success by numerical growth. This way of thinking is certainly seductive, like a bowl of peanut M&Ms sitting on our desk. We just have to indulge every now and then, right? Yet there are dangers in this indulgence. First is that judging by this superficial standard is addictive. Seeing large crowds in attendance tends to make us dependent on large crowds for happiness. Once we are used to seeing them, living without them gives us the shakes.

Closely related to this addiction is the common belief that a certain leadership personality is the key to success. If you don't think this is a bone-deep belief, research what search committees are looking for and the candidates' resumes. Even if we don't buy into the numbers game, we may believe that a successful pastor excels in preaching, and if he does that well, it's enough. But this belief tends to downplay how the pastor must model personal discipleship for the church. Good preaching is not a guarantee that a pastor can make disciples who make disciples.

This brings us to the big lie infecting our churches. The average church member in the average church doesn't truly see himself or herself as a minister. They believe they are just part of the supporting cast for the big show, the Sunday Service. While a church may talk to members about doing ministry, ministry boils down to inviting people they know to the Sunday Services so they can join the church. In other words, the average church has no expectation for ordinary members to actually make disciples themselves.

The reason members are failing to make disciples is not lack of teaching or training. It is because pastors and leaders are not making disciples, nor are they expecting the people in their churches to do so. Certainly, there are exceptions, but they are rare. In general, the lack of disciple-making pastors and churches is what immobilizes the international church. And that is why we never get to Ephesians 4:15–16: "Instead, we will speak the truth in love, growing in every way more and more like Christ, who is the head of his body, the church. He makes the whole body fit together perfectly. As each part does its own special work, it helps the other parts grow, so that the whole body is healthy and growing and full of love" (NLT).

You see, the goal is not to remain immature. The goal is to grow, become mature, and take on the mature life. Notice that this is a communal process. It is more than just one or two individuals making disciples. It is a disciple-making church, the body fitting together perfectly as every member does his or her gifted work.

Notice in particular what members are to do: "we will speak the truth in love." An honest, loving speech like this requires a special environment, or it will tear the community and its members apart. It requires both disciples who have a deep understanding of the gospel and a gracious sensibility created by the Holy Spirit. Without these elements, our churches can be very dangerous places. The members will be broken in their sin, and they will end up breaking everything in their path. To grow members to disciple-making maturity and become disciple-making churches, we need to create environments where we can speak the truth in love. We can only grow to maturity as a church if members can confess their sin and expose their brokenness and still be loved and accepted, for hiddenness is the great enemy of spiritual maturity.

The Great Enemy

From 1935–1940, Dietrich Bonhoeffer led a seminary community of young preachers in Nazi Germany. The seminary did not have government support, and it was closed by the Gestapo in 1937. Yet it continued as an underground seminary for the next three years. During this time, Bonhoeffer penned a short jewel of spiritual insight explaining the lessons he and his students had learned living in this community together. The book is called *Life Together*, and in it, Bonhoeffer shares several key ideas that should form the foundation of any Christian community. One of the most important is the idea that we must never be alone in our sin: "Those who remain alone with their evil are left utterly alone. It is possible that Christians may remain lonely in spite of daily worship together, prayer together, and all their community through service . . . for the pious community permits not one to be a sinner. . . . We are not allowed to be sinners. Many Christians would be unimaginably horrified if a real sinner were suddenly to turn up among the pious. So we remain alone with our sin, trapped in lies and hypocrisy, for we are in fact sinners."[44]

Bonhoeffer expresses the sad truth that in many of our churches, we are not *allowed* to be sinners. Even though church is the one place on earth where sin should be confessed and grace extended, it often isn't. In many churches, people cover over and hide their sins. Or they confess "acceptable" sins while hiding worse sins for years. The goal of our enemy is simple and clear. If believers keep their mouth shut and hide their sin, they will continue to suffer guilt and live in defeat and shame.

Our churches need to recover the practice of speaking the truth in love. This means being honest about sin yet creating a culture of grace and love. The moment we come out of hiding, we begin to live in the light of forgiveness and fellowship (1 John 1:7–9). Speaking the truth in love means that we grow through conversations, specifically talking about sin and struggles and asking for help. But we must use the proper words to do this. Paul instructs, "Don't use foul or abusive language. Let everything you say be good and helpful, so that your words will be an encouragement to those who hear them" (Eph. 4:29 NLT).

The Bible speaks of the church as a community with trusting relationships and a gracious environment. Grace requires us to treat one another as God has treated us, which means better than we deserve. We grow to maturity as we learn and practice mature communication skills, for example talking about who God says we are instead of using the world's labels and identities or the lies we believe about ourselves.[45] God says that every believer is gifted, every one has an important contribution to make, and every one is a saint and minister. One believer cannot say to another, "I don't need you" (1 Cor. 12:21). Everyone must be treated as someone God values.

But this does not just mean being nice to one another. It means listening to others when they confront us and getting rid of the bad habits that harm others. Paul lists several bad habits of the heart that need to be exposed and confronted, "Get rid of all bitterness, rage, anger, harsh words, and slander, as well as all types of evil behavior" (Eph. 4:31 NLT). Getting rid of these things is not something we do in a vacuum. The process begins with God's word entering our minds, then requires speaking his words to one another and putting them into practice in our community of believers. Putting off harsh words and putting on kind words is a habit that we must acquire and develop with the help of the Holy Spirit.

Bonhoeffer goes on to say, "Just as our love for God begins with listening to God's word, the beginning of love for other Christians is learning to listen to them."[46] Listening to others might be the greatest gift of love we can give them. And listening is always necessary because we cannot really help someone until we understand his or her need. Bonhoeffer further points out, "Christians who can no longer listen to one another will soon no longer be listening to God either; they will always be talking even in the presence of God."[47] If we cannot learn to listen in silence, then we cannot properly learn to speak. In fact, our speech will be distorted and driven by our own unmet needs. Our communication will be about us and getting our needs met, not helping others.

Again, let me stress that what is required here is not just being a *nice* person. We get angry when our sin is confronted. We grow defensive. We do not like it when people speak about our business. But this confronting is a necessary part of our discipleship, how we learn how to live our life as though Jesus was living it. Speaking the truth in love also requires being willing to receive the truth in love. Bonhoeffer reminds us, "Nothing can be more cruel than the leniency which abandons others to their sin. Nothing can be more compassionate than the severe reprimand which calls another Christian in one's community back from the path of sin."[48]

Some religious communities are like a group of drowning people who won't do what is necessary to save themselves because no one wants to go first. But speaking the truth in love is love at work, and it is necessary work.

Growing into maturity as a community is not possible unless the parts of the body are working properly. Only then can our churches grow into wholeness and health. The big lie will continue to survive as long as pastors and church leaders avoid the discipleship process. Preaching alone will not change our churches. Good leadership methods won't do it, either. Change requires disciple-making pastors making disciples who make disciples and form authentic communities that can model this process to others. This is a communal project.

What Is Spiritual Maturity?

We can define the goal in several ways. I've hinted at a few already. Here, I simply offer three characteristics of personal spiritual maturity. Dallas Willard describes a spiritually mature person this way: "the apprentice is able to do, and routinely does, what he or she knows to be right before God because all aspects of his or her person have been substantially transformed."[49] Here are practical and observable benchmarks that indicate a person is growing into Christlikeness.[50]

1. Mature Christians don't defend themselves when found to be wrong. In fact, they are thankful to be found out and will fulfill the Proverb, "Correct the wise, and they will love you" (Prov. 9:8 NLT). This response stands out in our world because we all want to defend ourselves, explain our motives, and rationalize our behavior. In addition, Christlike people do not defend themselves against false accusations. They say what is needed to establish the facts so that justice can be done, but they are not obsessed with defending their reputation. If wronged, they accept it and entrust final justice to God. In this they follow the model of Jesus who made himself of no reputation.[51] Our reputation is something we give up when we decide to follow Jesus.

2. *Mature Christians don't feel they are missing something by not sinning.* "It is better to be godly and have little than to be evil and rich" (Ps. 37:16). Mature people do not love sin. This does not mean they are no longer subject to temptation or that they are perfect. It means they aren't attracted to the temporary and soul-destroying pleasures of sin. They do not feel deprived, as if God is withholding something good from them. It does not pain them that evildoers—or even the distracted semi-Christian population—live in riches and enjoy much recreation. The mature man does not think he is missing out by not lusting or engaging in pornography. The affections of the mature have changed, and their heart is attuned to a better sort of joy. They have developed a taste for other pleasures and find happiness in holiness. This shift is key to leaving behind sinful behaviors.

3. *Mature Christians find it easier and more natural to do God's will than to not do it.* They take seriously what Jesus said, "Take my yoke upon you. Let me teach you, because I am humble and gentle of heart, and you will find rest for your souls. For my yoke is easy to bear, and the burden I give you is light" (Matt. 11:29–30 NLT). Being formed to the full measure of the stature of Christ means that we *want* to do his will because our will is being shaped into his will. Increasingly, we do not find it as difficult to obey. In some areas, obeying is easier and more joyous than doing anything else.

I realize that some do not believe this attitude is possible, and I admit that I was once among them. I am not denying the ongoing struggle of the Christian life. We are still engaged in war and must fight intense spiritual battles. But ultimately, obedience is *what we want* in our hearts. We must do a lot of dying on the journey. Jesus tells us to lay down the burden of religious performance, take up his yoke, and walk with him. He also promises us that his yoke will be light weight and easy to bear. Living in the grace of God and doing his will is not onerous.

Release the Saints

Have you ever heard of Nupedia? In 2000, Jimmy Wales and Larry Sanger believed they could revolutionize the way people access knowledge. Their idea was to develop a new online encyclopedia. Years ago, door-to-door salespersons tried to sell the Encyclopaedia Britannica, a set of nicely printed volumes of the most up-to-date information on a wide variety of subjects. This series became one of the bestselling (but perhaps least read) of all time. Wales and Sanger's idea was to gather knowledge by having the best and the brightest professors, historians, and researchers write articles and after careful editing, uploading the material to a website.

But after three years, they pulled the plug on the project. The work was incredibly tedious. And they constantly got stuck in the editing phase, locked in ideological conflicts. After three years of work, they had only been able to post twenty-four articles. In desperation, Wales and Sanger wondered if they could fix their problems by developing a feeder system for Nupedia. Instead of generating the articles themselves, they would enlist ordinary men and women who were passionate about a subject to voluntarily submit articles. This way, they didn't have to pay or prod people because they would want to write the articles. By the end of the first year, Wales and Sanger had posted twenty thousand articles. That project has become known as Wikipedia. It now has over twenty million articles and is the most accessible encyclopedia on earth.

Sadly, many churches around the world operate like Nupedia. A few hired experts produce some results. But the work is tedious, slow, and will never achieve the intended goal. And the problem is obvious. Churches are not intended to work like a Nupedia. They are designed to work like Wikipedia. We must remove the bottleneck by restoring the priority of discipleship.

Paul's plan presented in Ephesians 4 depends on two things. First, leaders must commit to equip ordinary saints to do ministry. Second, each saint must participate. But leaders must give up their fear of losing control, and saints must face their fear of embarrassment or failure.

The primary function of spiritual /educational leadership is to equip others to lead and minister, not to perform the ministry personally. What if spiritual leaders in churches and other ministries became experts in equipping others and considered the rewards of doing so enough to satisfy their longing for significance? This is a long-term project. It won't happen overnight. And it will require many brave souls. But it needs to happen if we want to see our churches restored to their true purpose as disciple-making communities.

I often say to people, "Think saints, not steeples." What do I mean by this? We can no longer think of the church building as the primary locus of ministry. We must find ways to activate the already present but not active saints in every domain of society. Don't think I'm minimizing the ministries in the gathered church. What I'm really saying is, "Think saints, not *only* steeples."

This isn't a silver bullet or a new idea. It's the vision Jesus gave his first disciples to be fishers of men, out in the world preaching and discipling new converts. It's his vision of the harvest, people in the world waiting to be discipled. "You know the saying, 'Four months between planting and harvest.' *But I say, wake up and look around. The fields are already ripe for harvest*" (John 4:35 NLT, emphasis added). In other words Jesus is saying, "Look at what you already have in front of you. If you simply take a look at what you already have, the strategy is simple. Take the people who are already living with the others they are to reach and equip them there." This is what our churches exist to do, and the work our leaders have been called to do. Jesus called us to make disciples who will reproduce. This is the plan, and our churches are the centerpiece, the places where disciples are made. *Churches exist for discipleship, and disciples are churches' gift to the world.* The question isn't *if* this will work; the question is, Will we do it?

8

THE PASTOR

Immanuel Kant remains a towering force in Western intellectual history because he addressed important questions and gave answers that pleased many. But his answers were not very good in his day and still aren't. This tiny man (with a very dull life) convinced the world that we can't really know anything with any degree of certainty. Kant also taught that religion is just a product of our mind, something we developed to cope with life and give it meaning. Religious belief is subjective, not able to be evaluated empirically, unlike scientific truth which can be tested and verified.

Given Kant's standard for proof, there is actually little anyone can really know, and certainly not much that is actually necessary for real life. But Kant indirectly played an important role in developing what some have called the devil's gospel. Jesus taught that the devil is a thief who comes to steal, kill, and destroy (John 10:10). Through Kant's teachings, the devil has attempted to steal from us that we can know, truly know, things that are not empirically provable like knowledge of God or the truth of the gospel.

As you might guess, doubt has led to a crisis of confidence. People wonder: *Can we really know anything at all?* Isn't religious knowledge a *lesser* form of knowledge? Doesn't it rely on faith, which is really just personal preference and wishful thinking? Sadly, many in our world believe all this, and this phenomenon largely explains why pastors are no longer considered custodians of knowledge, nor are they looked to as authorities. At one time religious knowledge was valued, and theology was considered the "queen of the sciences." But no longer.

Yet God has not changed his calling of pastors. As Paul so profoundly states when speaking of himself and another pastor, "This is how one should regard us, as servants of Christ and stewards of the mysteries of God" (1 Cor. 4:1 RSV). Pastors and teachers are uniquely called to steward the truth about God, a body of knowledge that is as serious and relevant as any other knowledge. While in the past, other institutions (schools, governments, communities) joined churches in retaining and passing along this knowledge, most of them have abandoned their post and have left the task to churches alone. Sadly, even families abdicate this role. Parents largely neglect their spiritual responsibility to teach their children and delegate it to church volunteers.

All of this means that pastors face two choices. Will they teach what has been passed down to them the past two thousand years? Or will they seek to change this repository of truth so it appears more relevant, often meaning what people want to hear? Most pastors don't choose one of the extremes I've presented here. They are the muddle in the middle, largely holding to basic doctrines but relying upon nice devotional tales, storytelling techniques, and interesting illustrations to reach people emotionally and motivate them. People love to be so moved, and speakers love to move them, so everyone walks away feeling good. Until the feelings pass and something new comes along.

Precious few are willing to attempt what many say is impossible—teach people to do everything that Jesus commanded.[1] The devil certainly doesn't want pastors to do this, because people who are taught to do what Jesus commanded gain knowledge that will destroy his plans. And he does not want to see his captives set free. So the most effective strategy he has is to convince the "stewards of the mysteries of God"—those called to be pastors and leaders—that the Great Commission cannot be done. Can every pastor become a disciple-making pastor? I believe every one can, in fact, must.

Distractions

Pastors are always struggling to decide how to best use their time. I am convinced that their most persistent daily obstacle is distraction. Pastoring is a type of work that is continually filled with choices. To use our time effectively, we must have a philosophy that guides our ministry and helps us set priorities. We need a picture of what we want to accomplish, something clear enough to us that we can remember it and explain it to others. Recently a pastor shared with me a daily mantra he has made as an antidote for distraction,

"I am a pastor who is making disciples who make other disciples." He recites this sentence to himself several times daily; his staff does as well.

Our vision should certainly include preaching, which is a key component of pastoral ministry, but we should broaden it to developing people in the way commanded by Jesus. Pastors have been entrusted with this responsibility, and as Paul points out, "Moreover it is required of stewards that they be found trustworthy" (1 Cor. 4:2 RSV). But there is a problem. To make trustworthy and faithful disciples, the teacher must first be trustworthy and faithful.[2]

Having served as a pastor and worked with pastors for many years, I know that many struggle with distractions and a boatload of expectations. In response, some prioritize preaching; others try to be good at helping people with their needs; and others run programs or focus on leading staff. The tendency is to become either a narrow specialist or a generalist who does just a little bit of everything.

On top of this, pastoral ministry is often specific and detailed because it focuses on individual people, and every person is unique. Pastors don't "generally" love people—they minister to specific individuals who have different needs, which requires a demanding level of attention and detail.

Finally, many pastors agree that making disciples is a good idea, but they have never committed to it in any *specific* way with *specific* people. They delegate the real work of discipling people to others who are often paid less, effectively deciding that this work is just not an essential task of their pastoral ministry.

But all of this reveals a deeper problem. As we have seen, a church's primary work is to make disciples. So if the pastor is leading the church to accomplish its mission, everything the pastor does must necessarily fall under this primary calling. Let me be up front: I am convinced that *not* making disciples is sin. And until pastors and leaders come to the point where they see anything other than total devotion to this task as a denial of their God-given calling and a gross sin, real change is unlikely to happen in their life and in their church.

So where does church change begin? In the soul of pastors. The word soul encompasses the mind, the spirit, and the will. Change for a church should begin in the pastors' soul because more than anything else, pastors need soul restoration that strengthens and satisfies. Why? To enable them to combat the allure of distraction and develop a single-minded focus. A satisfied soul is not easily discouraged or distracted. It is undeterred in pursuit of the goal. Have you ever been so thirsty or hungry that you could not concentrate on a conversation or task? A similar thing happens when our soul is dissatisfied. We look for other things to fill us, and these distractions end up dominating our ministry.

Pastors are just like everyone else, of course. But their soul matters because they directly affect the rest of the congregation. An unsatisfied pastor's soul makes for an unsatisfied congregational soul. If pastors are satisfied and clear about their calling and purpose, they can resist the spiritual fast food that the culture offers. They will have the patience and perseverance needed to make disciples. They can resist the temptation to adopt supposedly fast-track spiritual growth methods to make the church grow. They aren't looking to make a name for themselves. They aren't hungry for the applause of others.

On the other hand, a gnawing emptiness in many a pastor's soul causes real problems. Some pastors know they need to be discipling others, so they launch program after program to grow their church. They operate in a continual crisis, and the only spiritual rest they have is in starting a fresh program or seeing a well-attended service on Christmas or Easter. The remainder of the time they are struggling, frustrated, and stressed. Every week seems really busy and really tough. They talk a great deal about how much they needed a retreat or some special, emotionally charged seminar or experience because they think these things fill them with new energy.

So how do we fight against this hunger for more? *The first thing I tell pastors is don't trust crowds. They are dangerous and fickle, and they lie to you.* I've found Eugene Peterson to be helpful on this subject. In a letter to a fellow pastor who had left a church to go to a bigger one, Peterson asked if this was really a good decision. "Classically, there are three ways in which humans try to find transcendence: through the ecstasy of alcohol and drugs, through the ecstasy of recreational sex, through the ecstasy of crowds. Church leaders frequently warn against the drugs and the sex, but, at least in America, almost never against the crowds. Probably because they get so much ego benefit from the crowds."[3]

Peterson goes on to describe the evils of living for the crowds. Just like excessive drink and depersonalized sex, living for the crowds takes us out of ourselves, and it feels transcendent—but does not bring us to God. In fact, it does the opposite. What is more, we never come face-to-face with the real person we are. We keep busy so we don't see ourselves in moments of dullness and boredom. But living for the crowd is an exercise in false transcendence.

Pastors cannot run from the crowds, of course. We are called to love and serve people, especially when they are like sheep without a shepherd. Instead, pastors must learn to cultivate a satisfied soul that rests in the love of Christ. Pastors who do are free to live like Christ, to serve others. A satisfied soul can take or leave the crowd and is devoted to making and developing disciples. The crowd becomes a congregation, and pastors truly become shepherd to their people, not just speakers or charismatic leaders.

But how do we as pastors make disciples? By starting small, with just a few people. Discipleship is not a program we launch. It is a lifestyle we embrace.

Ready for Discipleship Journey?

I once spoke with a pastor who had just attended a conference with his staff on discipleship. He was highly motivated, so he approached me for advice. "After this week, I need to do something," he said. "I have eight of my pastors with me, and we need to go home and come up with something to impact our congregation. What do you suggest?"

I waited for about thirty seconds before answering. Then I told him to wait a bit more while I thought and prayed about his situation. After several minutes, I answered him. "Nothing," I said. "Don't start any programs, don't make announcements, and don't do anything public."

He seemed puzzled and confused. "What do you mean, Bill? Do nothing at all?"

I explained, "You should go home, get around a table with your eight pastors, and ask them to go with you on a personal journey of discipleship for one full year. Then if you think your desire is real and that you truly have something to offer the church, invite others to join you on the journey."

I said this because I knew that journeying with his eight pastors would require patience, self-discipline, restraint, vulnerability, submission, grace, trust, confession, and a great deal of bonding. This year-long activity would be an act of courage as well, because in the eyes of most people, it would not look like they were doing much. It would just be eight people, not some flashy new program or event to sign up hundreds.

But this is where we start and "make our bones" as a disciple-making pastor. It's the hard thing we *must* do to find out if we are really into disciple-making for the long haul. Start small. Disciple a few. And you will reveal the state of your soul as you open your life up to others. You will be exposed in ways you otherwise would have never been on display. In my experience, most pastors just aren't ready for this.

More Than Good Intentions

By now you should realize I believe that all pastors are called to make disciples. I also believe that virtually all *desire* to make disciples. In some way, most believe they are already doing so. But like other work in life, you know if the work of discipleship is being done by the fruit it produces. Our desire to make disciples is much like our desire to be fit, eat right, get plenty of sleep, and develop a less stressful schedule. The desire is there, but if we lack an intentional plan, we end up out of shape, overweight, cranky, and stressed. And we make excuses to avoid living with the constant guilt. We need an intentional plan for disciple-making. If we have no plan, there is no chance of discipleship happening. There will be no fruit.

Some will offer excuses at this point, and many of these are true. They will say they never get around to disciple-making because of other pressing issues. Most pastors find the daily realities of overseeing a congregation prove to be the greatest obstacle. But having a reason doesn't mean you have a valid excuse.

When it comes to disciple-making, pastors are like the soil in the parable of the sower.[4] Many hear the message and just don't understand it. For years, pastors have taught that making disciples means evangelizing the world. They skip over Jesus' imperative in the Great Commission to "make disciples" and pay little attention to the sentence, "Teach these new disciples to obey all the commands I have given you" (Matt. 28:20 NLT). That was something for Christian educators to figure out.

Other pastors get excited about making disciples and enthusiastically try, but they run into problems. As soon as it gets difficult and the price becomes too high, they drop the idea. Sure they may dabble in it a bit from time to time, but it is not the focus of their ministry.

A third category of pastors are those who hear the call to make disciples and give it a go, but the mundane and the ordinary nature of the work causes it to lose its appeal. These pastors get sucked into quicker, easier, programmatic approaches. They hear something is working in another church, and they switch plans, abandoning the daily, ongoing work of personally forming disciples. It's not that these pastors are distracted. They just grow bored.

The fourth category of pastors are those who hear and understand. The seeds of disciple-making take root, and they produce a harvest of thirty, sixty, or even a hundred times as much through a commitment to make disciples who make more disciples who make still more disciples.[5]

THE DNA OF A DISCIPLE-MAKING PASTOR

The DNA of discipleship is implanted by the Holy Spirit and developed by reading Scripture. It is further nurtured by the influence of those who teach us. Jesus said it well, "The student is not above the teacher, but everyone who is fully trained will be like their teacher" (Luke 6:40). Sometimes it is nurtured through the enthusiasm of another who advocates disciple-making as a way of life and work.

I was blessed to have been taught from the start that the Great Commission should be the centerpiece of my pastoral ministry. I was also inspired by the example of John Wesley. His philosophy was to begin by getting people to behave in a certain way and let belief and reason follow. Working this out in my own ministry only deepened my conviction to prioritize disciple-making. I also read widely and was influenced by many books. Seminary was an important piece in the equation, not so much for teaching me the philosophy of discipleship, but for teaching me how to study and research, which I have used for the rest of my life. But my most important learning was in churches, working with people, seeing what they needed, and adapting to circumstances.

Over time, the DNA for multiplying disciples developed within me. What is this DNA? It has eight key components, listed below. Most of these are covered at some point in this book.

1. A pastor's first priority is growing every member of the church to be a mature, reproducing disciple.
2. Every person called to salvation is called to discipleship.
3. The gospel expects all disciples to make other disciples.
4. All ministry activities should be evaluated by their contribution to growing mature, reproducing disciples.
5. The method should be Jesus' way of personally making disciples who make other disciples.
6. Success should be measured not by how many disciples are made, but by how many disciples are making other disciples.
7. Our churches exist for making disciples, and disciples are God's gift to the world.
8. The ultimate goal of making disciples is world revolution. When the gospel is preached to all peoples, the end will come.[6]

To summarize all of this, I borrow the wise words of Pat Morley. "A disciple-making pastor has a *vision* to disciple every person in his church, a *determination* to make it happen, and a *system* for sustaining it."[7]

SO WHERE DO YOU BEGIN?

Let's say you are on board. You want to be a disciple-making pastor, that fourth type who catches the vision and wants to commit to the journey. Where do you begin? How do you rewrite the contract you currently have with your congregation, shifting your focus and reforming your calling?

How do you begin communicating what it means to be a Christian who is a disciple of Christ?

Well, since the most visible point of contact you have with your congregation is preaching, you must begin in the pulpit by preaching the biblical gospel. As I laid out in earlier chapters, the gospel you preach must make it clear that *everyone called to salvation is also called to discipleship; there are no exceptions, no excuses.* Because this gospel is not commonly presented, doing so may be a new starting point that will require you to rebuild the gospel, word by word, from the ground up. This must be done slowly and carefully.

In 2007, Willow Creek Community Church published its REVEAL report.[8] Willow Creek commissioned a study of their people as well as several other churches in the Willow Creek Association. The study showed they had not been very effective at developing mature, reproducing followers of Jesus. When I first heard of the report, I had a luncheon with Dallas Willard. We discussed a wide range of issues that day, but just before I left, Dallas asked me if I had read the REVEAL study. I told him I had not read it yet. Dallas shared that he had read it and had an opinion about it, but he first wanted me to read it and tell him what I thought. Then he would tell me his opinion.

Digging Deeper

A LETTER FROM DALLAS WILLARD

December 27, 2007

Dear Bill:

I regret being so slow to respond, and I hope you will forgive me. In fact I had to get through a heavy patch of paper grading, and then got obsessed with a couple of difficult chapters in what I hope will be another book. I think your observations on REVEAL are right on. You were very gentle, as we should be, and I think I will be, too. In fact, I would like to be rather indirect. I love and admire the folks at Willow Creek, as I imagine you do, and would like not to offend them in any way. If they were to ask me for my opinion, I would be more direct and thorough. But they haven't, and so I shall simply say a few things from which implications about the report can be drawn.

The main difficulty for "church life" as we know it, and one which proves to be practically insurmountable for most churches, is posed by *the way people are brought into the church. Or, I should say "ways,"* *for in fact they come in a number of different ways or with diverse under-* *standings of what it means.* (Usually no one carefully works through their understanding with them.) *What really matters here is how they* *understand what they are committed to by being there.* That means, among other things, what they have agreed to let the staff do with them. As a result they standardly suppose that if they attend the main services with some regularity and contribute some amount of money, they are doing their part, and the pastor has no further real claim upon them. A small percentage of church members might think they should take some extra courses or seminars if they are in line with their interests, and a smaller percentage still might do some teaching or some custodial or committee work. *But these activities almost never* *have any effect upon their growth in what a candid reading of the New* *Testament would suggest it is all about:* for example, actually taking on the character of love as seen in 1 Cor. 13 or 1 John 4. Or putting off the old person and putting on the new, as Paul puts it in Col. 3, or "putting on the Lord Jesus Christ," as in Romans 13:14 (really, 8–14).

And then the church, quite naturally, can do very little with people who are there with such shallow understandings of what being a Christian is all about. They wind up thinking that involvement with the church's activities will lead to spiritual transformation. But they do not really expect it to happen, and they do nothing that would be likely to foster it. Really, they cannot. Their hands are tied by the background assumption of what it is to be a Christian. And if they challenge that assumption, they are apt to be accused of switching the goods advertised, adding to grace, and of outright heresy. This is because of what they heard as the gospel when they came in the door.

The teaching about salvation that is now an American cultural artifact is that you confess faith in the death of Jesus on your behalf, and then you join up with a group that is trying to get others to do the same. That is all that is essential. So it is thought and taught. "Spiritual growth" is not required on this scheme, and there is no real provision for it. Salvation is free, which means you need do nothing else but "accept." Then you too can sing Amazing Grace. Just observe who sings "Amazing Grace" now, and in what circumstances. You don't really even have to accept it, just sing about it. Not even that. It is wholly passive.

To deal with this situation, one has to start with what you preach as the message of salvation and what you take salvation to be. Salvation is spiritual transformation, which is not an option for those with special interests. Grace is situated in that "salvation." If you had a group, and you wanted to see such salvation in them, you would have to start from the beginning and teach closely. Do inductive Bible study on "grace" and all of the other central terms of our church discourse, and build your preaching and teaching around what you discover. Remember to include "repentance" and "faith." You would probably lose a lot of people, and have to rebuild your work. This has been done with great success in past times. The earliest church is the best illustration of the painful process and of the success that can accompany it. Genuine discipleship in the church context of today is very much like discipleship to Jesus in the Jewish religion of his day.

Grace, faith, repentance, and salvation are not church things. They are life things, and spiritual transformation is something that happens only when people intelligently and resolutely take their whole life into the kingdom of God. *I believe that the REVEAL study does not proceed along these lines, but hopes to make "church" work for honest transformation into Christlikeness without changing the fundamental assumptions.* Undoubtedly I am wrong about many things. I pray for God to teach and empower us all to do his will his way.

Best blessings in Christ,

Dallas

A couple of weeks later, I finished reading the report and sent Dallas an eight-point email covering my thoughts and opinions on the study. I will never forget what he told me in his emailed response (for more, see the letter in the Digging Deeper section). He shared that he was not very optimistic about Willow Creek solving their self-identified problems and becoming a disciple-making church. His reason? "For every person seated in a pew, there is a gospel represented. Some people hold different gospels at different times for different reasons. Unless they [Willow Creek's leaders] are prepared to rebuild their gospel and retrain their people in a gospel that embraces discipleship, I am not optimistic that they can turn the ship around."[9]

What Dallas was suggesting, as I have been, is a necessary recovery of the gospel. As I shared in chapter 1, this requires restoring the understanding of salvation that characterized evangelicalism from its beginnings to Luther. How will this be done? As Dallas said (quoted earlier), "It would primarily be a work of *scriptural interpretation and theological reformulation*, but modification of time-hardened practices will also be required. *Radical changes* in what we do in the way of 'church' will have to be made."[10]

Considerations from Willard's Letter

- A major problem is the various ways people are brought into churches.

- We must again ask, "What does it mean to be a Christian?"

- What claim and authority does the pastor and church have on a member's life?

- What can be done in teaching, training, and transforming if it is limited by a shallow understanding of the gospel and discipleship?

- The contemporary gospel is an American cultural artifact, namely, you can become a Christian and not follow Jesus. Discipleship is optional.

- The gospel will need to be carefully rebuilt from the ground up, and it must change some of our fundamental assumptions.

Recovering the gospel from the ground up is the "scriptural interpretation and theological reformulation" that Dallas refers to. Preaching gospel to the congregation and teaching them new ways of thinking and following Jesus is the "modification of time-hardened practices." Inevitably, we will receive pushback when we get to the "radical changes in what we do in the way of 'church.'" In other words, this will not be easy!

What makes this recovery especially difficult is that for so long, pastors and preachers have depended on packaged explanations of the good news. If you are starting from scratch and building your understanding from the Scriptures, you may find yourself challenged and experiencing some discomfort. To help you, let me suggest that you begin with five steps.

1. Study 1 Corinthians 15:1–28. This is the best "skeleton" for understanding the gospel. It covers the story at the heart of the message: Jesus was born; he lived; he preached; he was crucified, died, buried, and raised; and he will come again to establish his kingdom, bring an end to sin, and judge the world. This is the basic story. Remember that it is a story that takes time to tell in context. I've added a few extra things into the story above, but more is usually needed for people to fully appreciate the significance of the teachings, life, death, and resurrection of Christ in context.

2. Refine the words in your salvation vocabulary. Be sure that you understand what you mean when you use words like faith, believe, trust, sin, grace, works, repentance, confess, obedience, and conversion. Study how the words are used in the Scriptures and how they are connected to the context.

3. Preach on the apostolic sermons in the Book of Acts. These sermons are the closest you will get to what the apostles thought the gospel was. Considering they had just spent forty days with the resurrected Christ after three years of observation and instruction, these sermons of the apostles are your most reliable source. The sermons are presented primarily in a Jewish context, so connecting the story of Jesus to the story of Israel is crucial to putting the gospel in the full context of redemptive history.

One sermon in Acts is helpful for understanding how to present the gospel in a non-Jewish context. It is Paul's sermon on Mars Hill, given to the Athenians recorded in Acts 17:16–34.

4. Preach from the four Gospels. Consider Scot McKnight's words, "I believe the word gospel has been hijacked by what we believe about personal salvation, and the gospel itself has been reshaped to facilitate making decisions. The result of this hijacking is that the word gospel no longer means in our world what it originally meant to either Jesus or the Gospels."[11] When you understand the gospel, you know the whole story of humankind, from creation to consummation. The Gospels tell story after story of Jesus, his power, glory, life, and teaching. They help us put together how and why Jesus came and what he did, and they contain his directions on what his disciples were to do after he was gone.

Augustine explained the Gospels this way: "In the four Gospels, or better in the four books of the one Gospel."[12] The authors of the Gospels saw themselves not as historians but as witnesses. So read them as witnesses, saturate your mind with the stories, tell them again and again, and then announce to the congregation, "This is the gospel!" The Gospels tell us that Jesus is the promised deliverer of Israel and of his coming, life, death, resurrection, commissioning his followers, promised return, and wisdom about life. It's all there.

5. Teach your people to recognize the popular "gospels" that are commonly taught. As I presented in chapter 1, at least six common gospels are preached today. It is important that your people learn to see and understand the biblical gospel, not just for what it is, but also for what it is not. So point out to them what each of the other gospels is saying naturally and where each naturally leads. For example if a congregation can see how the consumer gospel will never lead to Christlike disciples, they will better understand how the biblical gospel does.

The process of learning the new, recovered gospel will inevitably create confusion and disorientation, so teaching must be done carefully. There is an old saying, "A mist in the pulpit is a fog in the pew." Back in the days before microphones, pulpits were set high above the pews to help project the preacher's voice. If you know anything about fog, you know that it tends to condense in lower regions. So the meaning of the saying is simple: if a preacher is confused, there is no hope for the congregation.

Keep this in mind as you trade out old illustrations and phrases that you've used for years and replace them with new ways of communicating that organically connect conversion with discipleship. What you do not want is a rebellion based out of accusations and misunderstandings. Remember what Paul said to Timothy, "A servant of the Lord must not quarrel but be kind to everyone, be able to teach, and be patient with difficult people. Gently instruct those who oppose the truth. Perhaps God will change those people's hearts, and they will learn the truth" (2 Tim. 2:24–25 NLT).

Also remember that we are not necessarily correcting heresies that lie outside the pale of orthodoxy. Much of the time, we are simply adding nuance, pointing out wrong directions in the way people are thinking, and clarifying confusing or misleading assumptions. What we have today is a *corruption* of the gospel that has greatly hindered our churches, but the gospel has not been lost completely. Correcting these misunderstandings will take kindness, gentleness, and patience—not accusations of heresy.

Implement Your Plan

After all of this comes creating and then implementing a plan. *Remember, if you don't have a plan, you don't really intend to do anything. And if your plan has no timeline, it falls short of actually being a plan.* In reading this book, you may be realizing that some things need to change in your life, your ministry, and your church. But just getting the concepts in your head and the verbiage right doesn't mean that you'll get the job done.

I know some pastors immediately try to make things happen. They push ahead, hoping that with hard work and enough energy, change will happen. Others are more cautious, relying on prayer but taking a passive approach. After all, if God wants change, he can bring change, right? As you think about your plan, think about your own attitude and which of these directions you tend to drift toward. To sharpen your thinking, it might be helpful to get a better grasp on the relationship between grace and discipline.

GRACE AND DISCIPLINE

"What God has put together, let no man rip asunder." These words were once the traditional conclusion to a Christian marriage ceremony. In marriage, man and woman become one, which is a great mystery. Marriage unites two different people—male and female—into one.

I think marriage is a fitting image for thinking about the relationship between grace and discipline. For some, grace seems to be naturally opposed to discipline, so the two opposites cannot be united together.

However, grace and discipline need each other and have a difficult time functioning apart. In fact, when either one of them functions apart from the other, the soul is damaged. We can draw this conclusion from the words of a man who was greatly disciplined yet also the great champion of grace.

In his second letter, the apostle Paul speaks to his young protégé, Timothy (who had the unenviable task of being his successor), of the pastoral duties and challenges that lay ahead. He gives his young disciple some sterling advice, "This is why I remind you to fan into flames the spiritual gift [of pastor or a related gift such as teaching or leadership] God gave you when I laid my hands on you. For God has not given us a spirit of fear and timidity, but of power, love, and self-discipline" (2 Tim. 1:6–7 NLT).

When Paul speaks of self-discipline, he has in mind the power to keep oneself in hand, what we call self-control. Some translations render this phrase "a sound mind," referring to the ability to think clearly under pressure. Timothy was under a great deal of pressure, so Paul mentions a discipline Timothy needed to stay focused and not get distracted. What Paul was asking of Timothy—to train reliable disciples who could teach others—requires a great deal of discipline.

At the same time, Paul knew that Timothy needed a lot of grace. Grace is God's favor and his doing for us what we cannot do for ourselves. So Paul begins the prescriptive part of this letter by saying, "Timothy, my dear son, be strong through the grace that God gives you *in Christ Jesus*" (2 Tim. 2:1 NLT, emphasis added). In Christ we find everything we need, including grace.

212

How do these two fit together? For Paul, being disciplined is not opposed to living in grace. We need both. As we live in the grace that God gives us, we will find the discipline we need to work hard. We will be motivated by God's vision, by his priorities, and our hearts will long to do his work.

THE NATURE OF THE TASK

Paul goes on to remind Timothy of what he has learned and seen Paul do in the various places they had traveled together. "You have heard me teach things that have been confirmed by many reliable witnesses" (2 Tim. 2:2a NLT). If you wonder what this teaching consisted of, remember what we read in Ephesians, Romans, and Galatians. These are the things Timothy heard Paul teach, for he tells us in his letter to the Corinthians that he taught the same things to everyone without much variation.[13] In fact, Timothy knew Paul's teaching so well that Paul sent him on special missions to teach exactly what Paul had taught him to say in his place. Timothy learned this teaching by watching and listening, and he set it deeper into his mind by teaching it to others.

Paul then instructs Timothy to "teach these truths to other trustworthy people who will be able to pass them on to others" (2 Tim. 2:2b NLT). Note that these new students must be willing and able to teach others and be trustworthy. Often we accept people into our churches on the basis of their willingness and look for volunteers who will help out when they can. But Paul is talking about something quite different here—that *only* people who have proven they are faithful should be taught and then be given the responsibility to teach others.

Some consider Paul's instructions to Timothy here as applying only to leaders, not to the average Christian. But I can find no restriction in the passage, and it fits what we know of discipleship in general, every disciple is expected to make other disciples. As we saw earlier, the entire saved population is under the command of our Lord's commission because all are to be disciples who follow him.[14]

So the instructions and method are clear. Simple mathematics shows that just as Paul taught Timothy to make disciples, Timothy can teach others to do the same, and Timothy's disciples can do the same *ad infinitum*. This, in a nutshell, is how disciple-making leads to world revolution and brings about the end of all things.[15]

We should acknowledge that teaching faithfulness and obedience to everything Christ commanded is frustrating work that requires more of what we don't have. This is where we need that unique mix of discipline and grace. We need lots of discipline, and the entire process must be bathed in God's grace. In other words, God will need to do a lot for us that we cannot do ourselves. But we need to do a great deal as well!

Some things God alone can do like put the interest and desire to follow Jesus in a person's heart. Or give people the willingness to be accountable and to submit their entire life to a Christian community. But some of God's grace requires the effort of individuals because it is manifested through loving others in a church community. These church members need to have the perseverance to stick with the process when people fail. And those who fail need encouragement from others to face their fears and doubts.

In a letter to the Corinthian church, Paul exhorts and speaks of his own experience using the analogy of running a race: "Don't you realize that in a race everyone runs, but only one person gets the prize? So run to win! All athletes *are disciplined in their training*. They do it to win a prize that will fade away, but we do it for an eternal prize. So I run with purpose in every step. I am not just shadowboxing. *I discipline my body like an athlete, training* it to do what it should. Otherwise, I fear that after preaching to others I myself might be *disqualified*" (1 Cor. 9:24–27 NLT, emphasis added).

I have highlighted some words to show that disciple-making is hard work: *discipline, training, athlete, disqualified*. But living productively for God also includes an element of mystery. We use all our human effort to the point of making our bodies into living sacrifices and our servants through discipline and hard training.[16] But God's grace comes into this discipline and effort through prayer, a willing heart, and obedience to what Christ has taught us.

One of my favorite sayings is, "Obedience is where the Holy Spirit meets us."[17] When we step out in faith, regardless of the degree of difficulty, God meets us with his resources. But if we are not willing to step out, we will never experience this meeting and won't even believe it is possible.

Athletes must follow the rules, otherwise they will win no prize. Often when our discipleship efforts don't produce fruit, the reason is that we broke the rules. For example, we allowed unfaithful people into the training environment. Or we didn't hold disciples accountable and watered down the expectation that they teach and affect others. Or we don't stick with them when they failed and wanted to quit. Or we were too easy on them under the guise of mercy. Or we ceased to love them by giving them relief from pressure when that was the last thing they needed.

Like farmers waiting for their crops to ripen, this work requires patience. When we work with people with dedication and discipline, we must also wait for God to work, and in time, he will produce a harvest.[18]

Implement Your Plan

This worksheet is an opportunity to get down on paper what you really believe about several of the key concepts we've covered in the book.

1.   What is a disciple?

The definition must be specific enough to enable you to answer the next question—"How do you make disciples?"—which is wholly dependent on your answer here. For example, let's say you define a disciple as someone who has five characteristics, something like:

    a.   A disciple is in conversation with God through the word and prayer.
    b.   A disciple reveals Christ daily by bearing fruit.
    c.   A disciple responds to God daily in obedience.
    d.   A disciple has joy and is contented in spirit.
    e.   A disciple loves others as Christ loved others.[a]

How to grow a person with these characteristics will likely require specific spiritual exercises and activities in a community of kindred spirits who all want the same qualities developed in them.

2.   How do we make disciples?

This answer requires you to think about how to provide environments, groups, and activities with trained leadership as well as schedules, goals, and other aspects of organization.

3.   What difference will these disciples make?

Describe how the world around you and at large will be impacted if your quest to make many more disciples succeeds. How will you know the plan worked?

[a] Taken from John 15:7–13.

Conclusion: Pastors Must Know God

At one time, John Wesley was a parish priest in the Anglican Church. He spent most of his life, however, as the pastor of a worldwide congregation. A statue of Wesley stands in the courtyard of his last parish on City Street in London. The inscription on the statue's base is, "The world is my parish." Wesley's impact was not only through his oral teaching but also his writing and organizing people into transformative groups and communities.

As we said at the beginning of this chapter, pastors are the custodians of the knowledge of God. They are the last group in our society who are free to teach this knowledge, and the responsibility to do it should weigh heavy upon them. Well-educated pastors are vital to the health and well-being of both churches and society. In his "Address to the Clergy," John Wesley said:

> Ought not a Minister to have, First, a good understanding, a clear apprehension, a sound judgment, and a capacity of reasoning with some closeness is not this necessary in an high degree for the work of ministry. Otherwise, how will he be able to understand the various states of those under his care; or to steer them through a thousand difficulties and dangers, to the haven where they would be is it not necessary, with respect to the numerous enemies whom he has to encounter. Can a fool cope with all the men that know not God, and with all the spirits of darkness? . . . Secondly, No less necessary is a knowledge of the Scriptures, which teach us how to teach others, yea, a knowledge of all the Scriptures; seeing Scripture interprets Scripture; one part fixing the sense of another. So that, whether it be true or not, that every good textuary is a good Divine.[19]

Knowledge of God is not just necessary for discipleship. It is essential for pastors and leaders because we are fighting a spiritual war against an enemy who opposes all that we do. As Paul teaches, "We are human, but we don't wage war as humans do. We use God's mighty weapons, not worldly weapons, to knock down the strongholds of human reasoning and to destroy false arguments. We destroy every proud obstacle that keeps people from knowing God. We capture their rebellious thoughts and teach them to obey Christ" (2 Cor. 10:3–5 NLT).

The war we fight is a knowledge war. Just like Elijah standing before the prophets of Baal, pastors stand with the Bible in their hand and speak truth to the reality of life. Though we no longer call down literal fire, our words spoken and taught should burn within people's heart. And as the winds of the Spirit blow upon the sparks of the Word of God, the flames of revival may yet again burn in our churches and in the world.

For many pastors in our post-Christian culture, speaking truth is becoming increasingly dangerous because popular cultural morality is considered superior to Christian morality, and the gospel of tolerance is celebrated.[20] Jesus Christ, the light of the world, has been replaced by human reason that rejects revelation. Pastors must battle against these ideas as they teach and disciple in their congregations.

Recently a pastoral friend of mine preached a sermon on human sexuality, presenting the straightforward teaching of the Bible, the same basic teaching that has been presented for two thousand years. His basic message was clear: if people are gay or straight, sexually active outside of marriage, and attend their church, they are welcome and loved by God and the congregation. But the pastor was also clear that God created sexuality as a gift for marriage between a man and a woman. He explained why pre-martial sex, adultery, divorce, and aberrant forms of sexuality are sin, which is rebellion against God.[21] His point was that we all are sinners, but he was clear that we cannot tolerate any sin or accept sin as the norm. His message was both honest and compassionate.

But soon after the message was posted, the pastor was excoriated on the internet and by the local press. Headlines on social media included, "Local pastor refuses to repent of homophobia" and "Extremist pastor says all gays should be killed." These dishonest headlines went viral, and the pastor and his family received death threats. According to cultural morality, disagreeing with someone's sexual behavior is considered judgmental, narrow minded, bigoted, and intolerant. Darkness indeed is being declared light and light is being consigned to darkness.

Disciple-making pastors must face challenges like this head-on. They must speak from God's Word when defining what is normal. In doing so they define the world and the church by explaining who we are and how we are to live to represent Christ. Pastors as teachers to the nations reveal knowledge that is a mystery to most and that cannot be understood from the outside—it is revealed, not figured out.

300,000 EVANGELICAL "POPES"

Pastors are one of the last groups of people in America who have authority and constitutional protection to speak the truth. This pastoral authority is much like that of the Roman Catholic pope. He has no standing army and possesses no power of state that anyone takes seriously. Yet when he speaks, his words are broadcast around the world and read in bold print on the front pages of newspapers. Pastors in America have access to around one-fourth of America's population on a weekly basis. People file into every kind of building, from cathedrals to store fronts with plastic chairs, just to hear their pastors speak. For the believing population, pastors still have power and authority.

But for the unbelieving populace, pastors are voices of opposition to contend with. They don't have political or governmental power, but they do have God's power. Pastors can explain to people why they are alive, what life is for, and how life should be lived.

Pastors need to hear afresh the words of the reformer Ulrich Zwingli as he appealed to pastors in the 1500s. In the midst of comfort and passivity, Zwingli cried out to them, "For God's sake do something brave!" The brave thing is to preach the gospel, and that gospel must include the expectation that *all* of God's people are disciples who are to make disciples. Yes, preach that we are charged using the words that bring spiritual life for eternity with God that begins now. But don't neglect to preach that Jesus calls people to be his disciples. And then do something beyond preaching. Lead your people on the journey of discipleship. Lead them out the door of your meeting place and show them how to live, to be witnesses, and to be relevant to the needs of those around them. Teach them to be the kind of people who light up the darkness, who live with moral clarity, who love others, and who live to serve others.

Doing all of this may require some changes in the way you live and lead. But don't you ask of your people every week to make similar changes? Don't set the bar low for yourself. Be a disciple who makes disciples. That is the calling of every pastor.

9

THE END

The thesis of this book is that all who are called to salvation are also called to discipleship. There are no exceptions, and we cannot offer excuses. I'm convinced that if churches believed this, pastors taught it, and people accepted it, the happy result would be a world flooded with Christlike disciples, which would transform the world.

Jesus tells us our efforts to share the gospel and make disciples will lead to "the end." When the world is reached with his good news, he will return.[1] The secular mind cannot understand this concept. Humans tend to think that the earth and the laws of nature are determinative, that we are temporary—here today and gone tomorrow. But the opposite is true. According to God's purposes and plans, human beings will last forever, while the world we see will not. The heavens and earth will be transformed, remade, and restored when the time is right. God in his foreknowledge knows when this time will come—when the full complement of souls are finally saved.[2] Paul says, "Some of the people of Israel have hard hearts" and reject the Messiah, "but this will only last until the full number of the Gentiles comes to Christ" (Rom. 11:25 NLT).[3] So while the Bible gives us some signs to guide us, God alone knows when his gospel project will be finished and the end will come.

That this world will end and a new one replace it is inevitable.[4] So we should ask ourselves, Will more people enter heaven and will the world to come be a better place because our churches accomplished their mission? If the answer to this question is not yes, then God has sent us on an illegitimate mission.

World Revolution

In his book *Renovation of the Heart*, Dallas Willard writes, "We must make no mistake about it. In sending out his [disciples], he set afoot a perpetual world revolution: one that is still in process and will continue until God's will is done on earth as it is in heaven."[5] As Christ's disciples, we are more than just residents in this world; we are revolutionaries. We have been sent, as Bonhoeffer says, into the "world come of age." We live in a world where science, philosophy, psychology, technology, and transportation have shrunk the world into a global village. This world is topsy-turvy, for light has been declared darkness and darkness declared light. In this environment, it is vital that we are not conflicted or confused about our mission, because we will receive a great deal of pushback.[6]

In reading this book, you may have picked up my affinity for Dietrich Bonhoeffer. Bonhoeffer was intellectual and aristocratic, and his understanding of revolution was elitist. He advocated for a completely free and trained pastoral nobility who could preach the Word of God and discern the spirits of the age. He wrote, "They would be a phalanx of the intellectual elite suitable to match wits with the 'spirit of the age.' They would form an aristocracy of responsibility—a nobility of righteous doers and prayerful pilgrims."[7]

While I love Bonhoeffer's idea and would have loved to have been included in his plans, I believe his ideas just did not go deep enough. These pastors would only have sparked a revolution among the intellectually gifted, and Bonhoeffer assumed that the masses would simply follow their intellectual leaders. The German masses had followed their Führer, Bonhoeffer reasoned, so why wouldn't they follow a righteous leader if Hitler was out of the way? We'll never know if Bonhoeffer's plans would have borne fruit, for his dream was cut short when the Gestapo closed his grand experiment, and most of his intellectual elite were drafted into the German army and sent to the Russian front to die.

Peter Drucker once quipped, "Culture will eat strategy's lunch every time." Bonhoeffer's plan was halted because the devilish Aryan heresy had a death grip on Germany. But Jesus' commission—his disciple-making plan to change the world—is far broader and more powerful. His vision is for a perpetual revolution that will continue, unabated, until God's "will be done, on earth as it is in heaven" (Matt. 6:10). Jesus' plan is flexible, able to adapt to different cultures and times and designed to grow, multiply, and spread across the earth. It is sustainable, able to last for centuries. Jesus' plan takes into consideration that to sustain a movement like this, the objective—the end goal—must be very clear.

Jesus warned his disciples to keep this clear goal in mind to guard against competing loyalties, "No one can serve two masters. For you will hate one and love the other; you will be devoted to one and despise the other. You cannot serve both God and money. . . . Seek the Kingdom of God above all else, and live righteously, and he will give you everything you need" (Matt. 6:24, 33 NLT).

With foresight into some of our current challenges, Bonhoeffer spoke approvingly of the development of what he called "religionless Christianity," meaning serious discipleship stripped of all the hypocritical and disabling baggage of institutional churches. The German Evangelical Church of the 1930s was a model of capitulation, compromise, and hypocrisy. By contrast, a flood of Christ's disciples sent into the morass that is society is a cure for its ills. But those disciples, above all else, must know God and be filled with the Holy Spirit. They must also know God's Word and have their minds and hearts stripped and freed from anything other than Christ himself.

Christ above All Others

Sociologist Peter Berger states "that the revelation of God in Jesus Christ (which is the object of Christian faith) is something very different from religion."[8] Jesus is bigger than any religion, even the Christian religion. C. S. Lewis wrote, "The church exists for nothing else but to draw men into Christ, to make them little Christs. If they are not doing that, all the cathedrals, clergy, missions, sermons, even the Bible itself, are simply a waste of time. God became man for no other purpose."[9] In the end, Jesus takes the preeminent position above all things. He stands apart and above all religions and philosophy because he is God, and no one else can compare to him.

This means that Jesus' disciples must follow him, not church institutions, theological systems, or their own cultural preferences. Some call Jesus the cosmic Christ because he can be seen and known despite all the impediments that religions have created in attempts to hide or change him. In this "world come of age," his disciples must show this Christ to the watching world. And the first place the world sees him is in the quality of life shared among his disciples.

The apostle Paul describes Christ in his cosmic position in a most glorious way.

> *Christ is the visible image of the invisible God.*
>> *He existed before anything was created and is supreme over all creation,*
> *for through him God created everything*
>> *in the heavenly realms and on earth.*
> *He made the things we can see*
>> *and the things we can't see—*
> *such as thrones, kingdoms, rulers, and authorities in the unseen world.*
>> *Everything was created through him and for him.*
> *He existed before anything else,*
>> *and he holds all creation together.*
>
> —COLOSSIANS 1:15–17 NLT

The wisdom of Jesus is unparalleled. His critical insight into society, the human heart, and this world's institutions shows the depth of his understanding. In a message that takes thirteen minutes to read, the Sermon on the Mount, he unmasked the world and took it apart. Jesus made it clear that human beings need a righteousness—a right way of living—that is better than that of the religious leaders of Israel (Matt. 5:20). As Dallas Willard comments, "His teachings, even mangled and broken, have an incredible power to disrupt human systems, including the ones that claim to own him. He is the misfit and this is available to all who would seek him."[10]

One of the strengths of the Christian movement is that Jesus is the strongest critic of our religious tendencies. Not only in the Sermon on the Mount but also in his words to the seven churches in Asia Minor, Jesus shows that he is prepared to discipline, rebuke, and correct his people.[11] After all, "Christ is also the head of the church, which is his body" (Col. 1:18 NLT). The church is not its own; it belongs to Christ. Willard states,

"Jesus is in his people, but he does not allow himself to be boxed in by them. He calls to us by just being here in our midst. There is nothing like him. The people in the churches also have the option of finding him and following him into his kingdom, though that may rarely be what they are doing."[12]

I marvel at what Jesus knows, which is far more than we know, even with our scientific knowledge and psychological study. Jesus created this world; he was here before there was any *there*. He made what we can see as well as what we can't, though the unseen portion of the world is just as real. It is where spiritual battles rage, and Paul describes it in several places.[13] When we consider Jesus' knowledge and understanding and the reach of his power and authority, we remember that he is not limited to working through his disciples. Jesus remains active both inside and outside our churches and has been at work all over the world for over 2,000 years.

Jesus' work extends into areas of life we, with our secular, Western worldview, don't typically think of as religious. He is Lord over medicine, philosophy, politics, and psychology. In a sense, we can say that all of life is inherently religious because all of life falls under the rule and reign of the risen Christ. Similarly Paul said to the Athenian council, "Men of Athens, I notice that you are very religious in every way, for as I was walking along I saw your many shrines. And one of your altars had this inscription on it: 'To an Unknown God.' *This God, whom you worship without knowing, is the one I'm telling you about. He is the God who made the world and everything in it.* Since he is Lord of heaven and earth, he doesn't live in man-made temples and human hands can't serve his needs—for he has no needs" (Acts 17:22–25 NLT, emphasis added).

Many people worship an unknown God. Reporter Sally Quinn recently wrote a religion column for the Washington Post online about the twenty-five million Americans who say they are spiritual but not religious. Quinn herself daily walks a spiritual labyrinth that is meaningful to her, but she does not focus on any specific god and does not think that goodness requires a god.

I believe that our discipleship needs to acknowledge that Jesus has been and continues to be at work around people like Sally, even though he is currently hidden from her. To fully extend our conversion to Christ into discipleship, we must integrate the rule of Jesus into all of life, which includes recognizing that he is so great and magnificent that we can't possibly fathom the comprehensive nature of his work. Like Paul in Athens, we must assess the situation, understand the culture, and then speak the truth of the gospel to it. The power of our message is not in a generic religion but in the gospel—Jesus and his story.

We Know God through Jesus

Paul's description of Jesus continues.

> For God in all his fullness
> was pleased to live in Christ,
> and through him God reconciled
> everything to himself.
> He made peace with everything in heaven and on earth
> by means of Christ's blood on the cross.
>
> —COLOSSIANS 1:19–20 NLT

There is no way to know God fully except through Jesus. And I have great confidence that Jesus will find every person who needs and wants him. Jesus is at work in public view and behind the scenes on broken and twisted systems, philosophies, and people. In the end, he will reconcile all things to himself. God will allow everyone into heaven who can stand it.

Now some people believe this means Jesus will bring everyone into heaven, but I disagree. While we cannot say that everyone will be saved, we *can* say that his sacrifice on the cross created the means for every person to be reconciled to God. We also know that, willingly or not, one day "at the name of Jesus every knee should bow, in heaven and on earth and under the earth, and every tongue acknowledge that Jesus Christ is Lord, to the glory of God the Father" (Phil. 2:10–11). We know that all judgment has been given to Jesus, and all of creation, the seen and the unseen, will eventually submit to him and come under his perfect scrutiny.[14]

The character of Jesus is the character of God.[15] There is more to the Triune God than Jesus, but our focus here is the fact that God as a whole has assigned Jesus to be our leader, guide, and example.[16] This means that if we wish to know God—who he is, his character and personality—we need go no further than a careful look at Jesus. To know God's will, we need consult no other source. Real discipleship is not to apostles or charismatic teachers, it is to Jesus alone. There is nothing he doesn't know, and he leaves nothing out of his instructions. He sends all of us to do his work that he has planned out using his perfect knowledge of all things, and he controls all things. When we want to see God, we look to Jesus and see God on the cross sacrificing himself for others. This is who we want to introduce to the world. Jesus is the good news.

What Makes a Revolution Successful?

In order for any revolution to succeed, it needs to be perpetually reproducing. It should penetrate all domains of society: entertainment, government, sports, the arts, media, education, the home, the church, and volunteer community groups, organizations. Some revolutionaries artificially attempt to do this, but successful revolutions occur naturally, penetrating all domains by the power of their message. This is why a revolution is more than just picketing outside a corporation or on the steps of Congress. You can make a statement this way, but it cannot be said that you have penetrated or transformed anything. Or consider doing street evangelism in front of a civic center during a convention. This activity is less effective than having advocates inside the organization actively promoting the cause.

Often our churches have attempted to bring change from the outside without penetrating the domains of society. We feel good about ourselves because we have done something, but what have we really accomplished? Most people ignore what we say. They only remember that we bothered them and may be thankful they are not like us.

Throughout church history, very capable Christians have made a variety of attempts to significantly impact the world. One such attempt was by the Roman Emperor Constantine. I believe we can learn from his mistakes and by doing so can avoid what some have called the Constantinian temptation. Scot McKnight defines this as "the temptation to get the state to combine its powers with the church's powers to accomplish, institutionalize, and legalize what is perceived to be divine purposes."[17] This temptation is still very much alive. Whenever church leaders abandon the ways of Jesus and rely upon the power of the state to accomplish their work, we are all in danger of succumbing to this temptation.

Through the edict of Milan in 313, Constantine declared Christianity to be legal in the Roman Empire. Several years later in 380, Theodosius made it the official state religion and joined the church with the state. Though their intentions were good, the result was compromise in the church and centuries of decline in Christian spiritual vitality. Over the centuries that followed, the European church became more oppressive as it compromised the gospel with the secular power, leading to the revolution called the Protestant Reformation.[18]

In the United States, we no longer have the marriage of church and state that was the norm in Europe. But we have the gospels of the left and the right.[19] Both versions fall victim to a variation of the Constantinian temptation. As McKnight says, "Leftists today worry about the Religious Right's blending of church and state, and not without reason, the Right worries that the Religious Left does the very same thing with its version of a naked public square. Any attempt to get the government or state to legislate what Christians believe and therefore to enforce Christian beliefs through the law is to one degree or another Constantinian."[20]

Both the Christian right and left attempt to get the government to promote certain behaviors and to prohibit others. Virtually everyone agrees that all law is based upon some type of moral norm. The question is which moral norms should be enforced through the authority of civil law, and which should be punished by the state. The Right wants laws prohibiting gay marriage and abortion, while the left wants laws that promote social justice and punish hate speech. But both sides err when they make civil law and governmental enforcement the end game. True change does not come through external laws but by transforming human character. We will not see lasting revolution when we pursue change by law because Jesus is not working to make us into moral and religious people. He is working to make us into people who do not hate or murder because we are not angry and who do not steal because we respect other people's property.

Again to be clear, I believe a good argument can be made for promoting morality through governmental action. And good people should promote goodness in and through the government. But we must not confuse having good laws with making good people. The goodness that makes our laws good is God, for God is the source of good.[21] A remnant of his goodness still resides in every human being because we have been made in God's image. But this goodness can be suppressed, which results in searing the conscience. Because of fallen human nature, we must not hope to change the world through the legal system and power of the government. The world can only be changed by the power of the gospel. McKnight quotes Carl Henry to support this point. "Christians have a biblical reason for seeking a predominantly regenerate society. But do they . . . have reason also to legislate all scriptural principles upon public institutions including government and schools? Will not Christians be disillusioned and in fact discredited if by political means they seek to achieve goals that the Church should ideally advance by preaching and evangelism?"[22]

History has shown that gains won by the religious right have been short-lived. For example while some laws have passed at the state level defining marriage as between a man and a woman and restricting abortion, for the most part laws have shifted to the left. And even when states have made laws that support conservative morality, the courts have struck them down.

While necessary work must be done in the political and legal spheres, our churches must not be confused about their calling and mission. We fight a spiritual battle, a war for people's character, and we rely primarily upon the influence that Jesus and the testimony of his disciples have—not external laws or political movements.

Have you fallen prey to the Constantinian temptation? Ask yourself, would things be better if our churches could take over our government? What if the international church ruled the world? Would things improve? My answer is a resounding No. I believe that *before the church can take over the world, Christ must take over the church*. Our churches are not ready for this level of power and authority—if they ever will be before Christ returns—because they do not have the maturity of grown up disciples of Jesus.

But what if our churches *did* improve their game? What if we did do a better job of developing Christlikeness in our members? What if we were as passionate as Paul about the work of discipleship?[23] Would it ever be a good idea for the church as an organization to have authority over the world in any way? I still think the answer is no, at least until Jesus returns and assumes his rightful place as ruler of God's kingdom on earth.[24] In any case, I highly recommend that we do not try to run the world before he arrives. But this topic leads us to another question. If successful revolution is not a matter of taking over the power of government and ruling politically, what does it look like?

Is the Church a Faithful Witness?

One popular idea of revolution is captured in a phrase coined by James Davison Hunter: the church is a faithful witness.[25] Hunter's view is that the church does not have the power to achieve political goals and grand notions of transforming the world. What's the alternative? The alternative I would recommend is to adopt the plan of Jesus to be a light to the world—in other words to make disciples who then make even more disciples (Matt. 28:18–20; 5:14–16). Obviously, this method is not one that brings change quickly. It takes time. It doesn't make the headlines. It is a person-to-person approach. We tell others the good news and people are publically baptized. Then we teach them to do everything Jesus taught us, including how to make more disciples, all until the story is told to all the earth. When this is complete, Jesus says that he will return and make things right.[26]

Being a quiet revolutionary is not flashy or complicated. It is simply living an authentic life and Christian witness embedded in society, preserving and illuminating God's truth until he returns to establish his kingdom.

I advocate that personal influence is the key to changing culture. Hunter presents a different approach, which involves cultural elites and powerful networks. Hunter and I agree that we are called to be faithful witnesses. But I see that the starting point is character change—disciples who make other disciples. Then when multiplication begins, it creates what Hunter describes as social or cultural change

Hunter presents four ways in which social change happens, which he sees as more determinative than commitment to make disciples and to teach everyone everything that Jesus commanded (Matt. 28:20). Jesus told us to make disciples and said almost nothing about society and networks. According to Hunter, *The key actor in history is not individual genius but the network*. New institutions are created out of networks. As an example, Hunter points to outlawing slavery in England. Most would contend that this victory was due to the character of William Wilberforce. Hunter, however, says it was due to the Clapham Circle, a powerful network of Christian abolitionists, of which Wilberforce was a member. I would say it was the character of Wilberforce which led to the advocacy of the Clapham Circle.

Hunter, a sociologist, has observed the following trends:

1. **The individuals, networks, and institutions most critically involved in the production of culture operate at the center where prestige is the highest.** Power is at the center, not on the periphery where the status is low. For example if the president of Harvard believes the right thing, he will have more impact than your local plumber.

2. **Long-term cultural change always occurs from the top down.** It is the work of the elites, the gatekeepers, who provide creative direction and management to the leading institutions of society. I believe that while there are examples of elites and gatekeepers changing society, change begins in the grassroots. One could argue that Pastor Rick Warren leads a powerful church and worldwide network and that is the reason people listen to him. That is true in its present manifestation, but Pastor Rick's influence is based on his character and being a faithful witness. First there was Rick Warren, and over a thirty-year period Saddleback Church became a major force, and then there was *The Purpose Driven Church* and *The Purpose Driven Life*. My point is you begin with the person, who then creates the effect, network, or movement that then a sociologist would recognize as elite or a center of power.

3. **World change is most intense when the networks of elites and the institutions they lead overlap.** According to Hunter, it is a consistent pattern that the impetus, energy, and direction for changing the world are

greatest where cultural, economic, and often political resources come together in a common purpose.[27]

To be clear, what Hunter is advocating is different from the Jesus way of transformation through personal evangelism and discipleship. If Hunter is right, then Jesus' plan is wrong, and our churches would be wasting time in attempting to change the world by working with ordinary people. The church's primary strategy should be targeting the key cultural players.

While Hunter may be somewhat correct on his first point, in that social elites do lead important institutions and networks, his remaining points tend to downplay the role ordinary people play in God's economy. Contrary to his second point, a certain carpenter from the backwater of Nazareth seemed to break this rule. Historian Randall Balmer writes, "My reading of American religious history is that religion always functions best from the margins of society and not in the councils of power. Once you identify the faith with a particular candidate or party or with the quest for political influence, ultimately it is the faith that suffers."[28] So while Hunter, a sociologist, sees the main potential for change at the center, Balmer says the church has done its greatest work out of the limelight, in the margins. In other words, the church has been at its best when it had the least.

On Hunter's third point, one could argue that grassroots movements actually bring about the greatest change. Hunter holds that the Renaissance, the Reformation, the Great Awakenings, the Enlightenment, the triumph of capitalism, and all democratic revolutions in the West began among elites and then percolated into the larger society. In other words, even if reproducing disciples are the salt of the earth and the light of the world, we will not see revolution until cultural elites get involved.

To be fair, I think Hunter would agree that Jesus didn't tell us to take over the world or dominate or control it in anyway. Our role is to be faithful witnesses until he returns and makes things right. But I believe Jesus has set the bar higher in his plan and kind of revolution, which Dallas Willard characterizes in this way: "We must make no mistake about it. In sending out his [disciples], he set afoot a perpetual world revolution: one that is still in process and will continue until God's will is done on earth as it is in heaven. As this revolution culminates, all forces of evil known to man-kind will be defeated and the goodness of God will be known, accepted, and joyously conformed to in every aspect of human life. He has chosen to accomplish this with and, in part, through his [disciples]."[29]

Willard specifically says here, "until God's will is done on earth as it is in heaven." This speaks of the revolution culminating at Christ's return, when he will defeat the physical and spiritual forces of evil. This is the time of judgment, when Christ finally establishes his rule over all and creates the new heavens and the new earth. So while we have a role in his revolution, we are not the ones to ultimately complete it. Our role is partial, yet crucial and significant because we are the means God uses in the revolution today.

We start the revolution, and Jesus finishes it. It is understood that we cannot ultimately seek to rule until Christ has returned, because he is the only one who rules. Balmer is right. Our churches will be suffering, persecuted communities until Christ's return, so the authority we have must be exercised from the margins of society. McKnight is also right in saying that political power is too weak. And Willard is right in reminding us that we have an important part to play as the church.

Above all, though, Jesus is right. The way we bring change is to be his disciples and to make disciples. What elevates making disciples above all else is the reality that only our churches can do this. If we don't make disciples, no one else will. Christians should be involved in politics, business, the media, and among the cultural elites. We should work among the poor and in the margins of society. But in all of our work, we cannot forget our primary mission. We have a unique calling to make disciples who make disciples. And this, above all else, must be our focus.

Digging Deeper
A QUESTION OF MOTIVE

We know Jesus has sent us as his disciples into the world to make more disciples. But the world is asking us a question about this mission: Can our message and our God be trusted? Is the offer of God's grace—that we can know Christ; be saved from the consequences of our sin; and gain eternal life in God—really legitimate?

At heart, Christians believe we serve a God who is just, righteous, and holy. But some presentations of God portray him as uncaring and even content to consign large portions of humanity to condemnation. Or they emphasize a God whose will is done regardless of human choice. Is there a way to think of God and his plan that emphasizes human responsibility while acknowledging our desperate need for a Savior?

Admittedly there is an element of mystery in all of this, and I don't claim to have solved this question. Regardless of our particular theological position on human choice and free will, at some level we must all acknowledge that our choices do matter. We may never get any closer to knowing the ultimate answer to this dilemma (which resides in God alone). But as a practical matter when making disciples, we must act and live as if our choices are real choices and that we are ultimately responsible for what we say and do. On this all can agree—whether Calvinist or Arminian. Even the most ardent disciples of determinism knows that they must choose to get out of bed, choose to wear certain clothes, choose to eat some kind of food, and even choose to possess a particular attitude. We all pray to God to help us make our decisions, but we know that our decisions are not made for us. We are responsible for them.

God's heart is revealed in the truth that he wants all to come to repentance and be saved (2 Peter 3:9). Therefore the fact that many will not be saved says more about the depravity of human sin than it does about the nature of God. God takes our decisions seriously. The price of our choice to reject God is the evil of sin. But we can also choose to repent and obey God and enjoy the blessings of engaging in relationship with our Creator. We can truly love and be loved. As Thomas Aquinas said, "God causes and moves our will, and yet without the will ceasing to be free."[a]

As you make disciples, don't fall for the extremes. On the one hand is the mistake of thinking that our salvation is entirely up to us, completely dependent on our knowledge, our will, and our choices. But salvation is always by grace—the undeserved gift of God. On the other hand is the wrong thinking that since everything is predetermined, our choices no longer matter. But our choices matter because God has chosen to bring his gospel to the world through us and has given us the responsibility of making disciples. There is no plan B. We must choose to walk in dependence upon God each day, relying upon his grace and working strenuously to making disciples who make disciples.

[a] Quoted in Brian Davies, *The Thoughts of Thomas Aquinas* (Oxford: Clarendon, 1992), 267.

The Gospel We Preach Determines Who We Become

The Jesus I believe in and the gospel I preach determines the kind of person I become and the kind of disciples I will make. I appreciate the words of E. Stanley Jones, "If God isn't like Jesus, he ought to be." Jesus is my motivation for discipleship. He is my teacher, my leader, my Lord, and my God; he is the exclusive revelation of God. The letter to the Hebrews puts it this way: "Long ago, at many times and in many ways, God spoke to our fathers by the prophets, but in these last days he has spoken to us by his Son, whom he appointed the heir of all things, through whom also he created the world. *He is the radiance of the glory of God and the exact imprint of his nature, and he upholds the universe by the word of his power.* After making purification for sins, he sat down at the right hand of the Majesty on high, having become as much superior to angels as the name he has inherited is more excellent than theirs" (Heb. 1:1–4 ESV, emphasis added).[30]

When we think of God, we should see Jesus on the cross. This is our God who sacrifices, lives, and dies for the sake of others. He cares in such a way that he holds nothing of himself back. "For this is how God loved: He gave his one and only Son, so that everyone who believes in him will not perish but have eternal life. God sent his Son into the world not to judge the world, but to save the world through him" (John 3:16–17 NLT). Ultimately, This is why we must respond to his command to go and make disciples of all peoples. Jesus gave his all; now I must give my all for him. All who are called to salvation are called to follow Jesus as his disciples. No exceptions. No excuses. Jesus held nothing back, and neither can we.

Recently a good friend of mine and fellow worker in the Bonhoeffer Project was working with some pastoral leaders in Bolivia. He taught them essentially the message of this volume.

1. All who are called to salvation are called to discipleship. No exceptions. No excuses.

2. The gospel we preach and believe dictates the kind of disciples we are and the kind of disciples we make.

3. If we attempt to make a Christlike disciple from a non-discipleship gospel, we will fail. We will make a disciple, but the wrong kind.

4. If we are truly saved, we will decide to enroll in Jesus' school and learn from him as his apprentice.

5. A disciple learns, grows, changes, and makes other disciples. Spiritual sterility is not acceptable.

6. Jesus' methods are just as important as his message. Our churches often accept his message but ignore his methods and create a non-discipleship Christianity that has no serious impact.

7. Our churches exist for discipleship, and disciples are God's delivery system to the world. When churches reverse this process

and attempt to get the world come to them instead of sending disciples to the world, the result is chaos.

8. Pastors should be evaluated and rewarded based on how many disciple-makers they produce and what kind of people their church sends into the world.

9. If our churches improve their game and increase the number of trained disciples they deploy into the world, more people will come into God's kingdom. More salt and light and more joy in Christ will be distributed, and more persecution suffered. But the sooner the mission is complete, the sooner the end will come.

10. Christ lives for others, the church is only the church when it exists for others. Any plan that does not create disciples who live for others is a failure.

The Bolivian pastors said to my friend, "We have always attempted to make disciples and have tried all the programs, but we always failed."

My friend asked, "Why do you think you failed with the best programs from around the world?"

"Because we didn't have the heart; we didn't understand why. Because we taught a non-discipleship gospel. We taught discipleship as an add-on to salvation."

Jesus tells us that making disciples is *his* way of rescuing the world: *his* plan, *his* method, and *his* dream for *his* church. Discipleship that follows the Jesus way will not fail because it is a mission that flows directly from the heart of God, the great disciple maker. As we follow his lead, we will see lives, churches, and communities transformed by the gospel.

NOTES

INTRODUCTION

1. More will be said about the more technical use of the word conversion in later chapters.
2. Dallas Willard, *Discipleship*, Oxford Handbook of Evangelical Theology (Oxford: Oxford University Press, 2010), 236.
3. John Stott characterized the gospel as being both a "gift and demand."
4. Dallas Willard, "Spiritual Formation as a Natural Part of Salvation," transcript of a talk given at Wheaton College, 2008, 19.

CHAPTER 1: THE GOSPEL

1. Dietrich Bonhoeffer, *The Cost of Discipleship*, Dietrich Bonhoeffer's Works, vol. 4 (Minneapolis: Fortress Press, 1996), 49.
2. Jonathan Pennington argues that the Greek word in the Septuagint version of Isaiah and the Synoptic Gospels (which derive much from Isaiah) translated "gospel" means basically "the restoration of God's reign on earth." This is counter to other Greek texts in the first century where "gospel" is used for the ascension of rulers like Caesar or kings.
3. Colin Brown, ed., *The New International Dictionary of New Testament Theology*, vol. 2 (Grand Rapids: Zondervan, 1976), 107.
4. Charles F. Pfeiffer, *Wycliffe Bible Encyclopedia* (Chicago: Moody Press, 1975), electronic media.
5. Rom. 12:1–16, 27.
6. See also Jude 3 (NLT), "But now I find that I must write about something else, urging you to defend the faith that God has entrusted once for all time to his holy people."
7. John 14:1–14.
8. 1 Peter 2:22–23.
9. 2 Cor. 5:15–16; 1 John 2:1–2.
10. Matt. 12:40; John 2:19.
11. Gen. 3:15.
12. 1 Cor. 15:9–58.
13. See The Faith Forum 20:12: *https://www.youtube.com/watch?v=ECMQ0Fn6Q0k.*

14. Scot McKnight, *The King Jesus Gospel*, revised edition (Grand Rapids: Zondervan, 2011), 74–75.
15. Gal. 1:8.
16. Dallas Willard, *The Divine Conspiracy: Rediscovering Our Hidden Life in God* (San Francisco: HarperCollins, 1998), 35–39.
17. Ibid., 403n8.
18. H. Richard Niebuhr, *The Kingdom of God in America* (Middletown, CT: Wesleyan University Press, 1988), 193.
19. The enemies of the prosperity gospel are as conservative as John Piper and as fervent as John MacArthur. Piper in recent years has preached entire sermons against it, and MacArthur held a conference titled Strange Fire to make a case against it.
20. Gal. 5:16–22.
21. Dallas Willard, *The Spirit of the Disciplines: Understanding How God Changes Lives* (New York: HarperCollins, 1989), 221.
22. Willard, *Divine Conspiracy*, 49.
23. Acts 1:5–8.
24. *http://www.goodreads.com/quotes/505050-the-two-most-important-days-in-your-life-are-the*.
25. Willard, *Divine Conspiracy*, 13.
26. Matt. 13:18–23.
27. Matt. 13:36–42. The burning up of the weeds or followers of Lucifer doesn't necessarily require eternal fire since the analogy is referring to what happens to wheat. It is clear that he mixes his language because weeds do not weep and gnash their teeth. The result is a sad one regardless of the interpretation.
28. Dallas Willard, "The Gospel of the Kingdom and Spiritual Formation," in *The Kingdom Life: A Practical Theology of Discipleship and Spiritual Formation*, ed. Alan Andrews (Colorado Springs: NavPress, 2010), 46.
29. Matt. 13:44.
30. Matt. 13:45.
31. Acts 1:6–8.
32. The first is Acts 11:26. The literal rendering is "the disciples were for the first time called Christians." The other references are Acts 26:28 and 1 Peter 4:16. Some extra-biblical evidence indicates that "Christian" was used by non-believers to describe followers of Jesus. But the term did not originate with Christ's followers.
33. George MacDonald, *Creation in Christ*, in *Guide to Prayer for Ministers and Other Servants*, Rueben P. Job and Norman Shawchuck (Nashville: The Upper Room, 1983), 60.

34. Matt. 4:19.
35. Luke 10:27–28.
36. Matt. 7:21–23.
37. John 8:31–32.
38. John 15:5–7.
39. Rom. 3:28.
40. Gal. 1:12–2:10.
41. See Gal. 1:8.
42. Robert Picirilli, *Discipleship: The Expression of Saving Faith* (Nashville: Randall House, 2013).
43. 1 Cor. 9:24–27; Phil. 4:9–13; 1 Tim. 4:7–11.
44. Gal. 4:19; Col. 1:28.
45. Matt. 13:19–23.

CHAPTER 2: THE CALL

1. A treatment of this period can be found in Bill Hull, *Jesus Christ, Disciplemaker* (Grand Rapids: Baker, 2004), 29–73. The other calls are Come and Follow Me, Come Be with Me, and Remain in Me. See discussion on these below.
2. *The Cost of Discipleship*, in *Dietrich Bonhoeffer Works*, vol. 4, ed. Wayne Whitson Floyd Jr. (Minneapolis: Fortress, 2003), 57.
3. Ibid., 59.
4. The Come and See period was about four months and is recorded in John 1:35–4:46. While this episode with Levi is recorded early in Matthew, it is placed after the Come and See period when calendared out in a harmony of the Gospels, and begins the Come and Follow Me period as recorded in Matthew, which is about ten months long. For further explanation, see Bill Hull, *Jesus Christ, Disciplemaker* (Grand Rapids: Baker, 2004). Robert Thomas and Stanley Gundry, *The NIV Harmony of the Gospels* (New York: HarperCollins, 1988) is a good resource for seeing the stages of Jesus' four calls to his followers: Come and See, Come and Follow Me, Come Be with Me, and Remain in Me. This four-fold call is derived not only from Scripture but was also noted by A. B. Bruce, *The Training of the Twelve* (Grand Rapids: Kregel, 1988), 11.
5. Alan P. Stanley, *Did Jesus Teach Salvation by Works? The Role of Works in Salvation in the Synoptic Gospels* (Eugene, OR: Pickwick, 2006), 220.
6. For example, Jesus fed 5,000 followers in John 6:1–15, but many disciples left him after hearing his hard teaching in John 6:60–70.
7. See Matt. 8:9; 12:50; John 15:13–15.

8. Mark 5:1–15.
9. Reading Mark's gospel, it's easy to forget that this initial period was probably much longer than it appears, because Mark tends to quickly summarize details. But from Matthew and Luke, we can estimate that this Come and Follow Me period was somewhere around ten to eleven months. Robert L. Thomas and Stanley N. Gundry, *The NIV Harmony of the Gospels*, revised edition of the John A. Broadus and A. T. Robertson, *A Harmony of the Gospels for Students of the Life of Christ* (New York: HarperCollins, 1988), 16.
10. The following paragraph has been gleaned from Stanley, *Works*, 226.
11. Ibid., 227.
12. See Matt. 10:39; 16:38; Luke 9:23–24; 14:25–27.
13. See Matt. 10:1; Luke 9:1–2; 2 Cor. 10:8.
14. C. S. Lewis, *Mere Christianity* (New York: Macmillian, 1952), 30.
15. Malcolm Gladwell, *The Tipping Point: How Little Things Can Make a Big Difference* (Boston: Little and Brown, 2002), 173.
16. John 1:39.
17. Matt. 4:19; Mark 1:16–18.
18. Bonhoeffer, *Cost of Discipleship*, 85.
19. Ps. 23:1–3.
20. See Mark 1:15; Luke 13:1–5; 15:7.
21. The Greek word translated believe is *pisteuo*, and it refers specially to faith. Salvation is the context of almost every use of the verb in John.
22. See Matt. 16:24–27; Luke 14:25–35.
23. See John 2:24.
24. Stanley, *Works*, 234.
25. See Rom. 2:12–16; 1 Cor. 3:12–15; 2 Cor. 5:10; Rev. 20:11–15.
26. See Rom. 1:16; 2 Tim. 1:8.

CHAPTER 3: SALVATION

1. Dallas Willard, "Spiritual Formation as a Natural Part of Salvation," transcript of a talk given at Wheaton College, 2008, 10.
2. This is another way of agreeing with what Paul saw to be his task, "So we tell others about Christ, warning everyone and teaching everyone with all the wisdom God has given us. We want to present them to God, perfect in their relationship to Christ. That's why I work and struggle so hard, depending on Christ's mighty power that works within me" (Col. 1:28–29 NLT).
3. See Eph. 2:10.
4. See Acts 2:38; 3:19; 7:2–53; 8:22.

5. Wayne Grudem, *Systematic Theology* (Grand Rapids: Zondervan, 1994), 713.

6. Ibid., 714.

7. The Lordship Salvation controversy in the 1980s was between John MacArthur in his book by the same name and some prominent faculty at Dallas Theological Seminary including Charles Ryrie and Zane Hodges. Ryrie and Hodges claimed that requiring repentance added a work to faith, while MacArthur claimed saving faith required repentance, commitment to a new life, and fruit to prove that new life was a reality. Some also teach that the gift of believing faith inherently includes the desire to repent. However if this is the case, why did John the Baptist, Jesus, Peter, and Paul include repentance as a requirement for salvation?

8. Karl Barth, *The Call to Discipleship* (Minneapolis: Fortress, 2003), 14.

9. See Rom. 4:3–5:11; Gal. 2:15–21.

10. N. T. Wright, *Justification, God's Plan & Paul's Vision* (Downers Grove, IL: InterVarsity, 2009), 25–26.

11. Eberhard Bethge, *Dietrich Bonhoeffer, A Biography* (Minneapolis: Fortress, 2000), 454.

12. Donald Bloesch, *The Crisis of Piety* (Grand Rapids: Eerdmans, 1968), 79.

13. Willard, "Spiritual Formation," 5.

14. Ibid., 6.

15. I first heard this from Dallas Willard in a message.

16. See Heb. 11:1.

17. See Mark 2:13–17.

18. This is not an issue of Reformed theology versus Arminian theology. Both believe that the Holy Spirit brings people to a point where they can believe. The difference is that most Reformed theologians believe that the number is limited, while the Arminian theologians hold that the ability to believe is extends to all people. The argument begins when one attempts to explain why person A believes and person B does not.

19. See Rom. 3:9–18.

20. Dietrich Bonhoeffer, *Cost of Discipleship*, Dietrich Bonhoeffer's Works, vol. 4 (Minneapolis: Fortress Press, 1996), 64.

21. Most Patristic Fathers held that salvation was not by works, yet that no one can be saved without them. See Alan Stanley's fine work, *Did Jesus Teach Salvation by Works? The Role of Works in Salvation in the Synoptic Gospels* (Eugene, OR: Pickwick, 2006), 20–60.

22. Augustine quoted by Stanley, *Salvation by Works*, 25.

23. Bloesch, *Crisis*, 77.

24. General thought taken from Ibid., 79, but not a quote.

25. Ibid., 82–83.

26. Walter Lock, *The Pastoral Epistles, A Critical and Exegetical Commentary* (Edinburgh: T&T Clark, 1924), 144.

27. Eric Metaxas, *Bonhoeffer: Pastor, Martyr, Prophet, Spy* (Nashville: Thomas Nelson, 2010), 246.

28. Willard, "Spiritual Formation," 11.

29. See 2 Cor. 5:17; Eph. 2:1–6.

30. Willard, "Spiritual Formation," 7.

31. Dallas Willard, "How to Save Your Life," speech at Westmont College, September 12, 2011.

32. Mark Johnson, *Morality for Humans: Ethical Understanding from the Perspective of Cognitive Science* (Chicago: University of Chicago Press, 2014), 161.

33. See 2 Cor. 5:17–20.

34. See Rom. 7:14–25; 1 Cor. 3:1–5; Gal. 5:16–23.

35. Dietrich Bonhoeffer, *Life Together*, Dietrich Bonhoeffer Works, vol. 5 (Minneapolis: Fortress Press, 2005), 32.

36. See Psalm 32:1–5; James 5:16.

37. Lewis Sperry Chafer, *He That Is Spiritual: A Classic Study of the Biblical Doctrine of Spirituality* (Philadelphia Sunday School Times, 1918; reprint Grand Rapids: Zondervan, 1967), 15–22.

38. Lewis Sperry Chafer, quoted in Stanley, *Salvation by Works*, 63.

39. Joseph Dillow, *The Reign of the Servant Kings: A Study of Eternal Security and the Final Significance of Man* (Miami: Schoettle, 1992), 151.

40. Ibid., 154.

41. R. T. Kendall, *Once Saved, Always Saved*, New Westminister Pulpit Series (1983; Waynesboro, GA: Authentic Media, 2005), 1.

42. Dillow, *Servant Kings*, 154.

43. Stanley, *Salvation by Works*, 316–17.

44. Malcolm Muggeridge, *A Third Testament: A Modern Pilgrim Explores the Spiritual Wanderings of Augustine, Blake, Pascal, Tolstoy, Bonhoeffer, Kierkegaard, and Dostoevsky* (Maryknoll, NY: Orbis Press, 1976), 69.

45. Ibid., 51.

CHAPTER 4: THE HOLY SPIRIT AND HOW PEOPLE CHANGE: PART 1

1. Mark 4:1–20.

2. Brian Davies, *The Thoughts of Thomas Aquinas* (Oxford: Clarendon, 1992), 267.

3. See Acts 2:1–41.

4. See 1 Peter 2:9.

5. Robert Picirilli, *Discipleship: The Expression of Saving Faith* (Nashville: Randall House, 2013), 144.

6. Ibid., 149–50.

7. Dallas Willard, *Renovation of the Heart* (Colorado Springs: NavPress, 2002), 226.

8. Eberhard Bethge, *Dietrich Bonhoeffer: A Biography* (Minneapolis: Fortress Press, 2000), 454.

9. Gordon Fee, *Paul, the Spirit, and the People of God* (Peabody, MA: Hendrickson, 1996), 75.

10. See also Matt. 5:15–20; 1 Cor. 13:1–3.

11. Meaning "church struggle."

12. Dallas Willard, *The Spirit of the Disciplines* (San Francisco: Harper and Row, 1988), 246.

13. See Matt. 28:19.

14. Col. 1:28–29.

15. Pronounced *kess-ick*.

16. 1 Cor. 3:1–3.

17. Characteristics of people who walk according to the flesh: 1. Walk according to the flesh (Rom. 8:1, 4). 2. Living under sin and death (8:2). 3. Live according to the flesh (8:5). 4. Set their minds on the flesh (8:5). 5. Carnally minded (8:6). 6. State of enmity against God (8:7). 7. In the flesh (8:8). 8. Cannot please God (8:8). 9. Have not the Spirit of Christ (8:9).

    Characteristics of those who walk according to the Spirit: 1. Walk according to the Spirit (Rom. 8:1, 4). 2. Live under the governance of the law of the Spirit of life (8:2). 3. Live according to the Spirit (8:5). 4. Set their minds on the things of the Spirit (8:5). 5. Spiritually minded (8:6). 6. Subject to the law of God (8:7). 7. In the Spirit (8:9). 8. Indwelled by the Spirit of God or of Christ (8:9).

    As found in Picirilli, *Discipleship*, 132–33.

18. These verses contain the verbal form εμαθον of μαθητευω, "to make a disciple." The NLT translates this as "learned." Later it uses "I know how," once again "I have learned," and finally, "For I can." Only the first case is the verbal form for the noun disciple used, but they are closely related and denote process. The last verse indicates that it takes spiritual power to learn and have it stick, which pulls together event, power and process.

19. Picirilli, *Discipleship*, 142.

20. Ibid.
21. See 1 Cor. 12:13.
22. See Acts 2:1–38.
23. For a complete discussion of this subject, see Bill Hull, *Straight Talk on Spiritual Power: Experiencing the Fillness of God in the Church* (Grand Rapids: Baker, 2002).
24. See Rom 12:2; Eph. 5:15–20.
25. Gal. 5:22–23.
26. The air-tight argument Paul presents in chapters 1–11 forces the reader to admit that the only logical, rational action is to turn oneself over to God for service. If God went to all that trouble to save us, empower us, and make us his own, then he is the best one to tell us what to do now. If this is not your conclusion, you need to reread the first eleven chapters of Romans.
27. Rodney Stark, *The Rise of Christianity* (San Francisco: Harper and Row, 1997), 13–21. Stark also conducted research among modern groups to determine why they converted to a religion. He found it to be separate issue as to whether they became seriously attached to doctrine and world view. He found that relationships and social cost were the main factors in conversion. In other words, the belief that "I could become one of them, I like them" was the main factor. The second major factor was that when there were more rewards than penalties for converting, then the convert would make the decision. This is characteristic of modern conversions in religion-friendly societies, not of the first century or where conversion will cost you much of what is dear to you. After those issues are settled, then teaching and doctrine become important.
28. Ibid., 18.
29. See 1 Cor. 2:1–16; 2 Cor. 5:17; Col. 1:26.
30. C. S. Lewis in Alan Jacobs, *The Narnian: The Life and Imagination of C. S. Lewis* (San Francisco: Harper One, 2005), 133.
31. See Jer. 17:9.
32. Willard, *Spirit of the Disciplines*, 142.
33. Ibid., 143.
34. See Gal. 5:16–17; Eph. 6:10–18; 1 John 2:15–17.
35. See Rom. 12:2, 1 Cor. 2:10–16.
36. While this statement may be sufficient for a believer, the secular mind doesn't accept it at face value. Some argue that God is the man behind the curtain, pulling the strings since the beginning, meaning that he created

this world and humanity and gave them a free will but then punishes them when they choose the wrong that he created with the right.

37. See Matt. 4:1–11; Heb. 4:14–16.
38. Matt. 4:1.
39. John 10:10a.

CHAPTER 5: THE HOLY SPIRIT AND HOW PEOPLE CHANGE: PART 2

1. See discussion of 2 Cor. 10:3–5 in Step 1 above.
2. See 1 Cor. 9:24–27; 1 Tim. 4:7–9.
3. This construct of ideas, images, and feelings comes from Dallas Willard, *Renovation of the Heart* (Colorado Springs: NavPress, 2003), 95–140. See also my exegesis in Bill Hull, *Choose the Life: Exploring a Faith that Embraces Discipleship* (Grand Rapids: Baker, 2004), 107–26.
4. Willard, *Renovation*, 41.
5. See Phil. 2:13.
6. Willard, *Renovation*, 127.
7. See Eph. 4:17–32; Col. 3:7–17.
8. *http://growingleaders.com/habitudes*.
9. See Phil. 4:9.
10. See Matt. 28:20.
11. See 1 Cor. 9:24–27; 1 Tim. 4:7–9.
12. See my discussion of this topic in detail in Hull, *Choose the Life*, 61–79.
13. Willard, *Renovation*, 156.
14. The Greek word translated "knowledge" is επιγνωσει. It is composed of two words, επι which generally means "upon" but in this case intensifies the second word, γνωσει "to know." This construction denotes interactive knowledge, or personal knowledge based on the relationship and interaction between two parties.
15. Growing in the knowledge of God means that grace is multiplied. This is clearer in the Greek because the word translated "grow" in 2 Peter 1:2 is πληθυηθειη, which means multiply.
16. While Gal. 5:22–23 is a standard, Peter's list is a good supplement.
17. See Phil. 2:13.
18. See 1 Cor. 9:24–27; 1 Tim. 4:7–9.
19. See 2 Peter 1:2–11.
20. John 13:35; 17:21.
21. William Law, *A Serious Call to a Devout and Holy Life* (Suffolk: Richard Clay and Sons Limited, 1906).

CHAPTER 6: WAYS AND MEANS

1. Dallas Willard, "Spiritual Formation as a Natural Part of Salvation," transcript of a talk given at Wheaton College, 2008, 19.
2. Ibid., 9.
3. Mike Breen, stated in a panel discussion at Exponential East, 2012.
4. *http://www.beliefnet.com/Quotes/Evangelical/J/John-Wesley/Give-Me-One-Hundred-Preachers-Who-Fear-Nothing-But.aspx.*
5. Robert Coleman, *The Master Plan of Evangelism* (Grand Rapids: Revell, 1963), 21.
6. I have much to say about this in Bill Hull, *The Christian Leader* (Grand Rapids: Zondervan, 2016).
7. Eugene Peterson, *The Jesus Way* (Grand Rapids: Eerdmans, 2007), 2.
8. Ibid., 4.
9. Ibid., 1.
10. Ibid., 6.
11. Ibid., 33.
12. Quoted in ibid., 33.
13. A. B. Bruce, *The Training of the Twelve* (1871; New Canaan, CT: Keats, 1979), 11–18.
14. Robert L. Thomas and Stanley N. Gundry, *The NIV Harmony of the Gospels,* revised edition of the John A. Broadus and A. T. Robertson *A Harmony of the Gospels for Students of the Life of Christ* (New York: Harper One, 1988).
15. Bill Hull, *Jesus Christ, Disciplemaker,* twentieth anniversary revised edition (1984; Grand Rapids: Baker, 2004).
16. John 12:23.
17. It actually says, "Jesus knew that his hour had come to leave this world and return to his Father."
18. Jesus seemed to be concerned that the Pharisees knew his popularity was growing greater than John the Baptist's. On returning to Galilee, he changed his route to go through the territory where the half-breed Samaritans lived, which Jews usually avoided.
19. Another obvious consideration is that Jesus' death had to match the prophetic calendar. The convergence of foretold events and people required his actions to have a certain pace.
20. This is based on a study of Robert L. Thomas and Stanley N. Gundry, *The NIV Harmony of the Gospels,* revised edition of the John A. Broadus and A. T. Robertson *A Harmony of the Gospels for Students of the Life of Christ* (New York: HarperCollins, 1988). The book has some apologetic essays regarding the validity of a harmony

of the Gospels. However, my guiding principle is that a harmony not replace the primary purpose of each Gospel which is to present Christ in a way that the reader will respond in belief and a life of discipleship to Christ. For this particular conclusion regarding the interim between Come and See and Come and Follow Me, see the timeline on 15–16 and the actual text on 54–55. Based on these passages alone, Jesus went to Galilee, Capernaum, and Nazareth. The fact that he then went to visit his disciples and called them to "follow me" is a strong argument that there was a period when they returned to fishing and he was doing ministry alone.

21. See the discussion on this issue in ibid., 57.
22. See Matt. 23:1–10.
23. See 1 Peter 5:5–9.
24. Matt. 10:1–42; Mark 6:7–12, 30; Luke 9:1–6, 10.
25. See John 6:14–15.
26. This topic is covered in chapter two among other general qualifications for becoming a follower of Jesus.
27. Count the pronouns, and you will be surprised how many times Jesus refers to his first disciples and to us, his present day disciples.
28. See Matt. 26:36–46; Mark 14:32–42; Luke 22:39–46.
29. See Matt. 26:31–35; Mark 14:27–31.
30. Dallas Willard, *The Great Omission* (New York: Harper Collins, 2006), 86.
31. See Bill Hull, *The Complete Book of Discipleship* (Colorado Springs: NavPress, 2006), 182.
32. Quoted in James R. Newby, *The Best of Elton Trueblood* (Nashville: Abingdon, 1979), 26.

CHAPTER 7: THE CHURCH

1. Quoted in Charles Marsh, *Strange Glory: A Life of Dietrich Bonhoeffer* (New York: Alfred A. Knopf, 2014), 384.
2. John 3:16–17.
3. Matt. 28:20; 2 Tim. 2:2. You don't get world revolution without intentionally expecting the fruit of a disciple to be another disciple so that the movement multiplies and spreads until the gospel is preached to every person in the world.
4. Eph. 3:10–11.
5. See Matt. 4:19; Luke 5:1–11.
6. John 6:1–15: Jesus allowed five thousand to slip away who were gathered to hear him speak. John 9:1–41: Blind man returned

home. John 11:1–25: Lazarus, Mary, and Martha, like most of Jesus' followers, followed his teachings but did not join his band of disciples as they traveled, and were not included as apostles.

7. Dietrich Bonhoeffer, *The Cost of Discipleship*, Dietrich Bonhoeffer's Works, vol. 4 (Minneapolis: Fortress Press, 1996), 202.

8. Dallas Willard, *The Great Omission* (New York: Harper One, 2006), xi–xii.

9. For a complete treatment of this subject, see Bill Hull, *The Disciple-Making Church* (Grand Rapids: Baker, 2010), 57 and following.

10. When they had 5,000 followers, Peter and John also stood before the religious council in Jerusalem and proclaimed the basic core of their teaching. See Acts 4:1–22.

11. Dietrich Bonhoeffer, *Life Together*, Dietrich Bonhoeffer Works, vol. 5 (Minneapolis: Fortress Press, 2005), 36–37.

12. See Gal. 6:1–2, James 5:16.

13. C. S. Lewis, *Reflections on the Psalms* (New York: Harcourt, Brace, Jovanovich, 1958), 94–95.

14. Rom. 12:1–2.

15. See Acts 8:1–4.

16. Eric Hoffer, *The True Believer: Thoughts on the Nature of Mass Movements* (New York: Harper and Row, 1951). While his book is not about religion, he does say Christianity is one of the kinds of movements that true believers will join.

17. News of documented cases is coming from Iraq, Syria, and other parts of the Middle East.

18. Dallas Willard, *Renovation of the Heart* (Colorado Springs: NavPress, 2002), 248.

19. Acts 19:1–41.

20. Acts 19:13–22.

21. Acts 19:8–10: the twenty-seven people are found in John Stirling, *An Atlas of Acts* (London: George Philip & Son Limited, 1966), 16–20.

22. Hull, *Disciple-Making Church*, 151–87.

23. Eugene Peterson, *Practice Resurrection: A Conversation on Growing Up in Christ* (Grand Rapids: Eerdmans, 2010), 29.

24. Acts 20:15.

25. 2 Tim. 1:7.

26. Ibid., 14.

27. See Rom. 1:18–21.

28. Eph. 4:1–6:18.

29. It is vital to keep in mind that Paul was obeying Christ's command to

teach all people to obey everything Christ commanded. Jesus taught Paul, and Paul taught the Ephesians, in person and through his letter that instructed them and now us.

30. See 1 Peter 1:6–9.
31. See Phil. 2:5–8.
32. See also 1 Cor. 12:28.
33. Eph. 2:20.
34. 1 Cor. 14:3.
35. Rom. 1:16–18; 2 Tim. 4:5.
36. Acts 20:28; 1 Peter 5:1–5.
37. Luke 6:40; 2 Tim. 2:15–16; James 3:1.
38. Rom. 12:4–8; 1 Cor. 12:4–12.
39. Jesus said, "When you produce much fruit, you are my true disciples. This brings great glory to my Father" (John 15:8 NLT).
40. See Matt. 11:28–29; 1 Cor. 2:9–16; 11:1; Phil. 2:2–14; 3:8–14; 1 Peter 2:21–24.
41. "The frontal lobes of the brain which are responsible for high level reasoning and decision making aren't fully mature until the early 20s, according to Deborah Yurgelun-Todd, a neuroscientist at Harvard's Brain Imaging Center. There's a portion of time when the child part of the brain has been pruned, but the adult portion is not fully formed. They are 'in-between.' They are informed but not prepared." *http://www.psychologytoday.com/blog/artificial-maturity/201211/the-marks-maturity*.
42. Basic idea from Peterson, *Practice*, 180–81.
43. Ibid., 180.
44. Bonhoeffer, *Life Together*, 108.
45. See Eph. 2:10.
46. Bonhoeffer, *Life Together*, 98.
47. Ibid., 99.
48. Ibid., 105.
49. Willard, *Renovation*, 226.
50. The three points here are derived from ibid., 226–28.
51. Phil. 2:5–8.

CHAPTER 8: THE PASTOR

1. Matt. 28:20.
2. See Luke 6:40; 2 Tim. 2:2.
3. Eugene Peterson, *The Pastor: A Memoir* (New York: Harper One, 2011), 157.

4. Matt. 13:18–23.
5. 2 Tim. 2:2.
6. Matt. 24:14.
7. Pat Morely, notes I took in conversation, August, 2014.
8. Greg L. Hawkins, Cally Parkinson, and Eric Arnson, *REVEAL: Where Are You?* (Chicago: Willow Creek Resources, 2007).
9. Dallas Willard, from my personal notes. There is more correspondence on this matter around the REVEAL from December 27, 2007.
10. Dallas Willard, "Spiritual Formation as a Natural Part of Salvation," transcript of a talk given at Wheaton College, 2008, 19, emphasis added.
11. Scot McKnight, *The King Jesus Gospel*, revised edition (Grand Rapids: Zondervan, 2011), 26.
12. Augustine, *Tractates on the Gospel according to St. John* 36.1.
13. 1 Cor. 4:17. He tells the Corinthians that he is sending Timothy to remind them of his ways in Christ, not only on a personal or character level, but also content.
14. See Matt. 28:18–20; 2 Cor. 5:17–22.
15. "And this gospel of the kingdom will be preached in the whole world as a testimony to all nations, and then the end will come" (Matt. 24:14).
16. See Rom. 12:1–2; Col. 1:28–29.
17. Dallas Willard, from notes, June 30, 2012, Long Beach, California.
18. Gal. 6:9.
19. John Wesley, "An Address to the Clergy," Wesley Center Online, *Wesley.nwu.edu*, 482–83.
20. This idea came from Dallas Willard, *Renovation of the Heart* (Colorado Springs: NavPress, 2002), 230–31.
21. Rom. 1:18–32 was the primary New Testament passage used in the sermon.

CHAPTER 9: THE END

1. See Matt. 24:14; 28:18–20; Rom. 10:5–15.
2. 2 Peter 3:1–13; Rev. 21:1–7.
3. Paul goes on to say, "And so all Israel will be saved. As the Scriptures say, 'the one who rescues will come from Jerusalem, and he will turn Israel away from ungodliness'" (Rom 11:26 NLT).
4. See 2 Peter 3:7–13.

5. Dallas Willard, *Renovation of the Heart* (Colorado Springs: NavPress, 2002), 14–15. "[Disciples]" is "trainees" in the original.
6. See John 16:33.
7. Quoted in Charles Marsh, *Strange Glory* (New York: Alfred A. Knopf, 2014), 378.
8. Peter Berger, *The Precarious Vision* (Garden City, NY: Doubleday, 1961), 163.
9. C. S. Lewis, *Mere Christianity* (New York: Macmillian, 1952), 30. Also found on Berger, *Precarious*, 60.
10. Dallas Willard, *Knowing Christ Today* (San Francisco: Harper One, 2009), 147.
11. See Rev. 2–3.
12. Willard, *Knowing Christ*, 147.
13. See Eph. 6:10–16. Jesus also revealed it through the account of his encounter with Satan in Matt. 4:1–11 and through the visions recorded in the Book of Revelation.
14. See Rev. 20:11–15; John 5:21–23.
15. Dallas Willard, *The Divine Conspiracy: Rediscovering Our Hidden Life in God* (San Francisco: HarperCollins, 1998), 334.
16. John 1:1–14.
17. Scot McKnight, *The Kingdom Conspiracy* (Grand Rapids: Baker, 2014), 260.
18. Many good histories have been written on this subject. McKnight, *Conspiracy*, 260, is a good place to start.
19. Both are described in chapter 1 of this work.
20. McKnight, *Conspiracy*, 262.
21. See Mark 10:18, where Jesus says that God alone is good.
22. McKnight, *Conspiracy*, 266.
23. Col. 1:28–29.
24. Some believe that when Jesus returns, he will reign from Jerusalem for a thousand years. Wouldn't that be interesting? Obviously, he will have the authority and the power to do so. But even then we are told that many will rebel. Does this mean that not even God himself can be completely successful in running the world while there is sin in it? See Rev. 20:4–10.
25. James Davison Hunter, in an address to Trinity Forum, June 21–22, 2003. Summarized by Jay Lorensen on June 10, 2006, in Leadership Movements: Marks of a Movement, *www.onmovements.com*.
26. Matt. 24:14; 28:18–20.
27. Hunter, Trinity Forum.

28. Randall Balmer, *God in the White House* (San Francisco: Harper One, 2008), 167, quoted in McKnight, *Conspiracy*, 267.

29. Willard, *Renovation*, 14–15. The first "[disciples]" is "trainees" in the original, and the second is "students."

30. See also John 1:1–3; Col. 1:15–20.

Bill Hull has devoted his adult life to pastoring, teaching, and writing about Christ's command to make disciples. Bill's primary means for pursuing his mission as a discipleship evangelist has been pastoring for twenty years, teaching in more than fifty countries of the world, and authoring more than twenty books. Bill is now the leader of The Bonhoeffer Project, which is devoted to the creation of disciple-making leaders. You can learn more about Bill's work at *TheBonhoefferProject.com* and *BillHull.net*.

Twitter: @BillHull

Facebook: https://www.facebook.com/discipleship.billhull

The Bonhoeffer Project

Bill Hull

Bill is co-founder of The Bonhoeffer Project. Bill's passion is to help the church return to its disciple-making roots, and he considers himself a discipleship evangelist. This God-given desire has manifested itself in 20 years of pastoring and the authoring of many books. Two of his more important books, *Jesus Christ Disciplemaker*, and *The Disciple-Making Pastor*, have been in print 20 years.

Brandon Cook

Brandon is co-founder of The Bonhoeffer Project and the lead pastor at Long Beach Christian Fellowship. He studied at Wheaton College (IL), Jerusalem University College, Brandeis University, and the Oxford Centre for Hebrew and Jewish Studies. He became convinced that his work—and the work of the church—is to become fully committed to discipleship and making disciple makers.

Goal

The goal of The Bonhoeffer Project is to encourage each participant to become a disciple-making leader. Once that decision has been made, then to provide the participant with the knowledge necessary to carry out a plan for making disciples who also will make disciples. The Bonhoeffer Project firmly believes that this is best done in a community of like-minded persons—that is why the project itself is a community.

Plan

Making disciples requires intentionality. William Law in his book *A Serious Call to a Devout and Holy Life*, made this point: the reason people don't change behavior is that they never really intend to do so. The intention to make disciples requires a plan and if you have no plan, you don't really intend to do it. The Bonhoeffer Project helps each participant craft a plan that is biblically sound and a good fit for their ministry context. Each of the ten gatherings will focus on a specific subject that is followed by a monthly project.

Contact

www.thebonhoefferproject.com